AFRICAN CATHOLICISM
AND HERMENEUTICS OF CULTURE

African Catholicism and Hermeneutics of Culture

Essays in the Light of African Synod II

JOSEPH OGBONNAYA

WIPF & STOCK · Eugene, Oregon

Wipf & Stock
An Imprint of Wipf and Stock Publishers
199 W. 8th Ave., Suite 3
Eugene, OR 97401

www.wipfandstock.com

ISBN 13: 978-1-62564-537-1

Manufactured in the U.S.A.   07/25/2014

To

Margaret (Peggy) O'Neill

Whose post-World War II overseas travels shaped her cross-cultural encounter, a requisite for World Christianity.

Contents

Foreword

LESS THAN FIVE YEARS after the conclusion of the Second African Synod and the release of its post-apostolic exhortation *Africae Munus*, a plethora of books and articles have been written commenting, highlighting important points, describing, explaining, chronicling, critiquing as well as appraising the synod.[1] Joseph Ogbonnaya's book joins this crop of scholars trying to make sense as well as suggest ways of implementing and advancing the synod decisions. The three themes of *Africae Munus*: reconciliation, justice and peace remain very vital for the survival of Christianity nay Catholicism in Africa.

The social history of Africa is bedeviled by centuries of slavery which robbed her of human resources to further her development. The artificial boundaries set up by various colonizing powers not only separated brothers and sisters but yoked together people with different cultures and history thus precipitating the

---

1. Worthy of note are: Agbonkhianmeghe E. Orobator, ed. *Reconciliation, Justice, and Peace : The Second African Synod* (Maryknoll, New York: Orbis Books, 2011; and its reviews by Scheid, Anna Floerke, "Reconciliation, justice, and peace: the Second African Synod," *Political Theology*, 13 no 4 Ag 2012, p 513–515; Oborji, Francis Anekwe, "Reconciliation, justice, and peace: the Second African Synod," *International Bulletin of Missionary Research*, 35 no 4 O 2011, p 228–229. Scholarly articles like Stan Chu Ilo, "The Second African Synod and the Challenges of Reconciliation, Justice, and Peace in Africa's Social Context. Part 2 A Missional Theological Praxis for Transformation," *Missiology*, 40 no 3 Jl 2012, p 249–260; McCabe, Michael, "Key challenges for international missionary institutes in Africa today in light of the Second Synod for Africa," *SEDOS Bulletin*, 42 no 7–8 Jl-Ag 2010, p 150–158; Bwangatto, Ambrose John, "Reconciliation and the Church in Africa: a Reflection on the Second Synod for Africa," *AFER*, 51–52 no 4–1 D 2009-Mr 2010, p 403–423; to mention but a few.

pernicious rivalry, ethnicity and violence that negate social integration and social engineering in many African countries. The ongoing neocolonialism and attendant international trade that favors
the industrialized countries coupled with corruption of all sectors
of African life perpetuate poverty and misery fuelling petty crimes
and other criminal activities making governance and implementation of the rule of law difficult in much of Africa. The overall
result is envy, hatred, ethnicity, favoritism, increasing crime wave,
superficial religiosity in African social, religious and political life.
Little wonder most people seek to escape from Africa to other
parts of the world. These form part of what Engelbert Mveng calls
anthropological poverty.[2] Reconciliation, justice and peace are
imperatives that will heal African social malaise. *Africae Munus*
is right on target in its proposals only they need interpretation by
theologians and other scholars which is what this book seeks to do.

In this new era of evangelization as the Church continues to
grapple with the challenges of modernity in a supposedly post-
Christian era in some parts of the world, Joseph Ogbonnaya's book
is timely reflecting the dynamics of Catholicism in Africa. Written
in the light of the Second Africa Synod's document *Africae Munus*, Joseph suggests a holistic approach to African Catholicism
integrating inculturation and liberation theology; the proper education of the civil society in critical thinking to challenge the corruption and maladministration that denies the common people of
Africa benefit from their abundant natural and human resources;
the healing of African psyche the distortion of which accounts
for anthropological crisis affecting the practice of Christianity in
much of Africa. Recognizing the contribution of the leadership of
African Catholicism to the promotion of social justice, the book
challenges the African Church to walk their talk highlighting areas
the church falls short of expectation especially with regard to the
clergy-lay faithful relationship and the danger of attraction to materialism. Of particular interest in this book is Joseph's recognition

2. Engelbert Mveng, "Impoverishment and Liberation: A Theological Approach for Africa and the Third World," Rosino Gibellini, ed., *Paths of African
Theology* (Maryknoll, New York: Orbis Books, 1994), 156.

of the importance of interreligious dialogue and broadening of vision of Catholics on the implication of salvation in Christ. In much of Africa this is necessary in the light of violence intolerance generates between Christians, practitioners of African traditional religions and Islam.

While in the 21st century, technology and globalization cannot be ignored without one being left behind, many African nations and churches are yet to pay adequate attention to the impact of globalization and its complexity on the economy, the social, personal and religious lives as well as public policies affecting existence in Africa. Joseph draws attention to this phenomenon and urges the Church to lead the faithful in the 21st century cognizant of the benefits as well as the dangers of globalization. Equally important in this regard is a shift away from what Joseph following the famous Brazilian educationist Paulo Ferire calls 'the banking concept of education' to liberationist education aimed at critical thinking. Since questions lead to search for answers, a liberation-oriented educational system will potentially arm African peoples to seek answers for bad governance and corruption that has kept them down preventing them from benefiting from their abundant natural and human resources. I highly recommend this book.

John I. Okoye
Bishop Catholic Diocese of Awgu
Nigeria

Acknowledgments

THIS BOOK IS THE product of years of research starting from my graduate studies at the University of Saint Michael's College in Toronto, Canada. The Second African Synod gave it final shape by providing themes that brought together my random thoughts on African Catholicism. I am grateful to Professor John Dadosky of Regis College Toronto, University of Toronto, Canada for introducing me to the thoughts of Bernard Lonergan, whose influence guides my thoughts on hermeneutics of culture. I am indebted to Professor Robert Doran of Marquette University, my academic mentor, whose writings on the integral scale of values have been foundational to my appropriation of theology and culture, as well as to my appreciation of the place of social history in cultural advancement, progress, and development. My thanks as well to Sylvia Chin for painstakingly reading through and revising the chapters of this book for publication.

I appreciate the generosity of my bishop, the Right Reverend John Ifeanyichukwu Okoye of Awgu Diocese in Nigeria for agreeing to write the foreword, and I thank Professor Bryan Massingale of Marquette University and for endorsing the book. The support of my senior colleague at Marquette University, Professor D. Stephen Long, was a source of valuable encouragement for me in the publication of this book. The collegiality of Marquette University's Theology Department creates an encouraging atmosphere for generating insights that I have very much appreciated during my research. I am thankful for the 2013 Summer Faculty Development Fund of Marquette University's College of Arts and Sciences, which freed me to devote my summer to the project. Finally, I benefitted from the review process of the Wipf and Stock editorial board, which helped me in the revision and expansion of this book.

Introduction

THE STUDY OF CHRISTIANITY in the non-Western world reveals a demographic shift in the center of Christianity from the Northern Hemisphere to the South. As the Holy Father John Paul II reveals in the synod document, *Ecclesia in Africa*, Christianity is on the rise in Africa as many people practice Christianity and consider their faith increasingly important in everyday life.[3] According to the Pew Research Center on Global Christianity, "the fastest growth in the number of Christians over the past century has been in sub-Saharan Africa (a roughly sixty-fold increase, from fewer than nine million in 1910 to more than 516 million in 2010) and in the Asia-Pacific region (a roughly ten-fold increase, from about twenty-eight million in 1910 to more than 285 million in 2010)."[4]

Thus, African Christianity is considered a "spiritual 'lung' for humanity" by Benedict XVI in *Africae Munus* (sec. 13). But the contradictory aspect of the massive African conversion to Christian faith is the grinding poverty level in Africa. This is contradictory because sub-Saharan Africa has abundant natural and human resources which, if harnessed and properly managed, would surely enhance the integral development of African peoples. Since the study of theology not only examines the origins of religion and seeks to apply them to the culture of its adherents, but also appropriates the Christian faith tradition to relate it to contemporary life, the African condition raises important theological and ecclesiological questions that demand urgent answers. One must ask: What role has theology played, and what form should it take

3. John Paul II, *Ecclesia in Africa*, sec. 38.
4. Pew Forum on Religion and Public Life, "Global Christianity," 15.

to ensure optimum integral development in the religious setting of sub-Saharan Africa, a region struggling with the dialectics of human development? What spirituality should theology and Catholicism in Africa foster in this age of globalization to usher in an African Renaissance that might enable sub-Saharan African peoples to take their destiny into their own hands? Has Christianity been integrated into the lives of African peoples, and to what effect? Since many people in sub-Saharan Africa have embraced Christianity, how has theology mediated the cultural matrix of Africa and of Christianity within that matrix? How has Catholic Christianity performed in sub-Saharan Africa? What role should theology play in the sustainable development of Africa as a continent?

This book is dedicated to answering these questions through an analysis of African culture, theology, and development from the perspective of African Catholicism. Its major contribution to scholarship is the formulation of spirituality for liberation in Africa in the light of Pope Benedict XVI's *Africae Munus*. Its proposals will be directed towards shifting theology in Africa away from the *fuga mundi* (flight from the world) spirituality; that is, passively expecting that in God's time things will improve such that African peoples will begin to enjoy reconciliation, justice, and peace. African theology with a liberation motif, which this work aligns itself with, seeks to integrate Christian social responsibility with practical measures to effect change in the socio-political, cultural, and religious attitudes that promote moral integrity towards the promotion of the common good. In view of the traumatic crisis of identity from which African peoples suffer (on account of centuries of subjugation and oppression with its attendant inferiority complex), this book draws upon the theological and philosophical analysis of Bernard Lonergan to suggest avenues for the emergence of African personhood called for by the Second African Synod's *Africae Munus*.

Therefore, the research objectives of this book are to examine African Catholicism's involvement in human promotion and to seek a new way of theologizing and being Christian that moves sub-Saharan African peoples to action against the massive injustices that keep them poor. First, this book explores African theology in relation to the sustainable and integral development of Africa. It questions what African theology has contributed towards this development besides the numerous charitable works that faith-based organizations have been doing through the assistance of foreign donors in Africa. Second, this book will formulate a theology for the integral development of sub-Saharan Africa with a liberation motif in line with Catholic social teachings. Such theology will be based on African cultural values, bearing in mind the problem of continuity and change in these values in the light of the various agents of social transformation that have impacted Africa over the centuries. This theology is informed by current dissatisfaction with approaches to theologizing in sub-Saharan Africa. Presently, theology concentrates on soothing the pain of the people with a promise of a better life in heaven, while not addressing the African condition here on earth. This book questions the spirituality formulated by such theology, even as it aims to present an alternative founded on solid spirituality founded on a strong sense of social justice and democratic principles. This theology aims at educating the people in their social and moral rights as human beings.

Third, especially in the light of the Post-Synodal Apostolic Exhortation of the Second African Synod, *Africae Munus*, the book will present a different way of communicating the good news in the light of the proposed liberation motif.

Background and Significance

The background of this study is the sad reality that the growth of Christianity in Africa includes the continuing condition of poverty in Africa. It is also framed by the dissatisfaction arising from the fact that as deeply religious people, African Christians run to God and the church as the sacrament of salvation for relief. Will they not be disappointed if their condition keeps deteriorating? The church will surely be seen as irrelevant if its ministry is unable to lift the people of Africa up from poverty, making it difficult for people to make sense of its promise of freedom as children of God.

Many scholars have chronicled the church's charitable efforts at improving the living conditions of African peoples. Josef Zalot's *The Roman Catholic Church and Economic Development in Sub-Saharan Africa* (1992) made excellent progress in this direction. Benezet Bujo's *African Theology in Its Social Context* (2006) examines the social context of Africa to suggest a communitarian theology requisite for mutual coexistence. Stan Chu Ilo's the *Church and Development Aid in Africa* (2011) uses Pope Benedict XVI's encyclical *Caritas in Veritate* to support development aid and the work of faith-based organizations (FBOs) in Africa. Other studies in this field, such as Emmanuel Martey's *African Theology: Inculturation and Liberation* (2001), show how the real hope for African theology lies in the dialectical tension between liberation and hermeneutics and in their potential convergence. Martey's focus is not on establishing a theology with a liberation motif, but on explaining the relationship between inculturation and liberation theology. John Parratt's *Reinventing Christianity: African Theology Today* (1995) is a comparative study of the various approaches of doing theology in Africa rather than on development of Africa. Elochukwu Eugene Uzukwu's, *God, Spirit, and Human Wholeness: Appropriating Faith and Culture in West African Style* (2012) is concerned with the language of God and specifically with how people of the West African region appropriate the Trinitarian doctrine through their traditional cultural religions. Emmanuel Katongole's *The Sacrifice of Africa* (2011) imaginatively fashions a political theology for Africa in the light of the Christian faith. Drawing from these earlier approaches at relating theology to works of charity in Africa, I aim at constructing theology for integral development through the integral scale of values: vital, social, cultural, personal, religious, from above downwards, and from below upwards.

This book draws from the experience of theologizing in an underdeveloped world to contribute another approach that reexamines the African condition through the liberation motif it suggests. It seeks to make theology relevant to the contemporary discourse of the peoples of sub-Saharan Africa. Drawing on *Africae Munus*, it argues the thesis that African Catholicism, to truly be "the spiritual 'lung' of humanity," must appropriate the Christian message to transform African attitudes and personhood to foster self-reliant commitment to integral development. This project is important for Christianity in Africa, for unless Christianity can fashion a theology that enables it to participate in transforming the African condition, it will become irrelevant to the people and die out. As Julius Nyerere, the late President of Tanzania, observes, "Unless the church, its members, and its organizations express God's love for man by involvement in the present conditions of man, then it will become identified with injustice and persecution. If this happens, it will die—and, humanly speaking, deserve to die—because it will then serve no purpose comprehensive to modern man."[5] This book is a response to such concerns and is aimed at making theology relevant to the socio-cultural, political, economic, and religious condition of the peoples of sub-Saharan Africa.

Methodology

Since this book is envisaged as a work in practical theology, it will adopt an empirical descriptive research approach characterized by inductive and deductive analysis. It will draw upon Bernard Lonergan's philosophical and theological analytical framework of social history, especially his idea of cosmopolis and the development of critical culture for the emergence of a superstructure of culture to reorient the cultural infrastructure, which breaks down on account of various negative factors called bias.[6] Its analysis will equally depend on the Post-Synodal Apostolic Exhortation

5. Nyerere, "The Church's Role in Society," Jon Pratt, ed., *A Reader in African Christian Theology*, 119.

6. See Lonergan, *Insight*, ch. 6–7 for analysis of constituents of society as well as its distortions as a result of various forms of bias. See also chapter 2 of my earlier book, *Lonergan, Social Transformation, and Sustainable Human Development*.

Africae Munus of the Second African Synod. The themes of the Synod—reconciliation, justice, and peace—are highly germane to the future of African Catholicism. Thus, through analysis of Africa's socio-economic and political conditions, this study seeks to actualize the social responsibility of African Catholicism without sacrificing its spirituality.

This book raises six central and interrelated questions. The first two, concerning the resiliency of African culture, will be addressed by an analysis of the social history of Africa in relation to various external agents of social transformation. The third question, which investigates the appropriation of Christianity through faith-based organizations in Nigeria, will analyze how religious values influence public life in Africa. The fourth question, concerning the involvement of theology in mediating faith and culture, will be answered through an examination of theology and the development of Africa. Specifically, the role of Catholicism in Africa will concretize the task of African Catholicism as the "spiritual 'lung' of humanity." Because Christianity in Africa cannot be relevant to the people if it is seen as foreign, the fifth question addresses the extent to which Christianity is at home in African culture. It recommends appreciation of African cultures as a way of making Christianity in Africa more indigenous. The reality of religious pluralism in Africa is indisputable. Consequently, the sixth question, aimed at achieving reconciliation, justice, and peace in Africa, addresses the question of religious pluralism as a challenge to integral development.

Accordingly, the book is divided into ten chapters. Chapter 1 introduces the Post-Synodal Apostolic Exhortation of the Second African Synod, *Africae Munus*. It lays out a summary of the outcome of the Synod in regards to African Catholicism and explains the hermeneutics of culture that this book will be engaged in. By highlighting the historical circumstances leading to the emergence of contemporary African nations, chapter 2 recognizes the loss of cultural integrity as a leading factor in the African misconception of statehood. Chapter 2 proposes that the way forward lies in attending to the integrity of the cultural values that influence people's everyday lives. Since this will be the task of the educated African, the cultural integrity of the superstructure will be mandatory. Chapter 3, recognizing that the creative minority of Africa is mired in squandermania arising from the hesitation to move from satisfaction to values, appropriates the Lonergan idea of cosmopolis and suggests means for integral development and responsible governance in Africa.

Since religion plays a central role in the African apprehension of reality, it is not surprising that religious claims dominate many public discourses. Therefore, mutual coexistence and development in Africa might be expected. However, a reality check finds the African peoples (especially of the sub-Saharan region) living in abject poverty, oppressed by corrupt leaders who collaborate with various international agencies to loot their countries' resources. Because it can easily be directed to evil, it is imperative to reexamine how religion, when distorted, can be detrimental to the integral development in Africa. Using Nigeria as a case study, chapter 4 presupposes the importance of religion in the integral development of Africa and seeks to find ways for religion to be a positive force in the transformation of the society.[7] Chapter 5 zooms in on African Catholicism to examine its role and constraints in African development in the light of the *Africae Munus'* designation of Africa as the "spiritual 'lung' of humanity." In the face of the dangers arising from globalization, chapter 6 presents theology's emphasis on human dignity as a tool for the preservation of cultural identity.[8] Bringing themes of development from Catholic social teaching into dialogue with contemporary theories of development, this chapter critiques the philosophical anthropological backdrop of development as mere economic growth. It suggests an integral developmental structure that takes care of human integral scale of

7. Chapter 4 is an improved version of my article, "Religion and Sustainable Development in Africa: The Case of Nigeria," *International Journal of African Catholicism* 3 (2012) 1–25.

8. Chapter 6 improves on my article, "Theology, Culture and Sustainable Development in Africa," *Association of Catholic Universities and Higher Institutes of Africa and Madagascar Journal* 2 (2012) 1–30.

values[9] in order to provide schemes of recurrence for the provision of the human good and the development of the human person. It also examines the implication of this for integral development of Africa. Chapter 7 proposes appreciating Africa's cultural values as a step towards a more indigenous African Christianity. In this way, chapter 7 envisages the formation of an African Catholicism that will not be seen as foreign and so will be better able to mobilize the people towards social transformation. Chapter 8 emphasizes the need for interreligious dialogue to advance mutual coexistence, without which the goals of the second African Synod for reconciliation, justice, and peace will not be possible. Chapter 9 proposes an ecclesiological imperative in the light of Vatican Council II as an appropriate replacement to the prevalent clericalized ecclesiology of African Catholicism in order to meet the task entrusted to African Catholicism by *Africae Munus*. In the light of reconciliation, justice, and peace, the three themes of *Africae Munus*, chapter 10 offers some recommendations on religious value, reconciliation, and education.

9. The integral scale of values is Doran's description of the relationship between the hierarchical values worked out by Lonergan in *Method in Theology*: vital, social, cultural, personal, and religious. The scale of values describes the dynamics of values characteristic of social history in society as well as theology of history. The mutual relationship of these values brings about integrated development that makes possible the provision of the human good in society. Exclusion or distorted relationships between these values results in distorted development as seen when economic globalization dominates other forms of globalization. See Doran, *Theology and the Dialectics*; Lonergan, *Method in Theology*, ch. 2; Ormerod and Clifton, *Globalization and the Mission*.

1

Introducing *Africae Munus* and Hermeneutics of Culture

A precious treasure is to be found in the soul of Africa, where I perceive a "spiritual 'lung' for a humanity that appears to be in a crisis of faith and hope," on account of the extraordinary human and spiritual riches of its children, its variegated cultures, its soil and sub-soil of abundant resources.

—POPE BENEDICT XVI[1]

THE SECOND SPECIAL ASSEMBLY for Africa of the Synod of Bishops was held from October 4 to 25, 2009. *Africae Munus (AM)*,[2] its Post-Synodal Apostolic Exhortation, focuses on the challenges facing Africa as a continent and Christians in particular. This is reflected in the Synod's overarching themes: reconciliation, justice, and peace. According to the *AM*, the challenges facing Africa stem from past oppressions that have traumatized the people, giving rise to a crisis of identity (*AM*, sec. 9). Some of these challenges include ethnocentrism, political acrimony, and inadequate eco-

1. Benedict XVI, *Africae Munus*, sec. 13.
2. Ibid., cited hereafter as *AM*.

1

nomic growth made worse by corruption (*AM*, sec. 26). These difficulties have been aggravated by disruption of the social order arising from the thirst for revenge, a feeble judicial system, timorous governments unable to enforce the rule of law, gross irresponsibility, a culture of impunity, and selfish pursuit of personal agendas contrary to the common good. These challenges have been exacerbated in modernity, resulting in an anthropological crisis (*AM*, sec. 11). In spite of these challenges, Africa celebrates life, welcomes children as gifts from God, and is highly spiritual (*AM*, sec. 9). The *AM* thus praises Africa as the "spiritual lung" of a humanity now passing through enormous crises of faith and hope (sec. 13).

This description has been regarded as praise for Africa by some, but bogus and contradictory by others. Is Africa a "spiritual lung" for humanity, especially considering the material poverty of Africa, and in what sense? Of course, as "incurably religious" [3] people who prize spirituality and integrate it into moral, social, personal, and economic life, Africans—especially in a world dominated by an almost post-Christian secularism—are indeed, for many people, a "spiritual lung" for humanity. Accordingly, "the African continent is vitally important for humanity; it supplies 'oxygen' that vivifies, regenerates, and assures the balance, health, and wholeness of humanity."[4] However, in order to benefit from these riches, Africa must fashion and design a concept of personhood attuned with reality, which should be a fruit of profound spiritual renewal (*AM*, sec. 11).

The inseparability of reconciliation, justice, and peace is indicative of their importance to the formation of an African concept of personhood that can solve the African crisis of identity mired in a history of subjugation and oppression. Peace is obtained through reconciliation and justice. Justice comes through reconciliation. Love of truth is the guide to bring about genuine truth through reconciliation, justice, and peace (*AM*, sec. 18). Without

3. Parrinder, *African Traditional Religion*, 27–28.
4. Soédé, "Enduring Scourge of Poverty," 183.

reconciliation, politics of acrimony reigns and a spirit of revenge perpetrates the cycle of violence.

Reconciliation obtained through justice and a willingness to forgive acknowledged wrongs is not only important, but is urgently necessary in light of Africa's past history of injustice, violence, and war. Healing is achieved in the spirit of forgiveness when reconciliation is obtained through justice (*AM*, sec. 18). For instance, Zimbabwe (formerly Rhodesia) suffered terribly during the minority rule that excluded the black majority and appropriated their lands.[5] According to David Kaulem, "The colonial humiliation of black people was very deep. There was clearly a need for many of the whites in Zimbabwe to shake off the ghetto mentality. They needed to begin seriously to develop a culture of human solidarity with fellow blacks in the country and abroad."[6]

However, President Robert Mugabe's Zimbabwe African National Union Patriotic Front's (ZANU-PF) later approach of seizing the lands of white farmers and reallocating it to cronies with little or no knowledge of industrial farming has not only resulted in unemployment, but has also led to the collapse of the Zimbabwean economy. According to *The Economist*'s Special Report on Africa: "Zimbabwe's economy has collapsed, along with its currency. Shops use dollar bills. In the absence of American coins, they give out bags of peanuts instead of change. The country's GDP is pretty much the same as it was three decades ago, despite extraordinary mineral wealth. The ground is full of bauxite, coal, diamonds, gold, platinum and nickel. Mining is still going on, but is of little benefit to ordinary people. Diamond mines are run by security forces to prop up the party of Robert Mugabe."[7] Instead of reconciliation, justice, and peace, Mugabe's government, filled as it

---

5. In addition to the land-grabbing, one could also recall the "perils of sex" in colonial Zimbabwe, a racist and gender differentiation policy that clamped many African males lured into sex with white women into jail and some were even killed (Pape, "Black and White," 289–306).

6. Kaulem, "Those of Us Who Stayed at Home," 150.

7. August, "Emerging Africa," 15.

is with bitterness, hate, and unforgivingness, divides Zimbabweans along religious, racist, and political lines.

The case is reversed in South Africa, where the Truth and Reconciliation Commission (TRC) was "established by the new South African government in 1995 to help heal the country and bring about a reconciliation of its people by uncovering the truth about human rights violations during the period of apartheid."[8] The TRC, characterized by openness and transparency, gradually healed the pains of South Africa's apartheid regime and reconciled the country's diverse races. According to scholars Emmanuel Katongole and Chris Rice, "the South African Truth and Reconciliation Commission (TRC) has drawn enormous attention, and people around the world are seeking to replicate it. But the unique gift of the TRC is not that it unveiled the truth about historic injustices, but that it did so within an atmosphere of mercy and forgiveness."[9] Such healing brought about a better society where the rule of law prevails rather than a society where strong men reign.

The *AM* outlines a path towards reconciliation, justice, and peace that includes: healing of memories (*AM*, sec. 21), care for the human person through authentic conversion (*AM*, sec. 20), and participation in the sacrament of reconciliation aimed at genuine conversion through personal experience of the truth of penance and forgiveness (*AM*, sec. 32). Others are a spirituality of communion (*AM*, sec. 34, 35) aided by the inculturation of the gospel (*AM*, sec. 36) and the evangelization of culture (*AM*, sec. 33, 37) in the light of the sacraments (*AM*, sec. 33), the Eucharist and the Word (*AM*, sec. 40, 41), and justice through prosecution of felons (*AM*, sec. 21). In order to further advance reconciliation, measures ought to be taken to promote the process of harmonious living (*AM*, sec. 20, 23). For this reason, the *AM* preaches respecting marriage and family life (*AM*, sec. 42–54), enhancing the dignity

---

8. *Encyclopædia Britannica Online*, s.v. "Truth and Reconciliation Commission, South Africa (TRC)," http://www.britannica.com/EBchecked/topic/607421/Truth-and-Reconciliation-Commission-South-Africa.

9. Katongole and Rice, *Reconciling All Things*, loc. 856.

of women (*AM*, sec. 55–59), creating opportunities for youths to actualize themselves (*AM*, sec. 60–64), and protecting, nurturing, and caring for children (*AM*, sec. 65–68). Interfaith dialogue with particular emphasis on dialogue with African traditional religion and Islam is an equally necessary measure towards achieving harmonious living (*AM*, sec. 92–93).

The search for reconciliation, justice, and peace is manifested in the theological and social responsibility of the church as well as in her public relevance in Africa (*AM*, sec. 22). The *AM* explains that balancing the tension between engagement with politics, which is not the immediate responsibility of the gospel, and avoiding political engagement as a theological escape from social responsibility makes this task difficult (*AM*, sec. 23). It is clear that in order to build a country of peace, a just social order is necessary. In Africa, it is the responsibility of the church to contribute to building a just social order through the formation of the conscience of the people. The aim here is to contribute to the good, to mutual coexistence, to honesty and transparency, and to the formation of personal self-identity courageous enough to actively participate in the political process for equality and the human good. Here education in civic responsibility is very important. A just social order will be created in Africa not through a political revolution, but through revolution of a different kind—a "revolution of love" (*AM*, sec. 26). Thus, the *AM* recommends that justice be achieved first by living in accordance with Christ's justice, and second by creating a just order "in the spirit of the Beatitudes" (*AM*, sec. 27) through a preferential option for the poor and the marginalized. The reason for this is not far-fetched. The endemic corruption in Africa has led to the dispossession of many by the few who appropriate the continent's resources. Here specifically, the church must speak out against the selfishness and greed of bureaucrats whose corruption perpetuates Africa's cyclic poverty despite its abundant natural resources. The *AM* asserts:

> God has given Africa important natural resources. Given the chronic poverty of its people, who suffer the effects of exploitation and embezzlement of funds both locally

5

and abroad, the opulence of certain groups shocks the human conscience. Organized for the creation of wealth in their homelands, and not infrequently with the complicity of those in power in Africa, these groups too often ensure their own prosperity at the expense of the well-being of the local population. Acting in concert with all other components of civil society, the church must speak out against the unjust order that prevents the peoples of Africa from consolidating their economies and "from developing according to their cultural characteristics."[10]

The *AM* recommends promoting the common good by guiding African leaders away from selfishness and self-aggrandizement and by educating them in the connection between rights and duties. In addition to preaching the Beatitudes, the church should make the voice of Christ heard by serving as the sentinel (*AM*, sec. 30), being the voice of the voiceless, and making the voices of the marginalized and the poor heard. To be vocal against social injustice "by rejecting people's dehumanization and every compromise prompted by fear of suffering or martyrdom" (*AM*, sec. 30) pits the church against those states which, in the pursuit of self-interest, oppresses or deceives the people, mortgaging their future and that of their children. Although the *AM* continuously emphasizes that the role of the church is not political, making the poor's voices heard will surely be construed by the political class as a challenge to constituted authority. The church could be accused of instigating the people against the state, but that is the role the church must play in the public sphere. The church does not fulfill this role by engaging in partisan politics, nor by neutrally sitting on the fence. The church is called to play an active role of informing the laity of their rights. The church as sentinel (*AM*, sec. 30); that is, the church's prophetic role can put it at risk of persecution in a continent where the pursuit of personal interest at the expense of the public good is rife.

Furthermore, the church is called upon to promote good governance in collaboration with other civil societies, without

10. *Africae Munus*, sec. 79.

which integral development will not be possible (*AM*, sec. 81–83). Interestingly, the *Africae Munus* moves from good governance to migrants (*AM*, sec. 84). Bad governance in Africa has precipitated massive migration of African peoples in search of the basic necessities of life outside their homeland, though God has abundantly blessed their continent with numerous natural and human resources. Often, Africans make up the bulk of the people who try to cross the desert into Europe in search of greener pastures for themselves and for their children. The condition of African migrants is rightly painted by the *AM* as suffering the abuses of "intolerance, xenophobia and racism" (*AM*, sec. 84), of low-paying jobs, and numerous other humiliations.

The *AM* also addresses the various members of the church by urging the faithful to work towards integral development by contributing to the common good. Bishops are advised to live exemplary lives and to provide leadership by remaining committed to Christ and avoiding such illusory distractions as nationalism and the idol of African culture. Priests are urged to be good pastors, shepherding the people entrusted to them by witnessing to life and the good news and by promoting integral development through grassroots civic education.

The role of the laity is spelled out in the *AM*'s idea of Christian professional life: witnessing to the gospel, contributing to the common good, and making a preferential option for the poor, for "in a word, it means bearing witness to Christ in the world by showing, through your example, that work can be a very positive setting for personal development and not primarily a means of making profit" (*AM*, sec. 130). The laity is also urged to participate in the various areas of human life, including politics (*AM* 131). Christians should, therefore, be involved in promoting good governance by being actively involved in public life (*AM*, sec. 81).

The task set for African Catholicism by *Africae Munus* is to balance engagement in the public sphere with spirituality aimed at genuine conversion and proper witnessing to the good news. Effectiveness in the discharge of this role depends on African Catholicism's ability to effect attitudinal change first in African

Catholics, and then to the broader societies of Africa. This conversion needs to spark a deep turnaround that can transform Africa's social, political, economic, technological, bureaucratic, and religious structure, which has been undergoing short- and long-term cycles of decay and identity crisis precipitated by a dysfunctional social history. The social transformation envisaged must be revolutionary, not political but moral—a revolution of love as described by *Africae Munus*. In order to be equipped for this task, African Catholicism needs to change its highly clericalized structure, its eschatologically-based theology, its one-dimensional *fuga mundi* spirituality, and its sexist morality in order to embrace the Vatican II idea of the church as "the people of God" committed to active engagement for the common good.[11]

Bernard Lonergan's philosophical and theological anthropology deals with social transformation from the perspective of the human good and the promotion of the common good in order to roll back the wheel of decline, especially the longer cycle of decline caused by general bias.[12] Therefore, I will approach African Catholicism's task using Lonergan's philosophical and theological construct applied to the concrete dynamics of African Catholicism in light of *Africae Munus*. The use of Lonergan's hermeneutical tools is informed by openness to ideas that promote human dignity, that foster schemes for the provision of the human good, and that recognizes every human being as intrinsically rational, irrespective of accidental differences.

One of the most significant contributions of Bernard Lonergan's philosophy and theology is his creative formulation of the

11. Paul VI, *Lumen Gentium*, sec. 9–17.

12. For Lonergan, the human good is the good human beings pursue. While not easily definable, its various components include "skills, feelings, values, beliefs, cooperation, progress, and decline" (Lonergan, *Method in Theology*, 27). The common good could be said to be recognition of the good and a committed resolve to pursue it for the wellbeing of everybody in society. There cannot be a common good without the human good. The human good is recurrently provided in society that has "good of order," that is, effective and efficient functioning of good social relations and practical intelligence (Lonergan, "Insight Revisited," 263–78).

invariant dynamic structure of human knowing. According to this structure, every person experiences, understands, judges, and decides. Even in the face of societal decay, there is possibility for healing, for restoration, and for social progress. As I have emphasized elsewhere:

> Lonergan's philosophical anthropology provides a general hermeneutic for understanding social development, breakdown and transformation . . . by being attentive to their experiences, by understanding intelligently, by judging reasonably and by deliberating responsibly, there is an "ever increasing progress." This is true of the subject and of the community. But decline cannot be underestimated, for human beings can be affected by bias, and therein the flight from understanding takes the place of genuine inquiry.[13]

In other words, Lonergan's philosophy and theology are requisite hermeneutical tools for addressing the tasks expected of African Catholicism by *Africae Munus*. My use of Lonergan is limited to his notion of the human good and to his clear distinction of the scale of values into vital, social, cultural, personal, and religious values. According to Lonergan:

> Not only do feelings respond to values, they do so in accord with some scale of preference. So we may distinguish vital, social, cultural, personal, and religious values in an ascending order. Vital values, such as health and strength, grace and vigor, normally are preferred to avoiding the work, privations, pains involved in acquiring, maintaining, and restoring them. Social values, such as the good of order which conditions the vital values of the whole community, have to be preferred to the vital values of individual members of the community. Cultural values do not exist without the underpinning of vital and social values, but nonetheless they rank together. Not on bread alone doth man live.

---

13. Ogbonnaya, *Lonergan, Social Transformation*, xx.

> Over and above mere living and operating, men have to find a meaning and value in their living and operating. It is the function of culture to discover, express, validate, criticize, correct, develop, and improve such meaning and value. Personal value is the person in his self-transcendence, as loving and being loved, as originator of values in himself and in his milieu, as an inspiration and invitation to others to do likewise. Religious values, finally, are at the heart of the meaning and value of man's living and man's world.[14]

Robert Doran, the editor of Lonergan's works, appropriates this scale of values by relating them from above downwards and from below upwards in what he calls the integral scale of values. The integral scale of values is the harmonious, complementary interdependence of the scale of values in a social order for individual, social, and religious transformation. In their *Globalization and the Mission of the Church*, Neil Ormerod and Shane Clifton appropriate Doran's work on the integral scale of values and relate it to the mission of the church. The church, they argue, exists not only to spread the good news but also to promote the functional efficiency of the scale of values aimed at advancing progress and development, for "inasmuch as the Church is concerned with working for the kingdom, it will be concerned with the problem of evil in all its manifestations. While its primary responsibility lies at the religious dimension of the scale of values, inevitably it is drawn into all other dimensions of the scale as well."[15] My choice of the scale of values in my analysis of *Africae Munus* is informed by my consideration of the Second African Synod's dedication to the public role of the Catholic church to integral development of Africa through promotion of good governance, through healing wounds of the historical past still traumatizing the African psyche (an anthropological crisis), and mutual coexistence in Africa.

Lonergan's hermeneutic tool is relevant here, especially his distinction of the scale of values, because if poverty is to be made

---

14. Lonergan, *Method in Theology*, 31–32.

15. Ormerod and Clifton, *Globalization and the Mission*, loc. 1129–36.

history as the international community envisions, vital values of basic infrastructures of life—food, clothing, and housing—have to be made readily available. This will be possible through a good social order respectful of rights and duties and in which members of society responsibly contribute to the optimum development of all. In such a structure—which we will call good of order—technology, economy, and polity harmoniously promote the common good. The vital values are recurrently provided and everybody is maximally happy. But of course, such social order as we envision for the constant provision of vital values depends on the constitutive meaning of such a society. It depends on society's cultural values, those symbols, stories, images, rites, rituals, and other practices through which humans express their social nature. Vital and social values are not free-standing; they need the backing of cultural values that give meaning to why and how of their function. Of course, human capacity for freedom, authenticity, and dignity crystallizes cultural values, which becomes the common meaning of a people under which social and vital values and institutions of society are able to provide for the human good. If these are true of Africa, the religious value of love of God evidently holds in Africa, a continent reputed as being "incurably religious."

Lonergan deals very well with progress, decline, and restoration, with the healing of anthropological crisis in history, and with the realities of pluralism, mutual coexistence, and the interrelationship of heterogeneous people. As will become clear, this book makes no attempt to force European or North American categories into an African theological construct. On the contrary, my use of Lonergan is as a hermeneutical tool to interpret the common meaning underlying African life and societies in an integral manner, especially in light of continuities and change in these societies in the context of modernity. Aylward Shorter, the socio-cultural anthropologist whose research has centered in Africa, highlights the importance of the integral scale of values. Indeed, Shorter warns against development agencies' neglect of Africa's cultural, personal, and religious values reiterates the importance of the integral scale of values:

> Development programmes have all too often ignored
> socio-cultural factors at their peril, and social upheavals
> have resulted which have brought lasting damage and
> unhappiness. National identity is far from being unrelat-
> ed to national efficiency or national solvency. This is the
> reason why political leaders work hard to promote socio-
> cultural integration and to foster a pride in indigenous
> culture which will motivate the citizens and stimulate
> co-operation with people of other traditions.[16]

Shorter's position emphasizes the interdependence of the scale of values so carefully delineated by Lonergan and appropriated by Doran as the integral scale of values. Our use of this category will be limited specifically to an African context in order to explain factors that help the attainment of integral development, as well as factors that distort the dialectic of community, giving rise to decline.

Hermeneutics of Culture

Certain approaches to the study of culture can at times give rise to the denigration of cultures other than one's own as inferior. Consequently, these approaches sometimes lead to negative attitudes towards others who, because they are different, may be regarded as inferior and uncivilized. Clifford Geertz, one of the most influential anthropologists of our time, identifies and warns against three such approaches. First, there is an approach that reifies culture, seeing it as perfect and completely whole in itself, "a self-contained 'superorganic' reality with forces and purposes of its own."[17] This approach identifies one culture as universal, the culture for all human beings. The second approach—closely related to the first—is a reductionist approach that sees culture as specified pattern of behavior identifiable in some community. From this viewpoint, cultures "consist in the brute pattern of behavioral events we observe

16. Shorter, *Toward a Theology of Inculturation*, 242–43.
17. Geertz, *Interpretation of Cultures*, 11.

in fact to occur in some identifiable community or other."[18] According to this viewpoint, not all human beings could be said to have a culture in terms of how they construe meaning and organize their lives. Third, a reactionary approach to both views is the cognitivist approach that sees culture as being in human minds and hearts. According to this school of thought, "a society's culture consists of whatever it is one has to know or believe in order to operate in a manner acceptable to its members."[19] This viewpoint regards a particular culture as classical and therefore outlines a long list of acceptable behaviors and beliefs that make one cultured. These approaches identify one culture, the European culture, as the classical culture and expects other cultures to become like them. All things considered, these three approaches focus on a single view of culture to their detriment, ignoring other important aspects.

A more comprehensive approach, Geertz argues, views culture in terms of meaning that guides people's lives either as individuals or as members of a social group. Actually, Geertz contends that without culture, human beings would be "unworkable monstrosities, with few useful instincts, few recognizable sentiments, and no intellect,"[20] adding that "culture is public because meaning is."[21] Thus, "understanding a people's culture exposes their normalness without reducing their particularity."[22] In other words, every society has its own culture and values by which they make sense of their lives and their environment. Geertz's position marks a shift away from the classicist notion of culture that approves only one culture for human beings irrespective of differences in language, lineage, and multiplicity of legal cultures. Christopher Dawson shares this understanding of culture, which he describes as "a common way of life—a particular adjustment of man to his natural surroundings and his economic needs."[23] According to

18. Ibid.

19. Ibid.

20. Geertz, "The Impact of the Concept of Culture on the Concept of Man," Cohen, ed., *Man in Adaptation: The Cultural Present*, 29.

21. Ibid., *Interpretation of Cultures*, 12.

22. Ibid., 14.

23. Dawson, *Age of the Gods*, xiii.

Dawson, the distinguishing aspect of human culture is human rationality, with which individuals overcome the blind fate of nature and environment:

> The formation of a culture is due to the interaction of all these factors: It is a fourfold community—for it involves in varying degrees a community of work and a community of thought as well as a community of place and a community of blood. Any attempt to explain social development in terms of one of these to the exclusion of the rest leads to the error of racial or geographical or economic determinism or to no less false theories of abstract intellectual progress.[24]

"In the formation of any culture," Dawson goes on to elaborate, "human activity and spontaneous cooperation with Nature take a leading part."[25] This is true of all cultures, of the different ways human beings fashion a way of life by engaging in varying social activities in adapting to their environments.

Lonergan shares Dawson's views. Culture, he reminds us, is the common meaning of a human community; that is "the meaning we find in our present way of life, the value we place upon it, or, again, the things we find meaningless, stupid, wicked, horrid, atrocious, disastrous."[26] Elsewhere, Lonergan adds, "and it is this common meaning that is the form and act that finds expression in family and polity, in the legal and economic system, in customary morals and educational arrangements, in language and literature, art and religion, philosophy, science, and the writing of history."[27]

Common meaning distinguishes each human community, narrates its history, and showcases their actions and their ways of conducting and ordering lives in their societies. Different communities may resemble one another in their common meaning, but there are also bound to be differences conditioned by their

---

24. Ibid., xiv.

25. Ibid., xv.

26. Lonergan, "Belief: Today's Issue," 91.

27. Ibid., "Natural Right and Historical Mindedness," 170–71.

various geographical and environmental factors and circumstances.[28] Thus, there are varieties of cultures just as there are varieties of peoples, and each culture selects what to emphasize and what not to emphasize. Each, from the point of view of another, ignores fundamentals and exploits irrelevances. Some cultures hardly recognize monetary values, while for others currency is at the heart of social organization. Technology appears to be ignored in some cultural contexts, while in others its complexity, while easing life, can make it all the more complicated. One culture might build an enormous superstructure upon adolescence, one upon death, one upon afterlife. Different ways of understanding adulthood can color different attitudes towards adolescence, placing emphasis on the inevitable psychological and physiological unrest characteristic of the period. According to the famous anthropologist Ruth Benedict, in Australia, adulthood means participation in an exclusively male cult. In central North America, adulthood means warfare. Among the Nandi of the lake region of East Africa, puberty rites mark adulthood by stressing distinct gender roles.[29]

Inasmuch as theories of culture have contributed to hermeneutics and literary criticism, Lonergan's contribution to the hermeneutics of culture particularly lies in his distinctions between two horizons of culture: classicist and contemporary notions of culture versus the transition from classicist to empirical notions of culture. Lonergan articulates the differences between these notions of culture in several of his writings. Specifically, in his 1968 essay, "Belief: Today's Issue," Lonergan classifies classicist culture as conceptualist, objectivist, and universally normative. On the contrary, contemporary culture is empirical, dynamic, historically-minded, and aware of the subject and subjectivity, yet emphasizes collective responsibility.[30] Classicist culture belongs to the approaches Geertz criticizes for treating a single aspect of culture as the totality, leaving behind other understandings. Lonergan asserts:

28. Ibid., "Post-Hegelian Philosophy of Religion," 212.
29. Benedict, *Patterns of Culture*, 21–44.
30. Meyer, "Introduction," 10.

Classicist culture contrasted itself with barbarism. It was culture with a capital "C." Others might participate in it to a greater or lesser extent and, in the measure they did so, they ceased to be barbarians. In other words, culture was conceived normatively. It was a matter of good manners and good taste, of grace and style, of virtue and character, of models and ideals, of eternal verities and inviolable laws. But the modern notion of culture was not normative, but empirical. Culture is a general notion. It denotes something found in every people, for in every people there is some apprehension of meaning and value in their way of life. So it is that modern culture is the culture that knows other cultures, that relates them to one another genetically, that knows all of them to be man-made. Far more open than classicist culture, far better informed, far more discerning, it lacks the convictions of its predecessor, its clear-cut norms, its elemental strength.[31]

The rapid change accompanying the transition from the classicist to empirical notion of culture, which has been made more real by modernity, has engendered varieties of crises, frustrations, disillusionment, disorientation, and unbelief both within and outside the church. As will be discussed in the next chapter, African Catholicism still grapples with the effects of modernity on African cultural values. The exaggerated classicist notion of culture as universal for humanity accounts for the mistakes of early Christian missionaries in Africa. As such, it continues to affect the African idea and structure of church as well as the church's relationship to African cultural values. The consequence, as we will see in chapter 7, is persistent syncretism and continued perception of Christianity as foreign by a good number of people in Africa. Lonergan recommends that the church make the gradual transition from classicist to empirical notions of culture by taking note of the social order and diversity of cultural contexts within which people accept the good news and become disciples of Christ. Lonergan notes that "the Church, if it is to operate in the world, has

31. Lonergan, "Belief: Today's Issue," 92.

to operate on the basis of the social order and cultural achievements of each time and place, that consequently its operation has to change with changes in its social and cultural context, that at present we have the task of disengagement from classicist thought-forms and viewpoints, and, simultaneously, of a new involvement in modern culture."[32]

This is equally the task of African Catholicism as it struggles to achieve the aims of the Second African Synod: reconciliation, justice, and peace. The interpretative tools for this task must be aware of and be ready to gradually shift from classicist to empirical notions of culture. It is particularly important to emphasize this because African Catholicism must be ready to integrate the culture of the people into the work of evangelization. In fact, its relevance and ability to heal the anthropological crisis Africans suffer depends on it. The root of Africa's problems are cultural; therefore to effect change, radical cultural action is imperative. Classicist notions of culture will not be able to accomplish this task. Only an empirical notion of culture, respectful of diverse cultural forms and of their validity for appropriating and communicating the Christian faith, can further the work of African Catholicism as envisioned by *Africae Munus*.

As Elochukwu Uzukwu argues in *The Listening Church*, "the retrieval and modernization of our African cultural matrix is the necessary route toward healing the political, economic, social, and religious misery of Africa."[33] In other words, African ecclesiology must advance the retrieval of Africa's cultural values. Uzukwu's position is borne from a careful analysis of the African condition and his quest for answers through a theology that will aid social transformation in Africa. Uzukwu faced the brute misery of life in Africa, where wars prevent people from farming their land and leave many unable to feed themselves, where diseases such as malaria and the plague of AIDS invade African towns and villages, and where bad governments that neglect the majority of the

32. Ibid., 98.
33. Uzukwu, *Listening Church*, 5.

African people and create so many more problems further exacerbate the African condition.

African contextual theology responds to African crisis by trying to propose viable models for the reconstruction of African societies. This is true of African theology of liberation, which has raised its voice since the 1980s to denounce the misery of the African peoples and identify its root causes. This theology, while blaming African problems on past colonial experience, proposes a fundamental element of change and development of African history and traditions. Uzukwu notes: "The Church [African Catholicism], aided by the reflection of her theologians, will become a more credible agent of change when the Christian life emerges from the realities of the African context and Christian theology responds to questions posed by the context and is nourished by local resources."[34] In the religious realm, Africans are setting aside the one-dimensional viewpoints of colonialism and missionaries and opting for an integral worldview that upholds a close relationship between human beings and ultimate reality originally embedded in their cultures. This takes the form of a reaffirmation of African cultural values. And so African theology of inculturation considers the totality of African culture, ancient and modern, as the context of theology. Inculturation theology is first and foremost a reaffirmation of African culture and identity, denied by Western colonialism and Christian missionary evangelism. Second, it acknowledges that the message of Jesus Christ, which must be carried and communicated culturally, has come to dwell among us. Third, it contends that the Jesus living among us is the church; fourth, that the church responds to this message through her liturgy, spirituality, discipline, ethics, and theology. African theology of inculturation succeeds in its proposed reconstruction of African societies by integrating cultural values to the rest of the scale of values.

Lonergan's distinction of the scale of values in *Method in Theology* into vital, social, cultural, personal, and religious values clarifies cultural values within the context of feeling as having to

34. Ibid., 3.

do with the meaning and values upon which human life operates. As Lonergan says, "Cultural values do not exist without the underpinning of vital and social values, but nonetheless they rank higher. Not on bread alone doth man live. Over and above mere living and operating, men have to find a meaning and value in their living and operating. It is the function of culture to discover, express, validate, criticize, correct, develop, improve such meaning and value."[35] In the dynamic structure of human knowing, cultural value is on the level of judgment directing humankind's search for meaning. In the integral scale of values developed by Robert Doran, through which he expounds Lonergan's scale of values, the analogical relationships that obtain among the three dialectical processes—dialectic of the subject, dialectic of culture, and dialectic of community—draw from personal, cultural, and social values.[36] Concretely authentic human subjects incarnate and achieve the common meaning of their community. Cultural values order the relationship of various groups in the community towards the provision of the human good for the common benefit of the community. Harmony in human society presupposes a cordial social order that allows everybody participate and contribute equitably in the production and distribution of goods and services according to each person's capability. This will be made possible by a culture that is critical enough to guide the human conscience toward the common good.

And so Lonergan's theory of culture—particularly the scale of values and Doran's appropriation of that scale in emphasizing an integral scale of values as a theory of history accounting for progress, decline, and redemption—is the analytic tool of culture for this book. The adequacy of this theory as a social analytic tool lies in its advancement of modern notions of culture that are generally respectful of cultural diversity, subjects and subjectivity, and the variety of contexts within which the Christian faith is appropriated, expressed, and communicated. This not only promotes the church's holistic mission to care for the poor, influence the social

35. Lonergan, *Method in Theology*, 32.

36. Doran, *What Is Systematic Theology?* 172.

order, challenge cultural values, enhance personal integrity, and further the establishment of authentic religion, but is also comprehensive in scope, dynamic in character, integrative of the dynamics of history, and makes effective the mutual self-mediation of church to various African cultural matrices. This is the method favored most by African theologians, as Elochukwu Uzukwu avers:

> African theologians today insist on the *historical or changing patterns of African cultures and civilizations* and distance themselves from ethnological accounts (emanating from colonial ideology) that viewed African cultures in essentialist or static terms. They also distance themselves from romantic and folkloric narratives of African cultures and traditions. A critical socio-historical approach to African cultures embodies the *memory of our cultural weakness*—a weakness manifest in a rudimentary technological culture . . . A critical approach enables a creative engagement with the project of cultural globalization facilitated by the incredible progress in information technology. Vigilant memory envisages a *living cultural tradition* which responds to contemporary needs, and a retrieving of dimensions of our heritage that carry the gain for *reinventing the African society.*[37]

---

37. Uzukwu, *God, Spirit, and Human Wholeness*, 8, emphasis mine.

2

Continuity and Change
in African Traditional Values

Like the rest of the world, Africa is experiencing a culture shock which
strikes at the age-old foundations of social life, and sometimes makes it
hard to come to terms with modernity.

—POPE BENEDICT XVI[1]

THE QUESTION OF CONTINUITY and change, especially in terms of
the impact of modernity on various peoples and cultures, remains
an ongoing conversation among social scientists and scholars of
other disciplines. In certain African countries, this question is
much more germane in view of the four centuries of slave trade
that robbed Africans of their human resources and dignity. Second,
decades of colonialism and Eurocentric missionary activities, as
well as Islamic conquests, further diminished their cultural values.
Third, ongoing decolonization has made Africa an epicenter of
raw materials used for the development of other continents, but
sadly, not at home. As articulated in *Africae Munus*, "Like the rest
of the world, Africa is experiencing a culture shock which strikes

1. *Africae Munus*, sec. 11.

at the age-old foundations of social life, and sometimes makes it hard to come to terms with modernity."[2]

One of the challenges facing Africans in the process of nation-building is the integration of the cultural values that give meaning to their lives. The traditional African sense of the sacred, fraternity and community, hospitality and compassion, is changing fast. This chapter, drawing on African cultural values and the challenges of continuity and change, looks into the political, social, and cultural effects of modernity on the African concept of statehood.

African Cultural Values

In spite of differences in culture and history of various African peoples, African cultural values are those aspects of human goodness Africans think promote the common good of the community. They include in the words of Oliver Onwubiko: "(i) Sense of community life; (ii) Sense of good human relations; (iii) Sense of the sacredness of life; (iv) Sense of hospitality; (v) Sense of the sacred and of religion; (vi) Sense of time; (vii) Sense of respect for authority and the elders; (viii) Sense of language and proverbs."[3] These cultural values form and guide the African attitude toward themselves as people, toward one another as members of a community, and toward others as visitors and residents in their communities. They form the backdrop of social and cultural life as well as the provisions of the basic necessities of life.

Because Africans are largely communitarian, they tend to promote the common good and adhere to the moral principles of truth and honesty, as well as to express a preference for being over having and for life over acquisitions and wealth. Because Africans

2. Ibid.

3. Onwubiko, *African Thought, Religion and Culture*, 13. African scholars like Idowu, *African Traditional Religion* (1973); Mbiti, *African Religions and Philosophy* (1969); Sofola, *African culture and the African personality* (1973); Davidson, *The African Genius* (1969), etc., have written extensively on these cultural values. Our concern will be with how they fashion African identity and personality.

are widely religious, the fear of God entrenches respect and makes these cultural values binding on every member of the community. African modes of production and distribution of wealth favors family life, especially extended nuclear family structures that make it imperative to care not only for the members of one's own family, but also to provide for one's blood relations and the common good of the community. These cultural values explain the social structure and provide a framework for the realization of the dreams and aspirations, goals and potential of members of the community, as well as assuring the survival of the community through the contribution of each person to collective progress and development.

African cultural values answer the metaphysical problem of the person and the community by emphasizing the person in the community. The person exists because the community exists; the community exists because human beings live together in it. The person existing isolated from the community atomically becomes an anomaly in the African societal structure. Embedded in the communitarian slant of African cultural values is a notion of community that socio-politically defines nationhood in terms of common interests, goals, and values. As Kwame Gyekye observes:

> The community alone constitutes the context, the social or cultural space, in which the actualization of the possibilities of the individual person can take place, providing the individual person the opportunity to express his/her individuality, to acquire and develop his/her personality and to fully become the kind of person he/she wants to be, i.e., to attain the status, goals, expectations to be, etc. The system of values which the person inherits as he/she enters into the cultural community and the range of goals in life from which he/she can choose—these are not anterior to a cultural structure but a function of the structure itself: they are therefore posterior to—indeed the products of the culture, i.e., the community.[4]

Gyekye's observation calls to mind the Igbo proverb that one tree does not make a forest. One person does not constitute

4. Gyekye, "Person and Community," 301.

a community; one's personhood derives from one's cultural community, from the interdependence arising from natural human sociality and intersubjectivity. Such community makes it possible for an individual person to realize his or her potential by providing not only the resources, but also the whole process of acculturation to inculcate cultural norms and values through various processes of education in the ways of community life. The members of the Commission for Africa observed this connection between the individual and community and describe culture as having to do with "how social values are transmitted and individuals are made part of a society."[5]

Thus, African cultural values promote the common good. Morally, the culture extols hard work, honors valor, and abhors ill-gotten wealth. It emphasizes honesty, righteousness, and justice. Crimes against humanity and spilling blood in any form are taboo and believed to be capable of drawing divine wrath. Therefore, the community ostracizes people who do not adhere to the communal sense of the sacred. Justice is meted out equally, no matter whose ox is gored. This is true both of communities with a centralized system of government and those without such structures, like the "stateless" communities.

These cultural values are at the hub of African identity.[6] They fashion the patterns of African lives: socio-political, moral and religious, economic and cultural, legal and judicial. They provide the lens through which we look at reality, our motivations and actions, our criteria of judgment and standard of evaluation, our social stratification, our medium of communication, our means of production and distribution.[7] They promote societal progress and

5. Commission for Africa, *Our Common Interest*, 28.

6. For example, J. M. Nyasani argues that "the existence of African identity is not in doubt" in view of the following values common to Africans even those in the diaspora—the African Americans: "hospitality, friendliness, the consensus and common framework-seeking principle, *ubuntu*, and the emphasis on community rather than on the individual" (Nyasani, *African Psyche*, 197–98).

7. I acknowledge the influence of Mazrui's categorization of the seven areas of cultural impact in my summary of African culture above. See Mazrui, *African Condition*, 47–48.

transformation by promoting each person's contribution to the common good of the community.

African cultural values enabled Africa to build and maintain such centrally organized states as the great empires of ancient Ghana, Kanem-Bornu, Mali, and Songhai; the great cities of the Western Sudan, Audagost, Gao, and Timbuktu; and long-distance indigenous trading networks in salt and gold promoting political and economic development dating as far back as the first millennium AD.[8] In addition, these values also gave rise to communities without such political structures; that is, "stateless" peoples like the Igbo of southeast Nigeria, the Tallensi of northern Ghana, the Tiv of Nigeria, and the Dinka peoples of Upper Nile. These empires and stateless communities, Basil Davidson notes, "were manifestly the product of early Iron Age growth. Having opened their way to cultivation, stock-raising, and mining, Africans had spread across the vast and thinly peopled lands of the interior, multiplied in numbers, evolved new ways of mastering nature, and embarked upon barter-trade with their neighbors and even with foreign countries. Already their situation was in one respect crucially different from that of their Stone Age forebears."[9]

What this means is that during the period of the Iron Age transformation, the dynamics of African civilization continued unabated in very different conditions in various parts of Africa through mutual interactions and external influences brought about by trade, conquests, and cultural affinities. All this was happening at a time corresponding to Europe's Middle Ages and Renaissance, thus displaying great potential in what Basil Davidson calls "the Mature Iron Age in Africa" between about AD 1000 and 1600.[10] These transformations brought about new techniques of farming (such as extending irrigation systems and soil conservation), mining (in gold, copper, tin, etc.), trading, health care (through herbal cures), and state formation.[11]

8. Davidson, *Africa in History*, 84.

9. Ibid.

10. Ibid., 107.

11. Ibid., 114.

"No Longer at Ease"

The major question now is how well these African cultures have survived the various agents of change through the continent over the centuries. Are African cultures resilient enough to retain their basic fabric while accommodating changes in modernity? Or is the social structure and the culture destroyed by these agents of social transformation such that we cannot really be talking of African cultural values in the traditional sense of the term? Whichever school of thought one aligns oneself with in this discussion, we can say that things are "no longer at ease"[12] in Africa. Things have changed for good in some areas and for bad in others. Some aspects of these cultural values are problematic in themselves and will pose serious problems in the march to modern nationhood and sustainable development. An instance of this is found in the unresolved issue of the person in the community and the uniqueness of each individual as a person. To what extent might a public official whose societal structure is communitarian balance the pull of extended family and the protection of the common good? If the indigenous African religious cultural values promote the human good by emphasizing the good of members of the community, do the modern cultural values arising from the three dominant religions in Africa—traditional religion, Christianity, and Islam—promote sustainable development or retard Africa's march to integral development? What is the African condition today?

The African Condition

More than thirty years ago, Ali A. Mazrui discussed what he calls the six paradoxes of Africa: the paradox of habitation, of humiliation, of acculturation, of fragmentation, of retardation, and the

---

12. Achebe's *No Longer At Ease* (1960), considered a sequel to Achebe's *Things Fall Apart* (1958), tells the story of the dynamics of social change in Africa, especially rural urban migration and the challenge of moral integrity in a corrupt society. This novel, along with Achebe's *Arrow of God* (1964), forms a trilogy on African culture. See Achebe, *African Trilogy*.

paradox of location.[13] Most of the paradoxes Mazrui referred to still exist in Africa. The paradox of habitation exists in Africa not only in terms of the harsh environmental issues that improved technological inventions have ameliorated, also in the various forms of misrule and dearth of opportunities that have intensified the brain drain robbing Africa of its best human resources. Africans still undergo the paradox of humiliation when they experience various forms of degradation arising from their color in spite of the abrogation of racial laws in our time. Going back to the era of slave trade, European colonization of Africa, and to subtle racial policies targeting Africa in the community of nations, Africans have reason to lose their self-confidence and suffer dispossession, having been humiliated, socially demeaned, and valued not much higher than other goods for sale. The inferiority complex arising from this dehumanization still haunts Africans to this day.

The paradox of acculturation manifests itself as Africa tries to come to terms with what Mazrui describes as "the triple heritage" of Africa: traditional cultures, Christianity (which he calls the West), and Islam.[14] The survival of African traditional culture in the midst of the powerful influence of Western culture, Christianity, and Islam says a lot about its resiliency. At times, these three heritages clash with each other, resulting in varied forms of conflict. Cultural contact has equally changed Africa's self-identity. In the new political institutional structure, many Africans see themselves in terms of nationality, tribe, religious affiliation, economic status, education, and rural or urban habitation. Such exclusive self-identity could generate various forms of nepotism and group bias as people favor those from their own ethnic background over others.

These changes have begun to affect the communitarian sense of African cultural values as individualism replaces a sense of community and as Africans unconsciously imbibe the varied

13. Mazrui, *African Condition*, xv–xvi.

14. Mazuri's book *The Triple Heritage* (1986) comprehensively deals with the implications of these heritages in the socio-economic, religious, and cultural as well as political life of Africa.

forms of capitalism. Wealth becomes more and more privatized; the land tenure system is changing as communal lands are put up for sale; political institutions change not only by the establishment of nations (by amalgamation of heterogeneous peoples), but also by rural-urban migrations as people from diverse regions settle together. These are interesting dynamics with far-reaching consequences for the integrity of African cultural values as Africa comes face to face with modernity. Mazrui's summary aptly describes some of the dialectics of the African condition:

> Christianity, western liberal democracy, urbanization, western capitalism, the rules of western science and the rules of western art have jointly exerted an unparalleled influence on the emergence of personalized identity in Africa. What emerges from all this is that the African has discovered himself as an individual, and a black man, and as a citizen of a particular modern African country, and indeed as a resident within the African continent, partly because of his historical interaction with western culture in all its richness and all its narrowness, in all its conquering aggressiveness.[15]

Mazrui leaves behind the Arabic influence that is pervasive in many parts of Africa, permeating the continent through Islam and sponsoring varying forms of charity. It introduces different ideologies through its petrodollar into African religio-cultural, social, and political life. Discussion of these matters will follow in a later chapter of this book.

Globalization and Modern Statehood in Africa

Various circumstances have led to the emergence of modern statehood in Africa and have impacted African cultural values and identity, including four centuries of illegitimate slave trade, the legitimate trade in palm oil and other raw materials during the Industrial Revolution in Europe, colonialism and wars of

---

15. Ibid., 68.

subjugation, and the amalgamation of formerly heterogeneous peoples into modern states.

The need for manpower in the New World (among other motivations) gave rise to four centuries of (trans-Saharan and trans-Atlantic) slave trade. The cruelty of the slave trade not only robbed Africans of personnel for their own technological development, but also of their self-pride and cultural confidence. Elizabeth Isichei, who has researched the impact of slave trade on the Igbo people of the southeastern Nigeria, mentions among other ills "the general insecurity which the practice of kidnapping engendered, which was both an evil in itself and productive of many others."[16] The slave trade discouraged long-distance trade, hindered the economic development of Africa, altered political institutions, gave rise to a disregard for human life, increased the sacrifice of slaves for religious purposes, and led to the corruption and distortion of religious custom. The abolition of the slave trade and the industrial need for raw materials also led to the trade in palm oil to Europe.

Colonialism not only caused many independent African nations to lose their sovereignty to various European nations, but also triggered the devastation of the cultural values of the African peoples and was responsible for the ensuing cultural identity crisis. The introduction of a different political structure robbed stateless African societies like the Tiv and the Igbo people of Nigeria of their egalitarian spirit by introducing a whole new system. Under the new political structure, although villages still retain their traditional systems, the judicial process in public policy takes very little notice of this traditional political structure. This is also true of the economic system, as well as of the social and religious life of Africans, all of which were dislodged by cultural contact with Europeans. The point here is that the various agents of social transformation and the different forms of cultural contact, as well as the attendant changes to the political structure and economic system, have often resulted in wanton greed and the corruption of African political, social, and economic structure and statehood.

---

16. Isichei, *Ibo People and the Europeans*, 55.

Thus the factors responsible for Africa's backwardness are systemic. We must look to a combination of external factors, such as the imbalance of trade and injustices of the international financial system's economics of exploitation.[17] We should equally consider internal factors like the unjust structures of governance resulting from abuse of state machineries by elite African bureaucrats and business moguls and their collaborators. Such internal abuses of the state by Africans negate African cultural values. The self-interest, greed, and corruption, the embezzlement of public funds, and the unimaginable avarice through which state institutions are abused to the detriment of the common good negate the communitarian societal structure of African cultural values. The dishonesty, cover-ups, tricks, schemes, and double standards contrived to deceive the unsuspecting public for the purpose of self-aggrandizement negate the African sense of the sacred. The increasing rate of murder, kidnapping for ransom, and other violent crimes to settle scores, cover up corruption, or eliminate political opposition contradicts the African sense of the sacredness of human life. For instance, in South Africa, the murder rate increased 4.2 percent from 15,609 murders in 2011–2012 to 16,259 killings in 2012–2013.[18] Nigeria has seen its own share of criminal violence, ranging from kidnapping to armed robbery to deadly Islamic militancy.[19] Of course, the failed state of Somalia is common knowledge in the Horn of Africa, where rising terrorist activities in Africa negate African cultural values. The frustration of people of other nationalities (tribes) with the son-of-the-soil syndrome, ethnocentrism, and nepotism negate the African sense

17. See Comeliau, "South: Global Challenges," and Amin, "Challenge of Globalization," for a sample analysis of the global challenge to the realization of integral development by the people of the Southern Hemisphere.

18. Africa Check, "FACTSHEET South Africa: Official crime statistics for 2012/13," https://africacheck.org/factsheets/factsheet-south-africas-official-crime-statistics-for-201213/.

19. For an analysis of Lagos, the former capital of Nigeria, as a snapshot of the rising crime wave in Nigeria, see Overseas Security Advisory Council, "Nigeria 2013 Crime and Safety Report: Lagos," https://www.osac.gov/pages/ContentReportDetails.aspx?cid=13917.

of hospitality, solidarity, and good human relations. The "important personality" syndrome that allows the political elite to maltreat and dehumanize their fellow citizens with impunity is a sad tale that not only negates the core African sense of brotherhood and sisterhood, but worsens the indignity and dehumanization Africans suffer through various forms of racism and discrimination. So while we lament how "Europe Underdeveloped Africa,"[20] we equally bemoan the underdevelopment of Africa by Africans.

As we struggle to find the reasons for the overriding pursuit of self-interest in a cultural system that was once predominantly communitarian, we must consider the remarkable changes that have been going on for centuries in African socio-cultural, politico-economic, and religio-spiritual life arising from various forms of cultural contact. The positive impacts of these changes are well noted, but one of the most negative of effects is the introduction of excessive individualism and a greedy, *après moi, le déluge* (after me, the flood) mentality into the psyche of the people. As articulated by Chukwudum Okolo, "Thus the problem of the African is himself, his values, life-priorities, his essential materialistic outlook on things which have characterized his political, private and public ways of life, his nearly exclusive pursuit of material progress and modernity which ironically are barriers to true progress and self-development."[21] This mentality, which continues to this day in wrecking many countries of Africa, is a carryover of the "get-all-you-can-get" attitude that came about partly as a reaction to the unjust colonial administrative system. According to Kwame Gyekye, "In postcolonial states in particular, governments are generally perceived as distant or objective entities whose activities have little bearing on the welfare and the daily lives of the citizens, and to whose activities the citizens, in consequence, have very little ideological and emotional attachment."[22]

In these situations, culture ceases to play its critical role of informing the African way of life. It ceases to function as a guiding

20. See Rodney, *How Europe Underdeveloped Africa*.

21. Okolo, *African Condition*, 14.

22. Gyekye, *Tradition and Modernity*, 195.

conscience to determine the norms of good and bad, of what is to be done and what is not permissible. Instead, culture caves in and rolls out the drum adulating what it ought to be condemning. The "get-rich-quick" syndrome becomes the norm. Traditional titles reserved for heroic individuals who have sacrificed for the good of the community are given to those who may have become wealthy through fraudulent means. The culture of impunity takes over the good of order; satisfaction takes the place of values; materialism and consumerism become self-transcendence and human self-actualization is stunted. Any attempt to uphold cultural values or to protect the common good is misunderstood as pretentious.

The consequence of this attitude is that after political independence, many African elite took over the role of the departed colonial masters, with all the privileges political power allots to itself. These included: constant availability of public funds to be used at one's discretion, expensing premier healthcare at the world's best hospitals to the state, limitless opportunities for the members of one's family and friends, control of the media network to do and say only what one wants, and the sycophancy and adulation of the low and the mighty. The insecurity associated with this state of affairs (for no one can stay in power forever) heightens a "grab what you can from the national cake" mentality. The material "success" of those who abused state power for self-enrichment and the lack of political will to check state corruption entrenched this syndrome as the "normal" course for people in political position. Due to this legacy of distorted statecraft, many African countries are today in various stages of decline.

However, it must be reemphasized that in spite of these distortions, African cultural values are not completely destroyed. The path to integral development for African peoples must attend once more to the integrity of their cultural values. The main question that comes to mind is how this is to be done in a modern world that is more closely knit together than ever before. Of course, these cultural values will not be pristine as they were before. Any changes in the life of Africans must be assessed in terms of how they promote the common good of the society to which they belong.

This is precisely what a communal societal structure based upon the African cultural values advocates. This position agrees with the two strands of solutions that Mazrui suggests will help Africa out of the current state of underdevelopment:

> Two strands of solutions are appropriate in addressing the development problems of the continent. The first strand is the imperative of looking inwards towards our ancestry, laying due emphasis on our native intelligence, collective wisdom, and the true essence of Africanity. This requires recognition of the value of our innate and traditional resources, which made our ancestors survive waves of onslaughts from foreign enemies and natural hazards . . . The second strand is an imperative of looking outwards to the wider world, which is the origin of the two foreign elements of the triple heritage. As Africa matures in its relationship with other world regions, it must stand ready to selectively borrow, adapt, and creatively formulate its strategies for planned development.[23]

Mazrui is neither recommending a return to nor the total obliteration of Africa's cultural past. On the contrary, he is suggesting an integrated solution that combines Africa's cultural values and endogenous and exogenous changes to the cultural values. Thus, African cultural values are to be upheld not in their pristine sense but as-is, refined and pruned in the light of the changes they have undergone. This of course demands a critical assessment of Africa's cultural traditions to be undertaken by Africa's present generation. Kwame Gyekye's work on *Tradition and Modernity* balances the views of Africa's cultural revivalists and anti-revivalists by maintaining that the refinement of a cultural tradition is necessary for cultural development of a tradition to the level of its time.[24] The responsibility of articulating these strands of solutions to Africa lies with educated Africans, who should critically examine everyday African cultural values in order to improve upon their inadequacies. Ordinarily, these critics should recognize the

23. Mazrui, *Tale of Two Africas*, 95–96.
24. Gyekye, *Tradition and Modernity*, 232–41.

inauthenticity inherent in the cultural systems of African daily life and stand prepared to make the sacrifices necessary to appropriate the resilient qualities of African cultural values.

Attention to the Superstructure of Culture

The superstructure of culture—that is, educated Africans—is responsible for the value structure of society. By virtue of training, formation, and study, educated Africans ought to have the critical minds needed to analyze the dynamics of societal transformation and weave together the variables of modernity shaping their societies. If this is the case, they can restore the integrity of Africa's cultural values and enable culture to play its critical role in society once more. The superstructure should be ready for the long haul; they are not to be stampeded into the fire brigade mentality of quick solutions and crash programs in response to issues. They must research, study, and implement solutions way ahead of distortions in cultural values.

The effectiveness of the superstructure depends on its integrity. If, as we have seen already about Africa, the superstructure of society is corrupt and lost in material pursuits and selfishness, then Africa has a big problem. The readiness with which the educated people, the specialists, and other intellectuals who ought to constitute the superstructure of culture join the mad race for personal aggrandizement is stunning. This mania, identified as "consumer or squandermania consciousness,"[25] is concerned only with short-term materialistic values. Such an approach to life already has a firm grip on the elite in many African nations. Sadly enough, according to Chukwudum Okolo,

> It is this sort of mental outlook and disposition which modern African leaders, broadly interpreted to include political leaders, intellectuals, and even many religious men and women, have brought into politics, the army, police, educational institutions, churches, etc. These [state and religious institutions] are generally run from

25. Okolo, *African Condition*, 17.

the perspective of material advantages or gain (personal, sectional, ethnic), not from the perspective of the common good, much less for the good of posterity. Hence the tragic fate of the African or the black man has continued unabatingly.[26]

The restoration of detached, disinterested intelligence among the superstructure of culture remains an imperative for Africa's achievement of integral sustainable human development. For this to happen, knowledge for its own sake must become a priority, and the cultural values of Africa's emphasis on honesty and the promotion of the common good must inform the backdrop of education in Africa. Mazrui captures this necessity well in his analysis of Africa's triple heritage, saying, "African political development must find ways to accord greater significance to indigenous African values of justice, fairness, equity, rewards and punishment, without which the endemic conflicts of our triple heritage will continue to undermine our developmental efforts."[27]

Therefore, attention must be paid to the superstructure of culture in order to promote the integral development of Africa. In order to do this, the education system in Africa must prioritize the superiority of the common good over self-interest. Citizenship education must focus on reorienting the public perception of statehood as belonging to the people rather than an informal structure to be abused to satisfy individual greed. In order to achieve this transformation, intellectual conversion of the superstructure's leaders and policymakers is mandatory. For this to happen, Africa's educated elite must overcome their biases, especially the unconscious bias lurking in the psyche (dramatic bias), underlying the shortsighted practicality responsible for the greed and avarice destroying African social system.

Such conversion will engender a commitment that imbues leaders with a sense of purpose and a readiness to sacrifice for the common good instead of greedy self-aggrandizement or ostentatious display of ill-gotten wealth. The benefit of this conversion will

26. Ibid., 18.

27. Mazrui, *Tale of Two Africas*, 89–90.

be living in a self-transcendent mode that will be a protection from being pulled down. Instead, African intellectuals will derive simple joy from their contribution to the community. This commitment will defeat the fear of failure that pervades the African endeavor and will celebrate that such achievements, no matter how small, have ripple effects to improve the life of the community, state, and nation. Instead of jealousy and envy, there will be humility and a readiness to learn from one another for mutual benefit. Patience, not despondency is needed here; hope and not fatalism must be the guide towards the future, for it is not easy to reverse the long cycle of decline. It is not without difficulty, especially when one considers how rooted these biases have become in a community of individuals who reinforce biases by grabbing for their own share of the "national cake." Leaders' community and family consider them fools if they fail to take the opportunity to grab for a slice while in public service. It takes time to reverse the cycle of decline, but the process of restoration has to start now. One of the approaches to this goal is the restoration of critical culture towards integral development and good governance in sub-Saharan Africa.

3

Critical Culture for Integral Development and Responsible Governance in Sub-Saharan Africa

> Africa's memory is painfully scarred as a result of fratricidal conflicts between ethnic groups, the slave trade and colonization. Today too, the continent has to cope with rivalries and with new forms of enslavement and colonization.
>
> —POPE BENEDICT XVI[1]

AFRICA IS CAUGHT IN a web of underdevelopment in a globalized economy, held captive by totalitarian oppressive regimes masquerading as democracies. Series of conflicts and uneasy calm, if not open conflict and violence, have led to wars in some African states. African leaders frequently champion causes that evidently are not for the common good, but rather for their selfish and often tribal interests. Thus anger, hatred, and revenge have overtaken a continent traditionally reputed for its values of brotherhood, hospitality, respect for life, and moral action. And these negative trends must change if Africa is ever to experience authentic development.

1. *Africae Munus*, sec. 9.

This ideal for a new African society is important, urgent, and necessary. Such an ideal society would respect the dignity of Africans as human beings, roll back the wheel of decline, engage in conflict resolution, promote human coexistence, and create conditions conducive to progress, development, and good order. In the quest for an ideal Africa, it is easy to get caught up in utopian ideals or to propose solutions that install totalitarian regimes to enforce good order or import systems from other places. Many ideological constructs have been tried in Africa. During the Cold War, Africa was the battleground for proxy warfare between Marxist-Communist ideologies and Neoliberal capitalist economic principles. In spite of the Non-Allied Movement by which Africa sought neutrality in the ideological conflict between the East and West, visibly Marxist regimes perpetuated unspeakable crimes against their own citizens while capitalist economic principles aimed at scooping out the resources of Africa in a wave of neo-colonialism in post-decolonized Africa. Africa remains a continent for the taking. Its resources have been appropriated to develop other places, but have yet to be harnessed to develop itself.

This chapter argues that the restoration of a culture that is critical of trends that negate African value system will be transformative of the entire African social system and thus revolutionize not only Africans' attitude about themselves as individuals, but also be the key to fostering commitment to the common good. Specifically, I emphasize areas of African life that must be healed if Africa is to overcome the crisis of underdevelopment. On the community level, healing ought to take place in the African psyche (battered by centuries of slave trade and decades of colonialism) that makes Africans consider themselves to be inferior. As mentioned in the previous chapter, African leadership needs to be healed through a reorientation of the superstructure of culture that will change attitudes towards the state to promote the common good of African peoples. As stated in *Africae Munus*, "Africa will have to rediscover and promote a concept of the person and his or her relationship with reality that is the fruit of a profound spiritual renewal" (*AM*, sec. 11).

The Dialectic of African Communities

As noted in the previous chapter, social life in pre-colonial Africa was either egalitarian or based on politically institutionalized structures. In decentralized egalitarian or stateless societies, social cohesion was achieved through custom and consensus. Life was predominantly communal with strong emphasis on family units, cultural values of brotherliness, hospitality, fellow feeling, etc. In more politically organized societies under "divinely ordained" kings and rulers, social life revolved more around laws, the authority of the kings, taxation and trade, and more sophisticated cultural practices. The Igbo of southeastern Nigeria and the Mbuti culture of the Democratic Republic of the Congo are examples of egalitarian societies reputed never to have had kings. Much more politically organized structures existed among the Benin of midwestern Nigeria, the Oyo of western Nigeria, and the Habe rulers of the pre-Islamic northern Nigeria.[2]

Present-day African countries are amalgamations of formerly independent heterogeneous city-states or stateless peoples haphazardly put together without consideration of language, lineage, cultural, or social affiliations. Consequently, as the 2004 "Report of the Commission for Africa" observes:

> Many traditional communities of people are now divided between two, three, or even four countries. Elsewhere disparate groups, some of whom were traditional enemies, are yoked together in uneasy union, many of them lacking a common language with which to speak to one another. Colonialism favored some groups over others, creating new hierarchies. The consequences of some of these divisions are alive today.[3]

Instead of resulting in a higher synthesis of mutual understanding and good order, what results is a conflict of opposites as individual and group bias is unleashed. Selfishness, greed, and group interest supersede the common good; patriotism scatters to

2. Mazrui, *Triple Heritage*, 69.
3. Commission for Africa, *Our Common Interest*, 17–18.

the wind as people without any common interest loot treasuries and cart away the resources of the continent. Allegiance is often tribal as people see themselves as tribe members first rather than primarily as citizens of their country.[4] This view is corroborated by Agbonkhianmeghe E. Orobator's 2007 analysis of the Kenyan post-election crisis: "In Africa one acquires identity by affiliation with an ethnic group, which guarantees cultural security and facilitates access to public resources."[5] This challenge will eventually dovetail into the ethnocentrism that African Catholicism must confront.

Group bias in Africa takes the form of different types of exclusion according to "We and Them" attitudes that have led to a plethora of violence and internecine acts resulting in wars. Wole Soyinka chronicles such exclusion in 1994 Rwanda, which resulted "in the massacre of three-quarters of a million people in under three weeks."[6] The Ivory Coast suffered the exclusion of many people of West Africa who had lived there as citizens under the totalitarian regime of President Houphouët-Boigny. Such exclusion culminated in the civil unrest that eventually left the Ivory Coast a ghost of its former self.[7] These exclusions, Soyinka goes on to explain, at times took the form of "racial categorization," or "failure to objectivize the problem of identity—racial identity."[8] The consequence was silence over racial conflicts, as happened in the Darfur on account of the race-inspired policies of the Sudanese government that resulted in the displacement, dehumanization, torture, and rape of millions of Africans.

The longer cycle of decline of many African nations began with the wrong notion of civil service and statehood dating back to the privileges that Africans observed civil servants enjoying under the colonial administrative structure. After gaining political independence, the African elites began by occupying the government

4. Ilo, *Face of Africa*, 138–39.

5. Orobator, "Church, State, and Catholic Ethics," 182–85.

6. Soyinka, *Of Africa*, loc. 149–50.

7. Ibid., loc. 162–75.

8. Ibid., loc. 274–80.

offices and residential quarters of their former colonial masters. Unfortunately, this bred a perception of civil service as an opportunity to maximize gain and personal profit. Many see the infrastructures of culture—social order, technology, the economy, politics, the legal system, and all institutions of government—as avenues for self-enrichment. The African elite largely lacks a committed patriotic engagement with their nations and peoples. Thus the cycle of poverty, maldevelopment, and underdevelopment continues unabated.

Another factor responsible for the African crisis of identity is the effect of the miseducation of Africans and inferiority engendered by centuries of slavery and colonialism. Chinweizu summarizes this situation succinctly:

> A quarter-century after Africa's political independence from European colonial powers, the colonial mentality still lies like a fog on the African consciousness. It befuddles African perception, confuses African thinking, messes up African feelings, and disorganizes African action. As a result, African efforts at nation building and development have yielded little. I believe that only when the fog of colonial mentality is burned off will Africa successfully grapple with its absurd and desperate realities.[9]

Although one cannot endorse apportioning blame for the woes of Africa on the West, as if Africans were not responsible for their own fate and could not have done things differently, it is worth noting that post-colonial African leaders have not been particularly different from the colonial overlords of the past. However, Chinweizu's assertion is tenable in view of the impact of miseducation on the African psyche, which partly accounts for the African misconception of statehood. It is necessary to reexamine the effect of such dehumanizing activities as slave trade and colonialism on African mentality, Africans' view of themselves as individuals, as well as attitudes towards fellow Africans. As the apostolic exhortation of the Second African Synod *Africae Munus* acknowledges,

---

9. Chinweizu, *Decolonizing the African Mind*, vii. See also ibid., *West and the Rest of Us*, xii.

"Africa's memory is painfully scarred as a result of fratricidal conflicts between ethnic groups, the slave trade and colonization. Today too, the continent has to cope with rivalries and with new forms of enslavement and colonization."[10]

The Impact of the Slave Trade and Colonialism on African Psyche

If there is any aspect of African life that is understudied, it is the impact of slave trade on the African psyche, on African self-identity and selfhood, and Africa's consequent self-presentation in the world scene. More than any other event in history, the commodification of Africans by the flesh trade is an identifying mark Africans carry both in their self-assessment of Africa and in the way other people identify them. According to Ngugi Wa Thiong'o, the impact of the slave trade on the African psyche as well as the economic, political, and social condition of Africans is enormous, and moreover, has serious moral implications that continue to haunt Africans to this day with "the negative perception of Africa and Africans by others, and the negative self-conception of Africa and Africans by Africans. Those two conceptions have common ground in the devaluation of African lives."[11]

Because of the conscious attempt to forget, to deny, to obliterate, and to refuse to take responsibility for the slave trade's heinous crimes against humanity, both the perpetrators and the victims subconsciously bury and suppress the trauma to the African mentality. The double tragedy of perpetration and suppression only deepens Africa's psychic wound and makes its healing difficult. The inferiority complex arising from the slave trade is passed from one generation of Africans to another, just as a superiority complex is passed on from one generation of Europeans, Americans, Asians, and Arabs to another with respect to Africans. In the case of the trans-Saharan slave trade, the Arabic superiority complex

10. *Africae Munus*, sec. 9.
11. Thiong'o, "Learning from Slavery," 6–7.

over Africans, whom they all too often consider to be inferior, accounts for the pogrom and continued genocide against the black
Africans of Fur in Western Sudan. Wole Soyinka draws the implication of this today:

> The yet unexpiated history of the trans-Saharan trade,
> that is, the centuries-old history of the relationship be-
> tween two races on the African continent, has coalesced
> into a master-slave tradition, one that established one
> part of the population as its subhuman sector, subject
> to permanent humiliation through neglect, double stan-
> dards of governance, uneven application of the law, and
> enthronement of impunity, leaving such a sector prone
> to elimination if and whenever it insists on a revision of
> its social status.[12]

The wounds of the slave trade had hardly healed when another form of subjugation occurred, further deepening the trauma
of the slave trade and accompanying dehumanization. Colonial
dictatorship subjected Africans to the orders and directives of foreign rulers. The occupying powers not only plundered the resources of the continent for the development of their own countries,
but also sowed the seeds of lasting discord through the reckless
partitioning and unjustifiable creation of artificial boundaries that
continue to intensify ethnic violence. The relatively young study of
decolonization recognizes the negative impact of colonization and
specifically addresses the "echo factor" question of colonialism;
that is, the other burdens and trauma arising from colonization
as well as the after-effects of anticolonial violence over the infrastructures of African culture.[13] According to Engelbert Mveng, the
late Cameroonian theologian, such conditions give rise to "anthropological poverty," or in other words, "the indigence of being, the
cause of which is the centuries of slavery and colonization that
has banished Africans from world history and the world map."[14]
Neo-colonialism continues to exacerbate anthropological poverty

12. Soyinka, *Of Africa*, loc. 1089.

13. Le Sueur, *Decolonization Reader*, 4.

14. Oborji, "African Theology, Roman Catholic," 18.

today. The paternalistic approach of Western and Arab countries toward Africa (which arise from a psychological and anthropological conviction that Africans are less than human, pre-modern, and superstitious) perpetuates Africa's anthropological poverty and impoverishes African human dignity at its deepest level. Furthermore, the effect of colonialism on the psyche of the people is at the root of the endemic misrule and dictatorial tendencies of many African leaders to this day. According to Theophilus Okere:

> After independence, the bad example of governance set by colonial rule was copied and continued, as Africans succeeded the colonialists, not as leaders championing the rights and pushing the development of their own people, but as black African colonialists sitting in the chair of Moses. Independence became a change of guard, a change of colors, with blacks merely taking up the relay from the whites. The new African masters governed the colonial way, that is, the exploitative way, the way of force and treachery and disregard for the people but all along without prejudice to the overall interest of the colonial power. The African *malin geni* was at its worst, as it adroitly manipulated every mechanism and every process designed to achieve good governance—population counts, elections, constitutions, and the armed forces and the media, in order to consolidate and perpetuate itself in power.[15]

The twin factors of Africa's underdevelopment, "the scourge of colonialism" and the "incompetence of a vast majority of most African leaders,"[16] are related, and the solution to both lies in healing the psyche of dehumanizing historical trauma.

The distortions of the dialectic of African communities run deep, permeating and fragmenting the social order and setting the institutions of governance against one another and against itself. Consequently, things go wrong in all corners. Although poor, the people have acquired tastes that can only be satisfied by imported

15. Okere, "Crisis of Governance in Africa," 6.

16. Okoye, foreword to *Philosophy, Democracy, and Responsible Governance*, x.

foreign goods. The widespread thirst for power and money, ignorance, and corruption make the masses vulnerable to the machinations of power-hungry and money-minded politicians who bribe their way into office by stealing the votes of the masses. Thus sham elections enthrone mediocrity at the altar of excellence as rogues and charlatans run the affairs of governance. Taken up by petty satisfaction and the immediate desire to accumulate needless wealth to loot and stack away in foreign banks, most African leaders are enslaved by their inability to compensate for their inner emptiness by amassing wealth, and confuse being with having. Good governance is confused with accumulation of foreign debts and loans that are often stolen and repatriated overseas according to the interest and benefit of the lenders.

Thus, according to Theophilus Okere, "Looked at from all angles, it seems clear that a majority explanation of the failure of governance in Africa is a lack of understanding or a misunderstanding of the meaning and purpose of government itself."[17] This is true not only of the politicians and bureaucrats, but also of the public realm, those members of civil society who see nothing wrong with politicians using public resources for private purposes. This weak citizen influence and oversight make it difficult for citizens to participate in the political process, in policymaking, or in holding the state and its functionaries accountable for irresponsible governance. The long-term effect is the political class acting with impunity with little regard for the citizens. Responsive and responsible leadership becomes skewed. Social reciprocities and intergroup tolerance are far from ideal.[18] Politicians privatize the state, and the citizens are only co-opted during elections and are bribed to vote in the often massively rigged elections that mock democracy and its institutions.

In order to restore the integrity of the social dialectic of African communities, genuine cultural values have to be promoted. This does not mean merely listing African cultural values as they are traditionally known, but restoring the meanings and values

17. Okere, "Crisis of Governance in Africa," 10.
18. Venter, "Democracy, Good Governance," 236.

upon which an intelligible, good, and just social order is founded. Genuine cultural values, in their infrastructural and superstructural form as critical culture, integrate the dialectic of community by holding in tension human primordial sociality and institutional forms of governance for the common good of the members of a community, state, country, nation, international communities, etc. The task now is the restoration of the integrity of African communities. This is to be undertaken with the aim of overcoming the biases that distort the dialectic of African communities—dramatic, individual, group, and general bias—by making culture uncritical. A possible approach is to heal the psyche of both the populace and African elites and bureaucrats. In the words of Chinweizu, we must work to "decolonize the African mind."[19]

The Process of Self-Discovery

Such healing of the psyche can unleash a set of transformations that will enable Africans to overcome the inferiority complex that is the heritage of their social history. In the first place, the feeling of being unequal affects African self-assertion and can be healed only by a realization of the basic *humanum* they share with all humans. As Kwame Anthony Appiah emphasizes, Africans must not only be proud of being black, but must recognize that the accident of skin color is not a determinant of human rationality.[20] Applying the cognitional structure of human consciousness developed by Lonergan, one recognizes that the immanent cognitional process of inquiry is common to humankind.[21] All human beings experience, understand, judge, and decide. This unity of consciousness and personal self-affirmation as a knower implies that the unity-identity-whole applies to every human being, Africans included.

Prior to World War II, Africans regarded anybody whose skin color was not black (often colonial Europeans) as "gods": as

19. Chinweizu, *Decolonizing the African Mind*.

20. Appiah, *Cosmopolitanism*, 6–7.

21. Lonergan, *Insight*, 353.

more creative, more intelligent, more capable of achievement than they were. World War II shattered that myth. African servicemen who fought alongside the white soldiers realized they were fellow human beings. That experience removed the pervasive fear that had restrained Africans from resisting colonialism. Hence, the processes of liberation intensified immediately after World War II as the Africans realized (through stories of their ex-servicemen) that they were as human as "the white" were. Once more it is necessary to affirm, using Lonergan's dynamic structure of human knowing as a means of healing the incipient timidity arising from centuries of subjugation, that being black does not mean being less rational. It does not mean either that Africans operate at the level of common sense while people of other races operate on the level of theory or interiorly differentiated consciousness. The project of decolonizing the African mind is the liberation of the psyche from the debilitating fear of inferiority complex that cripples their creativity. This apparently simple fact is nonetheless complex, for some people are still bent on perpetuating the hackneyed, superannuated, and supposedly abandoned but still unfortunately pervasive view of Africans' inferiority to members of other races. M. Shawn Copeland clearly articulates such viewpoint in modern society:

> In a negrophobic society, black ontological integrity suffers compromise. On the one hand, massive, negative, transgenerational assault on black bodies has ontological implications. In such a society, blackness mutates as negation, nonbeing, nothingness; blackness insinuates an "other" so radically different that her and his very humanity is discredited. Then, black identity no longer offers a proper subject of sublation, of authentic human self-transcendence, but a bitter bondage to be escaped. Blackness becomes a narrative of marginality and a marginal narrative.[22]

Psychic healing, as a process of decolonizing the African mind, aims at liberating Africans from internalizing negative

22. Copeland, *Enfleshing Freedom*, 19.

constructs about themselves so that they do not succumb to an ancestral inferiority complex in their relation to people of other races.

In the second place, and closely related to the first, is the issue of cultural authenticity and ethnicity. It is a challenge to the social order of modern African states to be faithful to one's cultural values or to promote mutual coexistence of other cultural identities. And yet this is precisely what nationhood implies and demands. While one must be faithful to the authentic values of one's own culture, modern nationhood demands the inclusion of other nations. Although the desire for cultural domination is often tempting, modern nationhood demands the pursuit and promotion of the common good to ensure the wellbeing of members of communities, states, nations, and countries.

Consequently, repeatedly bemoaning the heterogeneity of Africa's social order arising from colonialism as an excuse for intolerance and violence no longer augurs well for the continent. In situations where border demarcations cannot be redrawn, as is the case in most African countries, the oneness of being African should be sufficient to promote mutual coexistence. Individual and group bias, and the resulting ethnocentrism and nepotism that disorganizes the social order and destabilizes African countries, are self-destructive. Differences in the nuances of cultural values notwithstanding, generally Africans share similar and interrelated cultural values that should be unifying rather than divisive. The problem of ethnocentrism is often political, arising from the uneven distribution of resources and infrastructural amenities. Instead of individual and group bias, often kindled by the political class playing the ethnic card to their own self-interest, civil society must be strengthened and united to demand the strong rule of law as well as good governance and accountability from the political class. This is the only way to challenge the unjust structures of governance in Africa, where leaders take the people for granted and always knows when to divide and distract the attention of the public from bad governance.

Unlike the general image of Africa as a place riddled with ethnocentrisms that make mutual coexistence impossible, African cultural values have a good sense of human relations. Traditional African societies revolve around the basic social value of "live and let live."[23] Underlying this social value is the inherent right of every person to exist as an equal member of a community. This "live and let live" mentality is not limited to oneself or one's community, but broadly includes the right of others in their own communities who form the broader community that constitutes a nation, continent, and even all of humankind. The Igbo of southeastern Nigeria express this notion well in their proverb: *"Egbe bere, ugo bere / Nke si ibe ya ebela / Nku kwaa ya,"* which roughly translates to "Let the kite and the hawk perch, and if one rejects the perching of the other, may his/her wings be broken."[24]

Therefore, African communalism that prioritizes the community and its common good over the individual and group interest is a good starting point for reorienting African societies and bracing against the challenges of ethnocentrism. In fact, this value has been variously articulated by eminent African scholars and leaders in such terms as Nkrumah's "Egalitarianism," Nyerere's "Ujamaa," Senghor's "Negritude," and Uzukwu's "hospitality," indicating "the predisposition for care by the African as posting of the self in a free and symbiotic embrace with the other."[25] In order to overcome the individual and group bias exacerbated by influence of individualism on the modern African societies, the riches of heterogeneous society should be emphasized by harnessing of the diverse human resources for the common good of African countries. Differences in language, lineage, and the multiplicity of legal cultures are good for African creativity.

23. Kanu, "Social Values in African Tradition," 149–61.
24. Afigbo, "Age of Innocence," http://ahiajoku.igbonet.com/1981/.
25. Njoku, "African Philosophy of Right," 66.

Developing Critical Culture

Beyond the dramatic, individual, and group bias responsible for Africa's underdevelopment, the pervasiveness of general bias wreaks havoc on Africa's sustainable development. The longer cycle of decline is precipitated by the political elite's willful ignorance of the consequences of their corrupt practices on their countries' economies. Either because of greed or as overcompensation for an inferiority complex, leaders of African countries are stuck in shortsighted practicality. Instead of long-term planning for the optimum development of their countries, self-interest overrides the common good. They corrupt the social order by exalting avarice beyond the wildest dreams of the imagination.

On account of the general bias of common sense—that is, preference for the practical and the concrete—the communitarian behavioral patterns of life and thought embedded in traditional African cultural values give way to individualism, self-interest, and group bias. A sense of immediate gratification holds sway, displacing the patience and perseverance that traditional African society recognized as better fulfilling the values of joyful self-actualization and communal wellbeing. The critical culture underlying African morality caves in to compromise and collaborate in sins against the common good for personal or group interest. Consequently, culture now adulates what it ought to condemn. The attendant maldevelopment of Africa is therefore not surprising. For as John I. Okoye rightly articulates, Africa has become "a society where mismanagement, corruption, nepotism, sectionalism and greed constitute the order of the day, and where these are not viewed with abhorrence goes deeper and deeper into entrenching these noxious vices by repetition in the psyche of its citizens. Such a society hopes in vain to reap the fruits of good governance or management of its collective power and resources."[26] This, in Lonerganian terms, is the longer cycle of decline, one that has been devastating the continent.

26. Okoye, "Question of Virtue," 17–18.

Evidently what is lacking among African leadership is a complete development of intelligence, which ordinarily overcomes these various biases. In the words of Boniface Nwigwe, instead of democracy, Africa is ruled by "*Mafia* governments." That is, "government[s] infested with power-drunken, self-seeking, ideology-barren, orientationless operative—usually selected by their kind and of course scarcely ever elected by the people."[27] Simply put, most African governments act in ways that give the impression of lacking insight into the art of governance, an understanding of statehood, and of the proper and right place of their fellow citizens. As Bekele Gutema so rightly argued, "the crisis of leadership in Africa therefore must be attributed to the crises of ideas."[28] What is needed is a reorientation of the political class towards the pursuit of the common good. Such solution must overcome the factors responsible for the distortion of the dialectic of African communities. It must be strong and convincing enough to change the superstructure of African culture, the ruling class. They must learn to value their countries above their personal interests or that of their various tribes and to overcome the endemic inferiority complex that makes them prefer to invest in foreign countries instead of their own. Any suggested solutions (and there are many available) must go beyond the artificial social order wrecked by ethnocentrism and dysfunctional institutions of government ruled by self and group interests.

I am inclined towards education of civil society to empower people through knowledge of their rights as citizens to make the political class accountable. For as long as the civil society in Africa is weak and divided, the public will continue to fall victim to misrule and suffer endemic poverty in spite of Africa's abundant human and natural resources. While this should not be construed as implying that civil society in Africa is not doing anything to demand accountability, as many of them do, the point is that a good number of people in Africa do not consider themselves as part of a democratic government. Hence, there remains a need for

27. Nwigwe, "Origin and Limits," 94.
28. Gutema, "Problems in the Emergence," 113.

sensitization on effective participation in governance such that the people will demand good governance as a right.

Third, education of the elite, which I envision to be more difficult, is aimed at changing leaders' understanding of the aims of governance as service for the common good. The education in question is aimed at healing the inferiority complex that they try to eliminate by amassing wealth through various forms of corrupt practices. *Africae Munus* highlights the role of African Catholicism thus: "In order to put this ideal into practice, the Church in Africa must help to build up society in cooperation with government authorities and public and private institutions that are engaged in building up the common good" (*AM*, sec. 81). Intellectual collaboration is needed to achieve this.

Education for Critical Culture

Underlying the challenge of leadership and good governance in Africa is a question of values, the question of keeping priorities in order and of consciously working for the common good of African nations. An education aimed at reorienting the culture, meanings, and values that guide African choices as citizens and as leaders does not mean supplanting African cultural values, but rather promoting them as traditional African values (in their pristine state) that enhance the common good. Such education must respect the role of the constitutive elements of society. This means, on the one hand, reappropriating the African social value of inclusivity that accommodates African nations' diverse ethnic groups as equal members of African communities. On the other hand, it means unifying the efforts of citizens to promote the national interests of various African countries to which they belong. Here, the value of God's love, inherent in African religious culture, must come into play.

The role of religion here is to critically assess the decisions and values underlying the choices African peoples make in promoting the common good. As "incurably religious" people, genuine religious practice promotes mutual coexistence and the adoption of values that lead to the promotion of the common good. The conversion of life made possible by authentic religious values results in responsible people who, through personal integrity, create conditions for cultural integrity at both the infrastructural and superstructural levels.

Achieving good governance in Africa first implies education that overhauls the social stratification underlying traditional African societies. The advantage of this approach to good governance will be the emergence of a robust, active, enlightened civil society whose people can no longer be satisfied with their place in the social order, but instead demand their rightful share in the nations' resources for their optimum development, fulfillment, and self-actualization. In the same vein, education for critical culture liberates the leaders of Africa from the false notion of superiority that cage them in constructing a hierarchical structure that separates them from their communities, thus enslaving them to totalitarian power. In this way, education for critical culture can bring about a totally new culture of citizenship and governance in Africa based on equality and justice and the promotion of the common good. Third, such education implies an appropriation of not only cognitional consciousness, but also moral as well as spiritual consciousness such that the patterns of experience that hold Africans in chains will be broken. By this I mean rejection of those patterns of experience that leave the bottom poor unable to see the corruption of the system that keep them poor. I refer to those patterned experiences that prevent ordinary people in Africa from conceiving an alternative to their present socio-cultural, political, and economic structures. This kind of education for critical culture could be compared to the arduous work of Paulo Freire in educating the peasants of Brazil to think of the vast possibilities open to them that the structures of governance hide through various forms of propaganda in order to keep them poor and marginalized. Education takes over the liberating powers of people's consciousness to help them bring about better societies for themselves by envisioning and formulating a pattern of experience different from the patterned experience they are allowed.

Education for critical culture is able to do this by helping people raise questions about their marginalization and oppression, enabling them to reject the "peanuts" given them by politicians who loot their treasury as the dividends of democracy. Such education, as Doran explains, brings people "to own, to appropriate, the fact that latent within them, suppressed perhaps by cultural conditioning, is a power of raising questions that can break the patterns of their experience, that can lead to insight; and the fact that insight into experience is already in an inchoate fashion a liberation from a particular pattern of experience and the beginning of a reshaping that will be more under one's own determination and not a function of someone else's demands."[29] Education for critical culture is the liberation of the psyche from oppressive patterns of experience, from conceiving of self merely as a body like an animal whose existence is characterized merely by survival in a human world. Instead, the psyche will be guided by freedom and responsibility.

In educating a people known to be very religious, it will be important to examine how religion contributes not only to the healing of the psyche, but also to Africa's development. The next chapter does exactly this using Nigeria, the most populous country in Africa, as a case study.

29. Doran, *Theology and the Dialectics*, 40.

4

Religion and Sustainable Development in Africa

The Case of Nigeria[1]

The Church's mission is not political in nature. Her task is to open the world to the religious sense by proclaiming Christ. The Church wishes to be the sign and safeguard of the human person's transcendence. She must also enable people to seek the supreme truth regarding their deepest identity and their questions, so that just solutions can be found to their problems.

—POPE BENEDICT XVI[2]

CONTEMPORARY DISCUSSIONS OF WAYS to develop sustainable human improvement show a reluctance to consider the influence of religion. The reason for this stems from divisiveness and intolerance among various religious groups. This occasionally results

1. This chapter is an expanded version of my article, "Religion and Sustainable Development in Africa: The Case of Nigeria," *International Journal of African Catholicism* 3 (2012) 1–30. See also http://epublications.marquette. edu/cgi/viewcontent.cgi?article=1231&context=theo_fac.

2. Benedict XVI, *Africae Munus*, sec. 23.

in violent conflicts that hamper (if not destroy) development projects, thus precipitating decline of the nations. Development institutions and agencies often refer to wars of religion and their attendant consequences as reasons for the neglect of religion in discourse, or for preferring civil religion devoid of creed, code, and cult—committed humanism—as partners in development. In addition, when religion is involved in alleviating hunger or other forms of suffering through faith-based organizations' forms of charity, contemporary development discourse finds itself in a dilemma as to what form their relationship with religion ought to be in promoting development, especially at the grassroots level.

Since religion (this chapter considers the three dominant religions in Africa to be Christianity, African traditional religion, and Islam) promotes an integral development that goes beyond mere economic globalization, this chapter defends the thesis that religion plays an important role in the sustainable development of Africa despite the (at times, violent) conflicts that arise from religious intolerance. Using Nigeria as a case study and drawing from Africa's religious worldview, this chapter urges religious groups in Africa to inculcate in their adherents the importance of hard work and industrialization in the quest for the sustainable development of Africa. I strongly believe African Catholicism can lead the way in this initiative by implementing the riches of the social teachings of the church.

Progress and Religion

Religion has always been involved in influencing the progress to a better world. In view of its innumerable adherents and its common belief in the dignity of the human person under God, religion is committed to the promotion of the human good, the provisioning of basic human needs, to guaranteeing protection of human rights, and supporting integral development of the globe. Thus, neglecting religion, the source of normative meaning that grounds the architecture of infrastructural and superstructural institutions of society, is misunderstanding the world process as a whole. As long as secular discourse continues to exclude religion in its analysis of globalization, progress, and the development of people, the results of its analysis will always be defective. As Max Stackhouse asserts, "The neglect of religion as an ordering, uniting and dividing factor in a number of influential interpretations of globalization is a major cause of misunderstanding and a studied blindness regarding what is going on in the world."[3]

At various times in the not too distant past, recognition of the indispensability of religion in the development discourse has given rise to changes of attitude that have led to a series of dialogues between religion and various agencies concerned with the promotion of sustainable development.[4] For instance, within the context of the food and energy crisis of the 1970s,[5] major world religions met at the 1975 Interreligious Peace Colloquium on Food and Energy and declared food and energy to be a basic human right. They issued a statement urging structural changes in world societies in order to alleviate hunger and malnutrition.[6] Lessons of that conference brought to the forefront the complexity of such simple acts of charity as feeding the hungry, as well as the interdependency of the basic organs of society for the realization of integral development—technological, economic, ideological and political will, and religious and cultural values—for world peace.

On another occasion, in face of the gradual onset of economic globalization accompanying the call for a New International Economic Order, select leaders of the major world religions—including

3. Stackhouse, *Globalization and Grace*, 57.

4. This however, does not mean that all involved in international development are convinced of religion's relevance to the development agenda. Some still think religion is divisive and dangerous, working fundamentally toward a different agenda driven by tradition and immutable theological approaches. Some people think globalization and modernization shakes and changes traditional religious structures, while others think technology and media bring new challenges and opportunities to faith institutions. A good number of technocrats also assume religious institutions are gradually withering because of secularism. See Marshall, "Development and Faith Institutions," 27–53 for a study of the uneasy relationship between religion and development.

5. Gremillion, *Food/Energy*, 7.

6. Ibid., 4.

Judaism, Islam and Christianity—met at the 1977 Interreligious Peace Colloquium in Lisbon, Portugal, to reiterate the importance of religion in the emerging world order. They proposed a comprehensive grasp of the politico-economic, religio-cultural, and ethnic faith communities and ideologies as necessary for achieving peace in the new human order, especially considering that all these transnational actors in the world scene are significantly affected by faith dimensions.[7]

Furthermore, the World Faiths Development Dialogue (WFDD) set up in 1998 continues the dialogue of religion and development agencies such as the World Bank and the International Monetary Fund (IMF).[8] The result of such dialogue has been an emphasis on "integral development," or development that is not merely economic but also includes the political, social, cultural, economic, and technological as well as the religio-spiritual aspects of human life. Such development must focus on the human person involved in development and promote overall individual development: social, cultural, personal, and religious. Institutions now appreciate the position of faith-based groups, recognizing that "economic development programs will not be sustainable, even within their own terms of reference, unless they incorporate the spiritual as well as the cultural, political, social and environmental dimensions of life."[9] James D. Wolfensohn, former President of the World Bank, foresaw the need for closer collaboration between the World Bank and other development institutions with religion in remarking:

> Religion is an omnipresent and seamless part of daily life, taking an infinite variety of forms that are part of the distinctive quality of each community. Religion could thus not be seen as something apart and personal. It is, rather, a dimension of life that suffuses whatever people do. Religion has an effect on many people's attitudes to

7. Gremillion and Ryan, *World Faiths*, 2.

8. For other examples of such initiatives in Africa, see Tsele, "Christian Faith in Development," 203–18.

9. Tyndale, "Religions and the Millennium," 216.

everything, including such matters as savings, investment, and a host of economic decisions. It influences areas we had come to see as vital for successful development, like schooling, gender equality, and approaches to health care. In short, religion could be an important driver of change, even as it could be a break to progress.[10]

As a result of such dialogue, there is a realization that people's religious faith helps shape their view of development and their life in general. Religion provides the unifying power that grounds the socio-political, economic, technological, cultural, and moral dynamics of a culture. This is particularly true of Africans, for whom life is an intricate web of the sacred and the secular.

Africa's Religious Landscape

In African thinking, there is no division between religion and life, body and soul, natural and supernatural, as one sees in Western thought. What this means is that humankind is best seen as a life force interacting harmoniously with life forces in the universe, namely: God, the deities, the founding ancestors of different clans, the ancestors and other living or dead members of the family and tribe. According to John S. Mbiti:

> It is religion, more than anything else, which colors their understanding of the universe and their empirical participation in that universe, making life a profoundly religious phenomenon. To be is to be religious in a religious universe. That is the philosophical understanding behind African myths, customs, traditions, beliefs, morals, actions and social relationships.[11]

Africans eat religiously, dance religiously, trade religiously, and organize their societies religiously, but this is done in a holistic manner, without any dichotomy between the material and the spiritual. Since Africans are "incurably religious," the major

10. Wolfensohn, "Foreword," xvii.

11. Mbiti, *African Religions and Philosophy*, 262.

question is whether religion in Africa helps or hinders sustainable development. If African religious values promote the human good by emphasizing the good of the community, do modern religious values arising from Christianity, Islam, and traditional religion in Africa promote or retard sustainable, integral development? A brief examination of Africa's underdeveloped condition will shed some light on the role religion plays in this area.

African Underdevelopment/Development

There are two ways of interpreting development in Africa: First, from the purview of underdevelopment, which emphasizes Africa's material poverty in comparison to other highly developed economies; second, from the viewpoint of Africa as part of the developing world. In the former sense, African underdevelopment reveals that the continent is almost synonymous with poverty, malnutrition, disease, political instability, violence, dependence, corruption, and injustice. In his 1986 book, *The Triple Heritage*, Ali Mazrui asserts: "Things are not working in Africa. From Dakar to Dar es Salaam, from Marrakesh to Maputo, institutions are decaying, structures are rusting away. It is as if the ancestors had pronounced the curse of cultural sabotage." [12] The 2005 report of the Commission for Africa corroborates this observation and asserts: "Today Africa is the poorest region in the world. Half of the population lives on less than one dollar a day. Life expectancy is actually falling. People live, on average, to the age of just 46. In India and Bangladesh, by contrast, that figure is now a staggering 17 years higher." [13]

The challenges of Africa's underdevelopment are systemic. Things are going wrong on all corners. There are problems arising from poor governance and economic mismanagement, corruption, and embezzlement of public funds. There are social upheavals arising from distorted border demarcations and the forced

12. Mazrui, *Triple Heritage*, 11.
13. Commission for Africa, *Our Common Interest*, 16.

combination of incompatible people. The consequence has been nepotism and ethnocentrism, as was tragically seen in the 1994 Rwandan genocide. Another problem is the decay of infrastructure or a total lack thereof, making it difficult for Africa to compete profitably in the global market. This leads to greater dependence on food imports at levels as high as 40 percent.[14] These problems are worsened by unequal relationships in terms of foreign trade, debt, and aid with the rich countries of the North.

As a developing part of the world, there are positive signs of improvement in African continent on the whole. Many African countries now boast of democratically elected leaders, although much still needs to be done to ensure free and fair elections for representational governance. There has also been greater regional integration since the creation of the African Union to replace the wobbling Organization of African Unity (OAU) and the peer review mechanism by which African heads of state can learn from one another through a program called the New Partnership for Africa's Development (NEPAD). The Commission for Africa reports:

> In one African country after another the first signs are emerging that things may be changing. Twenty years ago it was commonplace for African countries to be run as dictatorships; today such governments are a minority . . . War has given way to peace in many places . . . Despite three decades of overall continental stagnation, growth exceeded 5 per cent in twenty-four separate countries in sub-Saharan Africa in 2003 . . . Everywhere there are the first signs of what could be a real momentum of change.[15]

There has also been improvement in the economy. As Canada's *Financial Post* reports of sub-Saharan Africa, "The region is shaking off economic chaos to become one of the most incredible success stories of the global economy."[16] In the words of Ngozi Okonjo Iweala, Managing Director of the World Bank and

14. López, "Dependence on Food Imports," 132–33.

15. Ibid., 12–14.

16. Pett, "Sub-Saharan Africa's Big Move up," http://www.financialpost.com/related/topics/Saharan+Africa+move/5389108/story.html.

two-time Minister of Finance for Nigeria: "There is growing conviction among sub-Saharan Africa's leaders that sustained growth will come from the private sector and increased integration with the global economy."[17] Thus, investment is replacing aid in Africa. For instance, foreign direct investment increased from the US$9 billion in 2000 to US$62 billion in 2008.[18] According to the International Monetary Fund, real gross domestic product (GDP) in sub-Saharan Africa increased 5.7 percent annually between 2000 and 2008, one of the fastest paces anywhere in the world.[19] According to David Pett, a columnist with the *Financial Post*, "The collective output of its 50-plus economies, meanwhile reached US$1.6 trillion, far greater than, say, global industrial power, South Korea."[20] The Commission for Africa equally believes that the African economy is growing as measured in GDP, testifying, "So Africa is not doomed to slow growth. Botswana is not the only indicator of that. In the last decade, sixteen countries in sub-Saharan Africa have seen average growth rates above 4 per cent, including ten with rates above 5 per cent and three with rates above 7 per cent."[21] The 2010 McKinsey Global Institute report on Africa's development, titled "Lions on the Move: The Progress and Potential of African Economies," similarly extols the economic development of Africa and its potentials. It estimates Africa's collective GDP in 2008 to be US $1.6 trillion (roughly equal to Brazil's and Russia's), Africa's consumer spending in 2008 to be US$860 billion, and the number of new mobile phone users since 2000 to be 316 million. It forecasts Africa's collective GDP by 2020 to be US$2.6 trillion and Africa's consumer spending by 2020 to be US$1.4 trillion.[22] It summarizes: "Africa's economic impulse has quickened, infusing the continent with a new commercial vibrancy. Real GDP rose 4.9 percent per year from 2000 through 2008, more than twice its pace

17. Ibid., FP6.
18. Ibid.
19. Ibid.
20. Ibid.
21. Commission for Africa, *Our Common Interest*, 76.
22. Roxburgh et al., "Lions on the Move," vi–vii.

in the 1980s and '90s. Telecom, banking, and retail are flourishing. Construction is booming. Foreign investment is surging."[23] The United Nations Economic Commission's for Africa "Economic Report on Africa 2012: Unleashing Africa's Potential as a Pole of Global Growth" approvingly restates the growth of African economies even in the face of global economic crisis. According to a summary of the report:

> While the negative effects of the triple crises in 2007–2009 still linger in food, energy and finance, the euro area sovereign debt crisis has further aggravated the structural imbalances in the world economy. Africa's swift and robust recovery in the aftermath of the global crises slowed to 2.7 per cent in 2011, with the political turmoil in North Africa. But even with the uncertainties in the world economy, the continent's growth rate is projected to rise to 5.1 per cent in 2012 and remain strong in the medium term. The growth resurgence has transformed Africa from the world's lowest growing region in the past to one of the fastest growing regions, raising its potential as a new pole of global growth.[24]

The United Nations Economic Commission's report for 2013 remains positive about Africa's growth, not only economically, but also politically, especially efforts at democratically elected government and the promotion of good governance. It is optimistic about industrialization of Africa by saving the money it makes in sale of its commodities to "promote value addition, new service industries and technological capabilities."[25] It declares: "Given its remarkable growth since 2000, the continent has been hailed as the next frontier for opportunity and a potential global growth pole. Political conflicts have declined, economic growth is robust and economic management, governance and political stability have improved."[26]

---

23. Ibid., 1.

24. United Nations Economic Commission for Africa, "Economic Report on Africa 2012," 170.

25. Ibid., "Economic Report on Africa 2013," 95.

26. Ibid., 4.

Unfortunately, however, African countries' increasing GDP has yet to translate into improvement for most of the people. For instance, while Nigeria's gross national product (GNP) has increased, poverty levels have paradoxically increased, throwing more people below the poverty line of less than $1 a day.[27] According to the National Bureau of Statistics,

> Relative poverty is defined by reference to the living standards of majority in a given society. In 2004, Nigeria's relative poverty measurement stood at 54.4 percent, but increased to 69 percent (or 112,518,507 Nigerians) in 2010. The Northwest and Northeast geo-political zones recorded the highest poverty rates in the country with 77.7 percent and 76.3 percent respectively in 2010, while the Southwest geo-political zone recorded the lowest at 59.1 percent. Among States, Sokoto had the highest poverty rate at 86.4 percent while Niger had the lowest at 43.6 percent in the year under review.[28]

This paradox of growth in the face of poverty and inequality is a result of inequity and injustice in Nigeria's socio-politico-economic distribution, wherein a small percentage of the population, (politicians and bureaucrats) allocate the resources of the country to themselves while the rest of the populace wallows in abject poverty. The role of religion in the sustainable development of Africa, particularly Nigeria, will be assessed based on the performance of Christianity, African traditional religion, and Islam in addressing

27. "Nigerians Living in Poverty Rise to Nearly 61%," http://www.bbc.co.uk/news/world-africa-17015873. The World Bank estimates the developing world's extreme poverty benchmark at $1 a day, stating, "The developing world has already attained the first Millennium Development Goal target to cut the 1990 poverty rate in half by 2015. The 1990 extreme poverty rate—$1.25 a day in 2005 prices—was halved in 2010, according to new preliminary estimates. According to these estimates, 21 percent of people in the developing world lived at or below $1.25 a day . . . In some developing countries, we continue to see a wide gap—or in some cases—widening gap between rich and poor, and between those who can and cannot access opportunities" (World Bank, "Poverty Overview," http://www.worldbank.org/en/topic/poverty/overview).

28. Kale and National Bureau of Statsistics, "Nigeria Poverty Profile 2010 Report," 4.

the socio-politico-economic issues bedeviling Africa. This will be a preliminary consideration of the role of African Catholicism in African development.

Religion and Development in Nigeria

The role of religion in the sustainable development of Africa has been both positive and negative. Positively, religion stands as a reliable institution that provides stepping-stones to sustainable development. According to Lamin Sanneh, "Although they were little prepared for it, the churches found themselves as the only viable structure remaining after the breakdown of state institutions, and as such had to shoulder a disproportionate burden of the problems of their societies."[29] Indeed, "from the days of the missionaries to the present, the church in Africa has focused its development strategy in two areas: education and healthcare."[30] And the church has done remarkably well, as detailed below.

Christian faith-based organizations (FBOs) like the Christian Association of Nigeria (CAN), along with Muslim FBOs like the Nigerian Supreme Council of Islamic Affairs (NSCIA), contribute to sustainable development of Nigeria in many ways.[31] In the face of the weakness of the Nigerian state and the inefficiency of its institutions to provide for the human good of its citizens, these faith-based organizations (FBOs) supplement and complement government's efforts towards improving the Nigerian standard of living. These FBOs are involved in pro-poor, charitable works that alleviate poverty, promote progress, and serve as agents of development in Nigeria. According to Omobolaji Olarinmoye:

> FBOs in Nigeria provide health and educational services through their hospitals, clinics and maternities, schools and colleges, vocational training centers, seminaries and universities. They own economic institutions, such as

29. Sanneh, *Whose Religion Is Christianity?* 15.
30. Ogbonnaya, "Church in Africa," 74.
31. Odumosu et al., *Religions and Development Research Programme*, 2.

bookshops, hotels, banks, insurance, mass media and ICT companies and are prominent owners of real estate in the form of sacred cities and prayer camps which cover thousands of hectares of land. The lands on which their hospitals, schools and orphanages are situated also make up part of their real estate portfolio.[32]

Specifically, research on religion and development in Nigeria in 2009 identifies the main Muslim FBOs to include "the Federation of Muslim Women Association of Nigeria (FOMWAN), the Nasrul-II-Fathi Society of Nigeria (NASFAT), and the National Council of Muslim Youth Organization (NACOMYO). The main Christian FBOs include Christian Rural and Urban Development of Nigeria (CRUDAN), the Justice and Peace Caritas Organization (JDPC), the Urban Ministry, the Christian Association of Nigeria (CHAN), and the People Oriented Development (POD) of ECWA."[33] FOMWAN, which enjoys consultative status in the United Nations, aims at stimulating the intellectual and economic empowerment of Muslim women, rehabilitating children and orphans, encouraging young girls to embrace education and access to adequate healthcare, and more. It embarks on these initiatives in partnership with the Nigerian government through the Universal Basic Education Program and Nomadic Education Programs. NASFAT, among other programs, seeks to tackle poverty and ensure sustainable income for the society. Thus, it supports small-scale businesses by granting loans to individuals and cooperative societies. CRUDAN partners with the government and other FBOs to promote rural and urban development, especially in the areas of "rural development, agriculture, water and sanitation, micro-finance and livelihoods development and training."[34] Established as an integral development commission, the Justice Development Peace Commission (JDPC), a pontifical council guided by the social teachings of the church, helps Catholic

32. Olarinmoye, "Faith-Based Organizations in Nigeria," 15.

33. Odumosu et al., *Religions and Development Research Programme*, 44–45.

34. Ibid.

dioceses in policymaking, specifically in areas of social development. It coordinates programs relating to social welfare, rural, urban and water development, animating integral development, and similar initiatives.[35] Established in all the Catholic dioceses of Nigeria and with branches in the parishes and zonal levels (small Christian communities),[36] JDPC sinks boreholes to bring good drinking water to communities, promotes good governance by partnering with government to monitor elections[37] and train police and prison officers,[38] grants small-scale loans to farmers and merchants,[39] provides housing,[40] builds hospitals, constructs and equips schools, advocates for widows, women, the unjustly imprisoned, and more.

This is equally true of African traditional religions as well as of Islam. Although not institutionalized like Christianity and Islam, African traditional religion contributes to the sustainable development of Nigeria psychologically. It provides a sense of security and assurance of assistance from the spirit of the ancestors who Africans believe serve as a protective shield against such evil forces as witches or wizards threatening to disrupt individual and

---

35. Ibid.

36. See the organizational structure of the Justice, Development and Peace, Catholic Archdiocese of Ibadan, Nigeria, http://jdpcibadan.org/index .php?option=com_content&view=article&id=37&Itemid=153#.

37. For more on the JDPC Onitsha Archdiocese's contribution to good governance, see "Justice Development and Peace Commission (JDPC) Onitsha 2011 National Assembly, Presidential and State Assembly Election Preliminary Reports," http://jdpconitsha.org/activities.html.

38. Aborisade, "JDPC Trains Police, Prison Officers," http://www.punchng .com/news/jdpc-trains-police-prison-officers/.

39. For instance, the Catholic Institute for Development, Justice and Peace Small Projects Fund (CIDJAP SPF) in the year 2001, through the UNDP/ Enugu State Government, solely disbursed N600m micro credit facility to communities in Enugu State as well as a N20m loan from a commercial bank. See http://cidjap.org/fund.html.

40. JDPC Enugu Diocese Nigeria, for instance, built in 1996 "Nwanne Di Na Mba Social Housing Estate low cost housing estate in an effort to tackle the housing needs of the people of the area," (Catholic Institute for Development, Justice and Peace, "Housing," http://cidjap.org/housing.html).

communal development. Therefore, when faced with the riddles of life and in moments of suffering or difficulty, a good number of Nigerians fall back on their traditional religious cultural beliefs. Although Christianity and Islam frown at the syncretism arising from mixing traditional religious practices with Christianity and Islam respectively, "millions of Muslims and Christians on the continent have managed to absorb into their system of values and beliefs certain contributions from ancestral indigenous creeds."[41] Furthermore, African traditional religions' tolerance towards other religious beliefs and practices will always serve as an example for Christians and Muslims as they struggle for mutual coexistence.

However, in spite of their laudable involvement in promoting progress and sustainable development, religions in Nigeria have in some ways been inhibiting sustainable development. Christianity and Islam are often antagonists, leading to ethnic and religious conflicts resulting in loss of lives and destruction of property. For instance, between 1980 and 2002, more than ten thousand Nigerians were killed and properties worth millions of naira were destroyed in riots between Christians and Muslims. Historian Toyin Falola presents the facts of countless tragedies to exemplify religious violence in Nigeria:

> In 1980, the Maitatsine crisis claimed thousands of lives (the government conservatively estimated the death toll at just over four thousand) and caused millions of naira in property damage. On the last day of October 1982, eight large churches were burned in the prominent city of Kano . . . A major riot in Kaduna that same year claimed at least four hundred lives. In 1984, violence sparked by Muslims in Yola and Jimeta killed approximately seven hundred people (including policemen) and left nearly six thousand people homeless. In the first week of February 1986 . . . at Ilorin, the capital of Kwara state, Palm Sunday turned disastrous as Christians clashed with Muslims, leading to the destruction of three churches . . . In March 1987, Christians and Muslims in key northern towns and cities such as Kaduna, Katsina, Zaria, and

41. Mazrui, *African Condition*, 54.

Kafanchan clashed with devastating consequences . . .
In 1988, Christians and Muslims turned the Ahmadu
Bello University in Zaria into a battlefield on which a
hundred people were injured and one person lost his life
. . . In 1991, the religious crisis in Bauchi state reached
the breaking point, leading to numerous deaths and
massive destruction . . . In 1992, large scale violence
returned to Kaduna state, with severe clashes in Zangon-
Kataf, Kaduna, and Zaria. Two 1994 incidents in Kano
and Sokoto revived the tension . . . In May and June
1995, a new crisis erupted in Kano, sparking sporadic attacks on Christians and southerners. In May 1996, eight
people lost their lives when police clashed with a group
of Muslim students.[42]

Similar religious conflicts, riots, and violence continue to
arise from clashes between Christians and Muslims occur in Nigeria almost every year, since "Rioting in 2001 killed more than
1,000 people, and subsequent outbreaks in 2004 and 2008 killed
another thousand. Smaller but no less vicious attacks in 2009
claimed dozens of lives."[43] The Jama'atu Ahlis Sunna Lidda'awati
wal-Jihad, a militant Islamic sect in Nigeria, has only intensified
this problem. This group, better known as Boko Haram, aims at
complete Islamization of Nigeria in a Taliban style, having claimed
up to twelve thousand lives and destroyed valuable government
and business properties since 2009. Its terrorist activities are crippling the economy of northern Nigeria, creating insecurity in the
country, driving away both foreign and local investors, and forcing government spending on security instead of much-needed
infrastructure. It should be noted, however, that as the Council on
Foreign Relations in a 2007 symposium on "Religious Conflict in
Nigeria" discovered, most religious conflicts in Nigeria also have
ethnic and political nuances.[44]

42. Falola, *Violence in Nigeria*, 3–4.

43. Handley, "Violence in Nigeria," http://www.time.com/time/world/ar-
ticle/0,8599,1971010,00.html.

44. Council on Foreign Relations, "Religious Conflict in Nigeria," http://
www.cfr.org/content/meetings/nigeria_symposium_summary.pdf.

Another cause for the upsurge of religious intolerance and violence is economic. According to Paulinus I. Odozor, "A cruel irony in Nigeria is that as the country discovers more and more oil fields, a sizeable proportion of the population sinks more deeply into poverty. The concomitant decline of investment in the education and economic well-being of people, especially the young, makes the latter easy prey for religious fanatics or lunatics who promise them something greater than themselves, whether in this world or in the next."[45] For instance, the present terrorist activities of the Jama'atu Ahlis Sunna Lidda'awati wal-Jihad stem from endemic poverty arising from bad governance and dissatisfaction with the structure of the Nigerian state. Although their violent activities have gained Nigeria notoriety as a haven of religious intolerance, across the religious divide of a Nigeria evenly split between Christianity and Islam, interfaith cooperation remains a commitment of many in the modern Nigerian state.

Religious fundamentalism, whether arising from Christianity, Islam, or African traditional religions, is an abuse of religion and therefore abhorrent. Genuine religious spirituality respects human dignity under God by advocating for peace and tolerance, justice, development, protection of lives and property, promotion of the common good, and the creation of conditions favorable to civil and religious freedom. The violence arising from religious conflicts brings the importance of interreligious dialogue to the forefront. In order to foster such dialogue, the Catholic Bishops Conference of Nigeria (CBCN) established an Interreligious Dialogue Commission in response to the demands of the Vatican II Council document *Nostra Aetate*.[46] The Federal Government of Nigeria equally established the National Religious Advisory Board (1986) and the Nigeria Interreligious Council (1999) with the goal of promoting interreligious dialogue for sustainable peace and religious tolerance. However, these international organizations are not taken seriously in Nigeria. The pursuit of self-interest and the influence of ethnic politics over virtually everything in Nigeria

45. Odozor, "Africa and the Challenge," 218.

46. See Flannery, *Vatican Council II*, 653–56.

accounts for this. Struggles for supremacy between the various religions in Nigeria breed such distrust that even when religious leaders gather for interreligious dialogue, mutual suspicion limits their effectiveness. The end results are communiqués that end up as empty platitudes, mere politically correct statements, and false promises of commitment to peace in the public's mind.

Religion also impedes sustainable development by tacit collaboration in corruption and mismanagement of the economy, mainly because religious leaders have failed to challenge the unjust structures that give rise to bad governance, corruption, and social malaise. Although some FBOs—like the Muslim Jama'tu Nasril Islam, the Center for Human Rights in Islam (CHRI), the Christian Justice Development and Peace Commission (JDPC), and the Ecumenical Commission of Justice and Peace—are socio-political organizations, they have not spoken with one voice against the cycles of injustice, greed, and self-aggrandizement of the political class that commandeers state resources for personal use. On the contrary, various religious groups have sought to benefit from the corruption and nepotism of the Nigerian system when a member of their religion gains a position of political power. In this way, religions in Nigeria are put in a position to be used at will by the political class. Little wonder that the Nigerian government can so easily sidetrack its citizens, even in policies aimed at alleviating poverty such as the National Economic Empowerment and Development Strategy (NEEDS) program.[47] Thus, instead of acting as an agent of development, religion has at times been an agent of decline, destruction, violence, and revenge.

Since it is not enough for religions to contribute to sustainable development of Nigeria merely by providing social services (which is what they have been doing up until now), religious leaders in Nigeria must figure out a way to honestly embrace peace and promote mutual coexistence by understanding one another's religious beliefs. Such an effort was made almost immediately after

---

47. See Odumosu, "Faith Based Organisations'" for details of government non-involvement with FBOs in the formulation of its economic and development empowerment program.

independence from the British early in 1970 in the form of symposia. The University of Nigeria in Nsukka launched a journal titled Nigerian Dialogue: A Journal of Inter-Faith Studies on the Relation Between Christianity and Non-Christian Religions in July of 1974. The journal promoted the kind of positive interreligious relations Nigeria needs, but could not continue, perhaps due to lack of funding. If such approaches had been allowed to continue, perhaps members of Christianity, African traditional religion, and Islam would have been equipped to tolerate one another and stem the tide of religious fundamentalism that has so often been responsible not only for the wantonly violent destruction of lives and property, but also for crippling the economy and setting back the clock of sustainable development and reversing progress gained through many years of arduous labor, planning, and creativity.

The Contributions of African Catholicism

Drawing from the riches of the Second Vatican Council, especially the "Declaration on the Relationship of the Church to Non-Christian Religions: *Nostra Aetate*" and from the social teachings of the church, as well as the "Post-Synodal Apostolic Exhortation: *Africae Munus*," African Catholicism can contribute to the renewal of religions in Africa. A change of attitude towards Muslims and African religious traditionalists can only be effected when Christians see them as human beings who, like them, worship one God and therefore regard one another as brothers and sisters. This spirit of mutual openness can remove all the prejudice and fear that breeds interreligious hatred and violence. Such a spirit can soften the space for genuine Christian-Muslim-traditional African religious dialogue. Jacques Jomier's advice to Nigerian Christians is applicable for Muslims as well: "If you pay attention to the values in the faith of Moslems, you will find many occasions to speak with some of them . . . If we remember; according to Vatican II, God calls them as he calls every man living in the world and if we remember that many of them have personal relationship with God during their prayer or during their daily life then it will be easier

to understand that the Moslems are our brothers and sisters."[48]
Africae Munus makes similar calls for ecumenical and interreligious dialogue, especially between African traditional religions and Islam:

> The Church lives daily alongside the followers of traditional African religions. With their reference to ancestors and to a form of mediation between man and Immanence, these religions are the cultural and spiritual soil from which most Christian converts spring and with which they continue to have daily contact. It is worth singling out knowledgeable individual converts, who could provide the Church with guidance in gaining a deeper and more accurate knowledge of the traditions, the culture and the traditional religions. This would make it easier to identify points of real divergence.[49]

Africae Munus equally enjoins esteem towards and dialogue with Islam, which we shall elaborate further in a subsequent chapter on interreligious dialogue:

> The Synod Fathers highlighted the complexity of the Muslim presence on the African continent . . . I call upon the Church, in every situation, to persist in esteem for Muslims, who "worship God who is one, living and subsistent; merciful and almighty, the creator of heaven and earth, who has also spoken to humanity." If all of us who believe in God desire to promote reconciliation, justice, and peace, we must work together to banish every form of discrimination, intolerance and religious fundamentalism. In her social apostolate, the Church does not make religious distinctions. She comes to the help of those in need, be they Christian, Muslim or animist. In this way she bears witness to the love of God, creator of all, and she invites the followers of other religions to demonstrate respect and to practice reciprocity in a spirit of esteem.[50]

48. Jomier, "Islam and the Dialogue," 4.

49. Benedict XVI, *Africae Munus*, sec. 92.

50. Ibid., sec. 94.

Another contribution African Catholicism can make is in the area of civic education. This education could inculcate a nationalist spirit of patriotism in Africans to help them love their countries, become genuinely involved in the political process, demand justice by holding their elected officers accountable, and promote internal peace. As will become clear in a later chapter, African Catholicism draws from the riches of the Catholic social teachings and *Africae Munus* to teach values that promote integral sustainable human development.

5

The Role of African Catholicism in the Light of *Africae Munus*

There is no doubt that the building of a just social order is part of the competence of the political sphere. Yet one of the tasks of the Church in Africa consists in forming upright consciences receptive to the demands of justice, so as to produce men and women willing and able to build this just social order by their responsible conduct.

—POPE BENEDICT XVI[1]

IN SPITE OF ITS numerous challenges elaborated in previous chapters, Africa is changing from its moribund state to active and fast-paced development in all sectors of life: the economy, politics, social order, culture, and technology. Wars are becoming a thing of the past. Dictatorship has almost disappeared. Democratically elected governance with massive popular participation is gaining ground and improving. Governance is getting better, and is beginning to be marked by a greater determination to improve the lot of the people. Efforts are being made to create conditions and opportunities for self-realization. Literacy rates are rising, with many

1. Benedict XVI, *Africae Munus*, sec. 22.

countries paying for primary and secondary education for their citizens. With greater tolerance and better civility in communal existence, the social order is much more cohesive than before. There is better distribution of goods and services to more people and concerted efforts to stem the tide of poverty and malnutrition.

The economy of many African countries is growing at a previously unimaginable pace. Interstate and African international trade has improved remarkably. Although a good number of people in various countries of Africa still live below the United Nations benchmark, life is better today than previously. Trade liberalization and the opening of African markets have created numerous employment opportunities for the teeming population. Accountability is required from politicians and citizens and journalists take them to task. According to *The Economist*'s special report, "Emerging Africa: A Hopeful Continent," it is clear that:

> Human development in sub-Saharan Africa has made huge leaps. Secondary-school enrolment grew by 48 percent between 2000 and 2008 after many states expanded their education programs and scrapped school fees. Over the past decade malaria deaths in some of the worst-affected countries have declined by 30 percent and HIV infections by up to 74 percent. Life expectancy across Africa has increased by about 10 percent and child mortality rates in most countries have been falling steeply. A booming economy has made a big difference. Over the past ten years real income per person has increased by more than 30 percent, whereas in the previous twenty years it shrank by nearly 10 percent. Africa is the world's fastest-growing continent just now. Over the next decade its GDP is expected to rise by an average of 6 percent a year, not least thanks to foreign direct investment. FDI has gone from $15 billion in 2002 to $37 billion in 2006 and $46 billion in 2012.[2]

While Africans acknowledge that a lot still needs to be done to improve the standard of living further, many Africans are escaping violent and premature death and hoping for the same for their

2. August, "Emerging Africa," 3.

children. However, Africa knows it is not yet where it ought to be in the committee of nations, and that it must tackle the challenges militating against integral development.

First, although corruption is a worldwide problem affecting the functionality of institutional and governmental bureaucracy, in Africa it cripples the efficiency of national institutions, often with devastating impact on national security. In many African countries, it is so endemic that it permeates all aspects of life: politics, economy, social order, culture, religion, and personal responsibility. On account of corruption, the wealth of resource-rich African countries does not trickle down to the masses, who continue to live on less than $1 per day in the midst of abundant natural and human resources. Therefore, for the overwhelming majority, Africa's growing economy is only on paper. They cannot see or feel its impact. It is only the few "big-men and women" close to the corridors of power who enjoy the economic boom and report high GDP growth to the international community. *The Economist* has this to say about corruption in resource-rich Nigeria, the most densely populated country of Africa:

> Nigeria is famous for corruption, yet at issue is more than thievery. Members of the elite systematically loot state coffers, then subvert the electoral system to protect themselves. Everybody knows it, and a few straight arrows in the government talk about it openly. Perhaps half the substantial (but misreported) oil revenues of Africa's biggest oil producer go missing. Moderate estimates suggest that at least $4 billion to $8 billion is stolen every year, money that could pay for schools and hospitals. One official reckons the country has lost more than $380 billion since independence in 1960. Yet not a single politician has been imprisoned for graft. The day that Nigeria works properly, the battle for Africa's future will have been won.[3]

Second, Wole Soyinka, the doyen of African literature and 1986 Nobel Literature Laureate, vividly describes political

3. Ibid., 9.

corruption in Africa in his personal narrative of the Nigerian crisis, *The Open Sore of a Continent*, as a grand scheme by politicians who rotate power among themselves so as to shield one another from scrutiny. Politicians operate under the inner conviction that:

> Privilege must never be abandoned nor conceded to others outside the hegemonic circle. The members meet and choose a flag bearer. His only concession to the rest of the nation is that he learns when to permit a trickle of the spoils of office, but not of power, to fall through his fingers where necessary, to douse the smoldering resentment of others—the enlightened, the rejected, or the merely ambitious.[4]

Because they know that whoever controls the center of political power controls the other sectors of national life, politicians leave no stone unturned to get themselves to power, abandoning ethical principles, rendering elections a charade, and making a mockery of democracy. In spite of the improved effort at good governance, this "winner-takes-all" money politics combines with economic corruption to rob Africa of the much-needed good governance, transparency, and respect for rule of law requisite for integral development. If this trend continues, the progress being made now will be reversed. As *The Economist*'s Oliver August asserts:

> In some countries economic growth has so far failed to translate into better lives. Poverty remains widespread and progress is fragile. Incompetent governments will continue to build roads to nowhere, many pupils will still be taught in overcrowded classrooms, plenty of fields will be polluted and farmers will be pushed off their land to make room for investors. Inequality has fallen in only half of Africa's fifty-five countries. Fresh conflicts may arise when new wealth buys more weapons and begets more cross-border jealousies.[5]

Something, therefore, must be done to avert a situation that will throw Africa back to the dark periods of gloom and doom

4. Soyinka, *Open Sore of a Continent*, 97.

5. August, "Emerging Africa," 16.

characterized by the backwaters of underdevelopment. Among other suggested means, this chapter examines African Catholicism's role in promoting peace and good governance, education of civil society, and the promotion of integral development. This must be done in the light of the Second African Synod's apostolic exhortation, *Africae Munus*, which advocates a form of political Catholicism to integrate spirituality with involvement in the promotion of human development through good governance.

The Role of African Catholicism

According to the *AM*, African Catholicism is charged with bringing about attitudinal change in the people of Africa from selfishness to the pursuit of the common good. Politically, the role of the church is not to get involved in partisan politics. It is to guide leaders to make an altruistic commitment to the common good by educating them to distinguish between rights and duties. It is to promote good governance by ensuring the conduct of free and fair elections. Morally, African Catholicism is charged with the formation of African conscience regarding respect for the dignity of human life. Politically, this demands emphasis on the importance of openness and the right of each citizen to participate in the democratic process not only during elections, but also daily through freedom of speech, of religion, of participation in civic society, and access to other human rights. Judicially, African Catholicism is tasked with promoting a culture that respects the rule of law both within the ranks of the church and in society. As an institution, African Catholicism is to shun a culture of "big men," by refusing to benefit from corruption and to model by example the equality of all before the law. Closely related to this, African Catholicism must advocate for independent judiciary and prison systems. It is to be involved in the rehabilitation and correctional purpose of the prison systems by continuous provisioning of pastoral care to prisoners, as well as campaigning for the elimination of capital punishment and reform of penal system.

Socially, African Catholicism is charged with the formation of African personality through the appropriation of the Christian message in the light of African cultural values. It has the responsibility of resolving the anthropological crisis of identity bedeviling Africa, with its unfortunate history of slavery, colonialism, oppression, denigration, neo-colonialism, maladministration, and more, all of which diminish African's notion of themselves as human beings before people of other races and nations. Just as Christianity preserved European culture and civilization during the dark ages, African Catholicism is expected to pioneer changes in the social order through the preservation of African cultures amidst the sometimes-negative influences of various agents of social transformation. Through the gospel message of love and commitment to peace, African Catholicism must promote mutual coexistence by confronting ethnocentrism and tribalism at its root. While the First African Synod, *Ecclesia in Africa*, proposed the church in Africa as the "Family of God,"[6] *Africae Munus* extends the implication of the family image as a recipe for addressing the challenges of tribalism, ethnocentrism, nepotism, and favoritism that ruin not only the social order, but also the continent's political and economic development as well as good governance in many African countries.

Since education contributes to integral development, African Catholicism is tasked with contributing to an education that integrates faith and reason, especially in the light of the ongoing worldwide crisis in education. It is expected to establish schools and universities not only to obliterate illiteracy, but also to provide quality education that arms the people to seek independence. Of course, education here must incorporate human rights in accordance with the social and moral teachings of the church.

Education partly addresses another important issue—the issue of healthcare. Primary healthcare is abysmally low or utterly lacking in most African countries. Perhaps on account of corruption and or lack of interest, Africans suffer and die from preventable diseases. The *AM* expects African Catholicism to play a role

6. Synod of Bishops, *Lineamenta*, sec. 39.

here, bearing in mind the moral teachings of the church. HIV/ AIDS demands the church's attention in counteracting the ambiguity and aggressive media endorsement of the use of the condoms as a preventive measure instead of fidelity and abstinence. African Catholicism must educate the people on the correct relationship with their bodies and encourage a high moral and responsible lifestyle in order to prevent infection. However, in addition to education, African Catholicism is to lobby for the availability of generic drugs at affordable prices to minimize the impact of HIV/AIDS infection.

Closely related to this initiative is the responsibility to educate civil society to become politically, economically, socially, religiously, and morally conscious of their role in effective participation in the progress of society. African Catholicism achieves this goal through her Peace and Justice Commission, through education of Christians in the Catholic social teachings, and through conscientization of the citizens on their rights as citizens. More so, African Catholicism uses the pulpit to preach committed engagement to the common good. Over and above all other approaches, African Catholicism's example of life—especially through a simple lifestyle following the example of Jesus—is the best way of educating the civil society on the way out of a life of aggrandizement, selfishness, and political corruption.

Spiritually, African Catholicism nourishes the faith of Christians in Africa by leading them to a personal encounter with Christ. This is her specific mission. She achieves this by presenting the Scriptures as the word of God, as a guide for a holy life further nourished through the Holy Eucharist. All of this implies a spiritual renewal and an exemplary life shaped by a commitment to the person of Christ through the word of God. According to the *AM*:

> Authentic hearing is obeying and acting. It means making justice and love blossom in life. It is offering, in life and in society, a witness like the call of the prophets, which continuously united the word of God and life, faith and rectitude, worship and social commitment. Listening to and meditating upon the word of God means

letting it penetrate and shape our lives so as to reconcile us with God, allowing God to lead us towards reconciliation with our neighbor: a necessary path for building a community of individuals and peoples.[7]

African Catholicism can fulfill these expectations by living in accordance with Christ's justice. She must bear witness to the courageous love of Jesus, her founder, and emulate the selflessness that led him to embrace the suffering, pain, and humiliation of the cross. The *AM*'s charge to African Catholicism is a demanding one that requires high moral integrity and power in terms of the network and influence of the church in Africa. First, African Catholicism must implement "political, social and administrative justice at home" (*AM*, sec. 27). The just structures she expects of the public and government must also be seen among her rank and file. She must bear witness by being salt and light herself (Matt 5:13–16). Second, just like any other church, she must be open to reforms, being ready to acknowledge her weaknesses and prepared to embrace conversion in those places where she falls short. Third, African Catholicism must be disciplined and united. The faithful must be able to speak and act with one voice in their prophetic function. They must denounce social ills and avoid compromising their position with attachment to material things, including "Greek gifts" by which bureaucrats buy them over to ignore the plight of the masses. Fourth, African Catholicism needs a strong institutional structure that integrates the clergy, the religious, and the laity, with each actively contributing to the public role of the church in society. This structure is important in view of the Vatican II ecclesiology of the people of God and the First African Synod document *Ecclesia in Africa*'s structure of church as a "Family of God" on mission. Furthermore, the spiritual, moral, social, cultural, economic, technological, and political task entrusted to African Catholicism cannot be accomplished without the expertise of all the people of God and members of African Catholicism.

7. Benedict XVI, *Africae Munus*, sec. 16.

So Far So Good

The various Catholic Episcopal Conferences of African countries must be commended for their active engagement in the politico-economic, socio-pastoral, and cultural-religious lives of their flock. They make their voices heard in the changes and chances of the events of their various countries. For instance, after the years of military rule that brought the country to its knees, and with the people disappointed at the massive rigging of the 1999 elections, the Nigerian Bishops' Conference authorized the Catholic Church's observation of the 2003 elections, declaring their commitment to Nigerians' right to decide who their leaders were to be:

> [W]e will continue to play an increasingly active and important role as a positive element within the Nigerian society. We direct every parish to begin a programme of basic education in the civic rights and responsibilities of its members, especially through the justice, development, and peace committees. If one does not know his or her rights, it is all too easy for government and others to take them away. In addition, we commit ourselves to a nationwide programme of education on the social teachings of the Catholic Church.[8]

The democratic national civic education programs embarked upon by the Justice, Development, and Peace Commissions addressed apathy among Nigerians created by the dreary years of military dictatorship and the disappointing civilian governments that failed to meet Nigerians' basic needs.[9]

In the aftermath of the 2007–2008 Kenyan conflict following the contested election that left many Kenyans dead, "the Kenya Episcopal Conference (KEC), called a crisis meeting just days after the election on 27 December."[10] In order to forestall a repeat, they

---

8. Catholic Bishops Conference of Nigeria, "Building God's Kingdom," in Enwerem, *Crossing the Rubicon*, 159–60.

9. Ibid., 165.

10. "Kenya's Churches Driving Peaceful Resolution to Crisis," http://au.christiantoday.com/article/kenyas-churches-driving-peaceful-resolution-to-crisis/3863.htm.

embarked on educating Kenyans on free and fair elections, urging them to participate actively and unitedly as citizens of one country. Part of their communiqué reads:

> Recent General Elections in our country have been characterized by violence, evictions, quarrels and discord. In 2007/2008, many lives of people were lost and thousands displaced. As your Bishops, we call upon you to look at the past and the present of our country Kenya and shape our political relationship and thinking in a way that harmony will prevail. We remind you that peace is a divine gift which we cannot afford to lose. In fact our stable economic, social and religious well-being depends on how much peace we have shown. We should avoid falling into the same pitfalls that almost destroyed our country.[11]

In response to social ills caused by the Public Order Act, by which the ruling government discriminated and attempted to muzzle the opposition, the Zambian Episcopal Conference warns the government against plunging the nation into chaos in a pastoral letter:

> For whatever reasons, we have observed over the years that each ruling party seems to have unlimited freedom to conduct public activities of any type on any day and at any time while opposition political parties and some civil society bodies are literally discriminated against whenever they try to conduct public activities . . . We call upon the Government to embrace the spirit and letter of democracy before the nation is plunged into chaos. The Public Order Act, in its current form, has no place in our statutes. It is both repressive and anachronistic. It needs to be repealed.[12]

The National Conference of Catholic Bishops of Congo, in response to the disputed election of 2012, passed a vote of no

11. Kenya Catholic Bishops, "Kenya's Commitment to Peaceful General Elections," 4.

12. Zambia Episcopal Conference Plenary, "Act Justly and Walk Humbly," http://www.lusakatimes.com/2013/01/27/the-public-order-act-in-its-current-form-has-no-place-in-our-statutes-catholic-bishops/.

confidence on the Independent Electoral Commission of Congo. They assert: "The Independent National Electoral Commission 'no longer enjoys the confidence of the population.'" The bishops asked for reform that would "include members of the civil society for more independence." They warned the authorities that "if they continue to rule by defiance, tensions that may seem under control at the moment could rise into a serious crisis that sooner or later will be difficult to resolve." They called on the "Congolese people, not to fall into pessimism, despair, violence, tribalism, or xenophobia, but to unite behind democratic and Christian values 'of justice and truth.'" They assert: "Our country is going through a time of uncertainty and anxiety. Our faith in God and our trust in man, created in the image of God, convince us that this uncertainty and anxiety can be overcome through a change of heart, attitude and practices. We must love our country, be willing to give up selfish interests and seek through dialogue the ways to build peace in DR Congo."[13]

In Rwanda, amidst the growing violence that eventually led to the genocidal killing of over 800,000 Tutsi and moderate Hutus, the Rwandan Catholic Bishops Conference issued a statement urging the government to negotiate with the rebels.[14] The pastoral letter states: "The Catholic bishops of Rwanda urge the Government and the Rwandan Patriotic Front to avoid the logic of war to settle their disputes. May they do everything possible to stop the bloody troubles in some parts of the country so that they do not consume the rest of the country."[15] This statement, which coincided with the demands of the Rwandan Patriotic Front, led to the murder of

13. All quotations from the National Conference of Catholic Bishops of Congo are taken from "Congolese Have Lost Confidence in the Electoral Commission, Catholic Bishops Say," http://www.congoplanet.com/news/1939/congolese-have-lost-confidence-in-the-electoral-commission-catholic-bishops-say.jsp.

14. "Rwanda: How the Genocide Happened," http://news.bbc.co.uk/go/pr/fr/-/2/hi/africa/1288230.stm.

15. Cowell, "Slain Rwanda Bishops Had Urged Peace Talks," http://www.nytimes.com/1994/06/10/world/slain-rwanda-bishops-had-urged-peace-talks.html.

the principal officers of the Bishops Conference two months later: Bishop Thaddée Nsengiyumva, 45, the president of the Bishops Conference, was reported slain along with Vincent Nsengiyumva, 58, the Archbishop of Kigali, and Bishop Joseph Ruzindana, 51, of Byumba.[16] In the effort to heal the wounds of the genocide through national reconciliation, the Rwandan bishops accepted the government proposal and urged their faithful to participate in the Gacaca courts. In a June 13, 2002 pastoral letter entitled "Justice for That Reconciliation," the bishops charged the faithful as Christians, while partaking in the Gacaca courts, to state the whole truth. That is, "Accepting the guilty to apologize to those they have harmed and victims willing to forgive."[17]

In Cameroon, whose president has ruled since 1982 through a mixture of intimidation and corruption, the National Bishops Conference of Cameroon stands as a lonely voice demanding transparency and social justice.[18] The consequence has been the murder and questionable disappearance of many members of the clergy and religious men and women. Thus, at the 18th Seminar of Bishops of Cameroon (10–16 January 1994), "the Bishops alluded to the violent disappearance of His Excellency Mgr. Yves Plumey, retired Archbishop of Garoua, the disappearance of some priests and religious, the poor and defenseless people, not forgetting the frequent aggressions perpetrated on Catholic Missions and the exploitations and abuse regularly carried out against the weak and defenseless."[19] The April 29, 1995 murder of Father Engelbert

---

16. Ibid.

17. "Message of Catholic Bishops of Rwanda," http://cpn.nd.edu/conflicts-and-the-role-of-the-church/central-africa/reconciliation/reconciliation-after-genocide. For the original French, see also les Evêques Catholiques du Rwanda, "Pour une Justice qui Réconcilie: Message des Evêques Catholique du Rwanda; Pour la Période des Guridictions Gacaca," Conférence Episcopale du Rwanda, Kigali, Rawanda, June 13, 2002, http://repositories.lib.utexas.edu/bitstream/handle/2152/5127/2437.pdf?sequence=1.

18. Allen, "Pope Addresses Corruption, Conflict in Africa," http://ncronline.org/node/12630.

19. "Some Declarations of the Bishops," http://www.leffortcamerounais.com/2008/07/some-declaratio.html.

Mveng in Yaoundé, Cameroon, led the National Bishops Conference of Cameroon, mourning the murders of fellow priests and the faithful, to rebuke the laissez-faire attitude of the government towards solving the crimes: "What revolts and worries the Bishops of Cameroon and our entire society, is the fact that no inquiry has yet revealed the perpetrators and accomplices of these atrocious crimes, outside of a few cases."[20]

These examples show that the leadership of African Catholicism is deeply involved in the search for social justice in various countries of Africa. In fact, unlike European and North American Catholicism, African Catholicism is not engaged in abstract arguments about doctrinal issues. Instead, it is meaningfully engaged in Africa's social history with the aim of contributing to the good governance, development, and wellbeing of Africans. It is committed to its prophetic function by fearlessly denouncing criminal acts as well as recklessness and corrupt government practices, sometimes to the detriment of their own lives. Through the social teachings of the church, African Catholicism aims at transforming the social, political, economic, and cultural life in Africa by imbuing them with the gospel values of love, peace, and justice for the integral development of Africa. The cooperation of the various Christian groups in Zambia brought about a regime change in an election that saw the defeat of Kenneth Kaunda and President Frederick Chiluba's election on October 31, 1991. Paul Gifford writes: "The role of the churches in making the elections possible, but also in gently promoting Chiluba, has not been sufficiently recognized. One cannot ignore the role played by labor unions . . . women's groups, and the international community, or gloss over the fact that the populace was generally alienated from UNIP by shortages. However, the churches played a considerable role in the change."[21]

Closely related to Zambia's experience, where African Catholicism, in collaboration with other Christian groups, influenced civil society to bring about peaceful regime change, is Ghanaian Catholicism's equally powerful contribution to social

20. Ibid.

21. Gifford, *African Christianity*, 197.

transformation. As articulated by Paul Gifford, "whereas the Ghana Bar Association and the Association of Recognized Professional Bodies could not hold out against the hegemonic instincts of the PNDC, the Christian Council and the Catholic bishops generally succeeded 'in maintaining their autonomy and integrity in the face of government hostility.'"[22] Another case in point was the Malawi Catholic Bishops Conference, whose March 8, 1992 pastoral letter, "Living in Our Faith," demanded multiparty politics and human rights reforms, set up a chain of events that brought down the thirty-year rule of President Hastings Kamuzu Banda:

> The letter denounced the government's rigid censorship of mass media, infringement on education, and frequent illegal imprisonment of hundreds of Malawians. Two days later, the Bishops were arrested by the government, and detained and interrogated for eight hours. Inspired by the letter, university students in Zomba began demonstrations that spread to other areas of Malawi. Police fired at the demonstrators and the students, who were reported to have "battled" with police.[23]

In Mozambique, the Catholic Church, through connections with the Catholic community of Sant'Egidio, mediated in a peace process that reconciled warring parties in the country. Thus, the Catholic Church brought to an end the devastating war that wreaked havoc on Mozambique. This is remarkable, especially considering the failure of the international community in this regard. After the peace accord, the Catholic Church, in collaboration with other Christian churches in Mozambique, continued to further the peace process and stability of the country by engaging in processes of disarming the nation and ridding it of dangerous weapons of war. Through its exchange of weapons (which were later destroyed) for beneficial materials like sewing machines,

22. Ibid., 109.

23. Carpenter, "Malawians Bring Down 30-year Dictator, 1992–1993," http://nvdatabase.swarthmore.edu/content/malawians-bring-down-30-year-dictator-1992-1993.

corrugated iron sheets, bicycles, and the like, the church contributed to social reconstruction in Mozambique.[24]

However, one question that comes to mind is this: Considering the efforts of African Catholicism, why are changes slow, and in some situations, hardly visible except in such church institutions like mission schools and hospitals? Reflecting on the Ugandan experience of African Catholicism's public exhortations and denunciations based on Catholic social teachings, Emmanuel Katongole expressed his frustration over how little weight the pronouncements of African Catholicism seem to carry in transforming the social order in Africa. He confesses:

> As I studied the official documents of Catholic social teaching as well as the pastoral letters of the Uganda Catholic bishops, I discovered that these offered a number of beautiful suggestions and recommendations to ensure stability, peace, and development. I was, however, frustrated that none of these seemed to have deeply challenged or offered a viable and concrete alternative to the endless cycle of violence, plunder, and poverty. In a word, it was as if these recommendations and pronouncements did not matter one way or the other. What added to my sense of frustration was the realization that even though in many parts of Africa the church, at least numerically, was a strong and powerful institution, it did not make much difference to Africa's social history of violence, corruption, and poverty.[25]

Katongole's experience cuts across Africa, and to be honest, is true of the world as a whole, for one could equally ask why, in spite of Christianity's efforts and the values of other world religions, is there still so much evil and injustice in the world? However, let us examine some factors that constrain African Catholicism's commitment to social justice and social transformation.

24. Van Butselaar, "Role of Churches," 96–115.
25. Katongole, *Sacrifice of Africa*, loc. 146.

Constraints against African Catholicism

In spite of their courageous appeals and denunciations of injustices in Africa, one of the reasons the voice of the church is not heeded in the public arena of African life is because of the church's feeling of utter helplessness in the face of brutal injustice and violence in Africa. For instance, at a National Workshop from April 15 to 19, 1996, the coordinators for Justice, Development, and Peace in Nigeria observed, "the hierarchy and the faithful often react to unjust structures and acts of social injustice with a feeling of utter helplessness and resignation. This reality tends to make the Church an irrelevant entity in Nigerian [and African] society and the social doctrine a mere abstraction."[26] Furthermore, most of the pronouncements of the church hierarchy are vague and phrased in ways that do not hurt or indict the government of the day or name the perpetrators of social injustice against the people. At times their communiqués appear to be repetitive, an endless recitation of social ills, a constant repetition of unchanging woes and distress. There is also a great chasm between the pronouncements of the African church hierarchy and actual commitment towards achieving a just society. They see their prophetic mission as speaking out, exhorting the leaders to consider the plight of the people, and appealing to Africans to remain calm. Even when they do make truly prophetic statements, they do not outline an effective program of action to carry them out. Consider the 1996 Catholic Bishops Conference of Nigeria's condemnation of military rule for stifling democratic ideals, restricting freedom, and concentrating power to the center. But no program was marshaled out to overcome militarization except calls for prayer, penance, and fasting.[27]

Is this really a way of being prophetic after the manner of Old Testament prophets like Amos, Jeremiah, and of course, Jesus Christ himself? In the context of the social and political oppression Africans go through, can the African church say it has played

26. See Aguigwo, *Problem of Poverty in Nigeria*, 184.

27. "Communiqué on 'Rays of Hope,'" in Schineller, *Voice of the Voiceless*, 329–33.

its prophetic role of not only pleading for social justice, but of directly confronting social injustice and being ready to suffer to ensure the enthronement of social justice? According to Augustine Nebechukwu, in such contexts, prophetic roles involve:

> The pursuit of justice for the poor and the disadvantaged . . . direct confrontation with the causes of social and political oppression . . . critical awareness of, and actual naming of the plague, i.e., the concrete issues that violates justice . . . denunciation of real persons, social, political and economic institutions or structures, or formalistic religious worship insofar as any of them violates justice. There is in a way no room for an unnecessary prudential and pleading approach in dealing with the evil of injustice . . . It involves suffering and persecution for the agents of such a mission. [Finally, it involves] the participation of Christians in political action as a major aspect of the prophetic mission of the Church.[28]

In other words, it is not enough to make pronouncements, which remain empty platitudes when they are not reinforced with direct intervening action and readiness to walk one's talk. In view of these requirements for a prophetic church, it is difficult to say with certainty that African Catholicism has been true to its prophetic mission. On the contrary, as articulated by A. E. Orobator: "A profusion of solemn avowals of the prophetic mission of this church exists, but the analysis above leads us to conclude that this avowed prophetism only finds expression as a purely exhortatory function, seasoned with ample doses of verbal militancy and expressed in occasional polite deputations or high-profile delegations to political leaders."[29] George Ehusani, former Secretary General of the Catholic Secretariat of Nigeria, out of whose office most of the statements of the bishops emanates, confesses that:

> When it comes to prophetic confrontation with unjust social structures; when it comes to challenging the evil status quo, the social teaching of the Church does not

28. Nebechukwu, "Prophetic Mission of the Church," 110.

29. Orobator, *Church as Family*, 86.

> seem to have "taken flesh" in the Nigerian context. The majority of Nigerians, even Catholics, are not even aware of the powerful pronouncements of the Church on issues of justice and human development, perhaps because the public statements of the hierarchy have remained largely on the level of pious exhortations, passionate appeals, and benign denunciations, but lacking any practical gestures of solidarity with the oppressed and distraught with the oppressor. The Nigerian Church cannot be said to have really done much that will amount to a confrontation with the unjust and inhuman regimes that have plagued this land for the greater part of her life as a nation.[30]

In other words, aside from the few exceptions detailed so far, African Catholicism has been a sleeping giant with regards to its commitment to social and political change in Africa. While reckoned as a powerful institution, its role seems at best insignificant, apart from communiqués from the Episcopal Conferences and often foreign-financed social institutions like schools, hospitals, construction efforts, etc. Certain external and internal factors could be seen as responsible for this problem.

Some External Constraints

First, it is important to understand that Catholics are not the religious majority in Africa. Although the number of Catholics grew 21 percent between 2005 and 2010, with an estimated 175 million of the population of Africa identifying as Catholic, people of other Christian denominations and other religions outnumber them.[31] According to the Pew Forum on Religion and Public Life's research, in 2010 there were some 470 million Christians living in sub-Saharan Africa. Muslims in sub-Saharan Africa numbered 234 million, and about 27 percent of Christians and Muslims believed in the

30. Ehusani, *Prophetic Church*, 109.

31. Corey-Boulet, "With 176 Million Catholics, Africa Gains Prominence," http://www.usatoday.com/story/news/world/2013/03/12/catholic-church-africa/1963171/.

power and efficacy of African traditional religions.[32] In 2011, Pew reported that Catholics in sub-Saharan Africa made up an estimated 16 percent of the 62.7 percent of Africans who identify as Christians.[33] So it is that the communiqués of the bishops and their pronouncements, while addressed to all Christians and all people of goodwill, are generally received by a small percentage of African population. As Anthony Egan notes: "Africa is not Catholic but a religiously pluralist continent. Despite its enormous role in social and educational ministry crossing Christian and faith boundaries, the church needs to tread lightly in its theological articulation of its self-identity, particularly in countries . . . where the church is a minority."[34]

Second, the church also lacks functional communications structures to disseminate its communiqués, for the access to both electronic and print media is controlled by the government and in most cases do not allow any dissident views to be aired to the public. Most Catholic-owned print media are not widely circulated. Furthermore, people are so poor that their immediate concern is survival—looking for basic, scarce, and expensive essentials of life. Many people, therefore, are not aware of the church's communiqués. Added to this is the fact that many Africans are illiterate and so are not able to read the communiqués' technical language.

The material poverty of African Catholicism constitutes a third constraint. The African church is not a self-reliant, self-supporting, self-propagating church. It depends on the income of its flock to finance the majority of its projects. As the people become poorer, maintaining the church becomes a heavier burden. Thus, some Christians abandon the church on account of its constant financial demands. In effect, the church lacks the resources to implement its justice and peace program. It depends on foreign

32. Pew Forum on Religion and Public Life, "Tolerance and Tension," i, http://www.pewforum.org/executive-summary-islam-and-christianity-in-sub-saharan-africa.aspx.

33. Pew Forum on Religion and Public Life, "Global Christianity," 4, http://www.pewforum.org/Christian/Global-Christianity-exec.aspx.

34. Egan, "Governance beyond Rhetoric," 96.

grants that often do not match its domestic needs. Paul Gifford, in commenting on the place of foreign money in the African church, is clear on this point: "Overseas links . . . bring resources, and the Catholic Church has enormous resources available to it, so much so that it always seems to be presumed that money will come from external resources; it is rare in Africa to hear Catholic appeals for money."[35] This is changing because as the Catholic Church in Africa increases, they now appeal locally for money for their domestic needs. Financial constraints limit the ability of African Catholicism to be truly indigenous. Most of the churches in Africa are still considered mission churches, depending on money from the Holy See. Consequently, their budgets and activities are more susceptible to scrutiny by the Vatican. This dependence and attachment to Rome's mother-church apron strings militates against the emergence of a truly African Catholicism. Could this have contributed to the exceptionally low profile of the continent-wide Symposium of Episcopal Conferences of Africa and Madagascar (SECAM) on sociopolitical issues out of fear for offending the Vatican as Latin American Episcopal Council (CELAM), the Latin American prototype of such a body, did with its preferential option for the poor?[36] Due to this crippling dependence on overseas links, African Catholicism can hardly be considered to be self-reliant. They will always be told what to do.

Over and above these external constraints, however, are some internal restraints arising from certain signs of contradictions within the African Church that threaten to obscure her prophetic pronouncements.

Signs of Contradictions within African Catholicism

The advice of the late Professor Barnabas Okolo, while exhorting the church to the task of transforming Nigerian society, applies equally to African Catholicism:

35. Gifford, *African Christianity*, 311.
36. Ibid., 310.

> The critical role of the church as the "artisan of a new humanity" in Nigeria would mean to rise above the unwholesome values of the society. The church should never be so affected by these values that its power and freedom to act are neutralized and rendered ineffective. If this happens, it gradually becomes the slave of the system rather than its transformer. For it cannot whole-heartedly nor effectively oppose the society if it shares exactly the same mentality and values as the society.[37]

The "unwholesome values" of contemporary African society include attachment to money, bribery, corruption, nepotism, embezzlement, the flamboyant display of wealth, abuse of power and authority, class distinctions, poverty, exploitation, etc. Since what divides the world also divides the church, as the saying goes, one wonders how different the African church is from African society. Can the church really step back from the dominant culture enough to have space to critique it? How and to what extent does the church's witnessing afford moral authority to make pronouncements on justice? A look at some of the internal contradictions of African Catholicism reveal some baggage that may inhibit African Catholicism from fully fulfilling its mission and bearing adequate witness to the gospel.

The Flamboyant and Ostentatious Lifestyle of the Clergy

The lifestyle of the clergy in Africa hardly shows any commitment to the poor. The clerical state today is characterized by pomp and pageantry. Under the influence of materialism and clientelism, the clergy and religious leaders of the African church are identified by a flamboyant and ostentatious lifestyle, outdoing one another in material acquisition. Ordination to the priesthood appears to have become a status symbol and a sure guarantee of social standing and job security. For instance, Paul Gifford reports on the perception of the Catholic Church as a business venture among the

37. Okolo, "Liberation Theology," 183.

Pogoro Catholics in Southern Tanzania.[38] Nigerian priests compete with each other for material success by displays of wealth. Many drive flashy, expensive cars that others of a similar age could not dream of owning until they retire. As Elochukwu Uzukwu, a former rector at the Spiritan International School of Theology in Enugu, Nigeria, observes, "In Nigeria, the way money and wealth are employed as principal indicators of success among priests has reached a level of scandal."[39] Anthony Ekwunife explains the situation with these words:

> In their lifestyles, one often fails to distinguish between the wealthy secular Nigerian or businessman and a priest. Hence some of the indices of a successful priest in Nigerian society today are: doctorate secular degree that is marketable; lucrative secular job or a commanding job in ecclesiastical or secular sphere; an executive car—Mercedes Benz, V-Boot, and what have you.[40]

The rectories are palatial when compared to other houses in their neighborhoods. Yet the priests are dependent on poor parishioners who tax themselves heavily to maintain their high tastes. Some Catholic priests now advocate for religious taxation, urging their flocks to contribute one tenth of their income for the upkeep of the clergy according to the scripturally justified practice of tithing. Because of their comfort, most priests have lost all passion; that is, the capacity and readiness to care, to suffer, to have compassion, and to feel the plight of their flock. Thus, clergy often find it difficult to speak out in defense of the poor—about whose situations they know little or nothing—for fear of losing the support of the rich political class that supports their parish financially. At present, these priests' bourgeois lifestyle alienates people who see them as privileged, wealthy, and as part of the greedy elites. In other words, African priests have not been able to "rise above the unwholesome values of the society," as Chukwudum Okolo advised.

38. Gifford, *African Christianity*, 312.
39. Uzukwu, *Listening Church*, 102.
40. Ekwunife, "Image of the Priest," 156.

Marginalization of Lay Employees

Side by side with the ostentatious lifestyle of the clergy lies the brazen poverty of the African church's lay employees. The catechists who man most of the remote outstations, the members of the Confraternity of Christian Doctrine who prepare candidates for the sacraments, the cooks and stewards at the rectories, and the secretaries and other staff of the diocesan secretariats, are poorly paid and work without benefits. While local churches in Africa may not have the means to pay the minimum wage, it is difficult to reconcile the poverty of these workers with the apparent show of wealth of their employers, the church hierarchy. Thus the condition of these workers casts doubt in the minds of the people about the church's willingness and ability to demand justice from the political class. Consequently, two classes of Christians are created within the African church: the few in a privileged clerical class and the marginalized lay faithful. The former have all the rights and privileges, while the latter are denied the basic necessities. One therefore wonders from what position of moral authority the African church could call upon the government to be just. As Pope John Paul II noted to the bishops gathered for the Special Synod for Africa:

> The Churches in Africa are also aware that, insofar as their own internal affairs are concerned, justice is not always respected with regard to those men and women who are at their service. If the Church is to give witness to justice, she recognizes that whoever dares to speak to others about justice should strive to be just in their eyes. It is necessary therefore to examine with care the procedures, the possessions, and the lifestyle of the Church.[41]

Apparently, not much came out of the First African Synod in this regard. This could be because most churches lack the resources, or due to lack of advocacy and supervision, for there is no standard salary and benefit scheme across dioceses and parishes for the welfare of the workers. Unfortunately, at times the churches

41. John Paul II, *Ecclesia in Africa*, sec. 106.

take advantage of the abysmal conditions of the poor, who are willing to settle for little or nothing in their desperation for work. Perhaps for this reason, *Africae Munus* picks up the issue and charges
African Catholicism to ensure just wages for their employees:

> I urge bishops and priests to be concerned for the hu-
> man, intellectual, doctrinal, moral, spiritual and pastoral
> formation of catechists. They should pay great attention
> to the living conditions of catechists, in order to ensure
> their dignity. Nor should they overlook their legitimate
> material needs, since the faithful worker in the Lord's
> vineyard has a right to a just recompense (cf. Matt 20:1–
> 16), while awaiting their due from the Lord, for he alone
> is just and knows our hearts.[42]

This demand applies not only to the catechists, but also to
all those employed in any sector of the African Catholic Church.
Pope Benedict urges African Catholicism to take this charge seriously in order to protect the church's credibility, saying, "It will
also be fitting to ensure that personnel in the Church's educational
institutions, and indeed all Church personnel, receive just remuneration, in order to strengthen the Church's credibility" (*AM*, sec.
134). The marginalization of the lay employees is indicative of a
bigger challenge facing the ecclesiology of African Catholicism.

Ethnicity within the Rank and File of the Clergy

Another sign of contradiction within the African church is ethnocentrism. This weakness is a result of carrying into the church
the rivalry and suspicion that festers among the different ethnic
groups in Africa. This negatively affects the administration of the
church and even, at times, affects relationships within the church
hierarchy. It also gives rise to accusations of marginalization by
ethnic minorities against those perceived to be in the majority.
Even within a local church among people of similar ethnicities,
selections of bishops, transfers of priests, appointments, and

---

42. Benedict XVI, *Africae Munus*, sec. 126.

promotions are viewed with suspicion as priests form cliques and accuse the bishop or one another of marginalization or favoritism. Even the appointments of bishops have become a subject of great tribal politicking. Bishop A. O. Makozi acknowledged this trend in observing, "The rate at which some Church members promote disunity is becoming very alarming to say the least. The creation of new diocese and the appointment of Bishops have become a game play in which ethnocentrism or tribalism has seemingly become the order of the day in certain sectors in recent times."[43] Archbishop Albert K. Obiefuna likewise noted the reality of ethnocentrism in the African continent as a whole when, at the African Synod of 1994, he complained that in Africa "the blood of the tribe was thicker than the water of baptism."[44] George Ehusani bewailed similar situations and called for immediate action to arrest its corrosive effect on the Nigerian church:

> Ethnicism in the Nigerian Church is a reality that must be honestly addressed by bishops, priests and religious, if the Church must be faithful to its mission of evangelizing the Nigerian nation and people. For too long in our history as a Church and in our mutual relations, we have chosen to sweep the matter under the carpet and present an image of organic unity and claim a matter of solidarity. Yet now and again, comments are made and actions are taken by highly placed persons and groups in the Church that indicate the reality of deep-seated resentment and bitterness, if not hatred, among members of some ethnic groups against others.[45]

This crippling ethnocentrism in African Catholicism brings about serious strains in relationships between and among bishops,

---

43. Makozi, "Bishop's Welcome Address," 15.

44. Quoted in Shorter, "Curse of Ethnocentrism," 29.

45. Ehusani, "Evangelising Ethnic Loyalty in Nigeria," 145. In 2004, the Catholic Institute of West Africa held its CIWA Theology Week on the theme of "Ethnicity and Christian Leadership in West African Sub-Region," acknowledging that the church is not spared the "intrigues and excessive particularisms arising from ethnocentrism" (Nwaigbo et al. *Ethnicity and Christian Leadership*, 327–29).

priests, religious, and the laity. Because it is swept under carpet, it eats deeply at the church's foundations, giving rise to frustrations, disgruntled priests and religious, and at times the inability of the lay faithful to live and work together. The case of Rwanda is a wakeup call for every Catholic in Africa as to how far ethnocentrism, when unchecked, can become an agent of the devil to destroy not only the church, but to waste human lives as well. That churches became killing fields in Rwanda as people who worshipped together every Sunday turned against one another while African Catholicism was unable to do much, remains an indictment on the nature and the public role of African Catholicism. Katongole clearly describes the failure:

> The case of Rwanda is very instructive. Christianity has played an active role throughout Rwanda's history, and before the genocide, close to 90 percent of Rwandans self-identified as Christians. Yet not only did many Christians, including church leaders, fail to offer any form of marked resistance to the call to eliminate the Tutsi in 1994, many killings took place within the churches, with Christians killing other Christians. The church had been so thoroughly socialized by the dominant vision of Rwanda as a society inherently marked by Hutu-Tutsi rivalry that the elimination of the Tutsi "cockroaches" was easily projected as a civic duty . . . The church, the Catholic Church in particular, not only became a dominant actor in Rwanda's social and political history; it also became the state's most reliable partner in elaborating, advancing, and defending the Hamitic story . . . Since the dominant discourse and practice of Christian social responsibility in Rwanda succeeded in securely locking the self-understanding and mission of the church within the dominant political vision of a tribalized society, when it came to the final showdown, the church simply performed the story so well that being a Christian made no visible difference.[46]

---

46. Katongole, *Sacrifice of Africa*, loc. 618.

The backdrop of Rwandan genocide was the perpetuation of the Hamitic story that the Tutsi ruling class were invaders who supposedly came from distant lands over centuries and imposed their rule over the Bantu people.[47] This story, arising from gross misunderstanding informed by miseducation of Europeans about Africa formulated by the colonists, destroyed centuries of social identity roles by which the three groups of people—Hutu, Tutsi, and Twa—had assumed complementary roles through division of labor under the king (*mwami*) for the common good of Rwandan people. This disinformation deformed Rwandan identity and cemented the Hutu-Tutsi rivalry.[48]

Related incidents took place in other parts of Africa. For example:

> In Kenya, where more than half the population is Christian, the post-election violence divided the country along ethnic lines, leading to the death of thirteen hundred people. Similar situations have been witnessed in Burundi, Ethiopia, Sierra Leone, and other countries. Evidently, Christian identity is often submerged by the social, economic, and political threats that prioritize identities based on manipulated fears created by politicians and the subsequent unjust structures in place.[49]

In this way, seeds of discord are sown in the local church. As the clergy fight one another, they become divided on issues of social justice as some ally themselves with corrupt government officials from their ethnic groups. This situation makes the search for social justice much more complex.

In spite of these challenges, there is still a general belief that "churches can play a role in breaking down ethnic barriers, since the intensity of conversion bestows a new identity which transcends other identities."[50] The attitudinal change this demands

47. Safari, "Church, State and Rwandan Genocide," 876.

48. See Katongole and Wilson-Hartgrove, *Mirror to the Church*, loc. 449–694.

49. Opongo, "Inventing the Creative Approaches," 81.

50. Gifford, *African Christianity*, 347.

of African Catholicism is an intensification of efforts towards preaching the value of human life beyond one's own kith and kin. African Catholicism can stem the tide of ethnocentrism by persistently teaching the human dignity that all people are endowed with as beings created in the likeness of God. This is important because, as has been discovered, African values honoring the sacredness of life hardly go beyond each African's kith and kin. Thus, while the lives of one's family members are sacred, the lives of other people, neighbors from another tribe for instance, are not as valuable. Therefore, such lives can be sacrificed in ethnic conflicts. Odozor aptly describes the importance of this change in not only stemming the tide of ethnocentrism, but also in Africa's social and economic advancement:

> Africa's cultural patterns, which tend to guarantee full humanity only to one's kith and kin, have had deleterious consequences even in the economic development of the continent. "This non-appreciation of the humanity of the other" figures prominently "in Africa's many ethnic clashes today." The point is that in spite of a glorious history of respect and hospitality for the known other within one's own group, African traditional societies were not able to elevate this regard for the known other into a universal norm of human rights that can assure every citizen, irrespective of his or her other affiliations, equal protection before the law . . . "In order to metamorphose into modern democratic [and economically viable societies] African countries must expand their understanding of citizenship and develop a sense of participation as essential for the development and sustenance of democracy" and of economically viable states.[51]

While attitudinal change might take time, vigilance is recommended on the part of African Catholicism. In this regard, as an agent of peace, the church is to set up mediation centers or bodies to facilitate the process of reconciliation as recommended by the *Instrumentum Laboris* for the Second African Synod: "The Church-Family of God is called upon to establish mediation groups

51. Odozor, "Truly Africa, and Wealthy!" 273.

at various levels."[52] *Africae Munus* bids the faithful to open up the treasures of love as the uniting force that binds human beings together. This, it hopes, will dissolve the divisions of race, tribe, ethnicity, wealth, and other differences among human beings:

> Beyond differences of origin or culture, the great challenge facing us all is to discern in the human person, loved by God, the basis of a communion that respects and integrates the particular contributions of different cultures. We "must really open these boundaries between tribes, ethnic groups and religions to the universality of God's love." Men and women, in the variety of their origins, cultures, languages and religions, are capable of living together in harmony.[53]

The day Africans begin to accord full humanity to other people beyond their kith and kin will be the day Christian faith will become the guide for interpersonal relationship in Africa. On that day the evil of ethnocentrism, which is plaguing African societies and African Catholicism, will be laid to rest and Africans will coexist in harmony.

The Task Ahead

The challenges facing Africa—and the solution to which African Catholicism can contribute—demand the grassroots mobilization of people of diverse backgrounds and social values to promote a better knowledge of their rights and responsibilities as citizens. This includes education to nurture a change in attitude from ethnocentrism to a positive view of people of other tribes. Hopefully, mutual coexistence for the greater good of all would ensue. The pervasiveness of narrow-mindedness and tunnel vision, as well as the consequences of violence and armed conflicts arising from unchecked negative ethnic sentiments, makes such an education not only important but necessary and urgent.

52. Synod of Bishops, *Instrumentum Laboris*, sec. 109.
53. Benedict XVI, *Africae Munus*, sec. 39.

The various forms of discrimination against people on account of race, religion, and skewed social stratification against the poor negate the Christian anthropology of the dignity of all human beings before God. This anthropology is at the root of the church's social teachings.[54] As local church united in communion with the universal church, African Catholicism is obliged, like all other local churches, to teach and profess this theological anthropology. Although African Catholicism may not be the majority in Africa, significant portions of the population are Catholics. The grassroots mobilization that will bring about attitudinal change has to start in the classroom. For this reason, Catholic social teachings on the dignity of all human beings, on the common good, on the principle of solidarity and subsidiarity, on the universal destination of goods, etc., have to form part of the curriculum of study in the formative years of African youth. It is clear that attitudinal change cannot happen unless people are convinced through experience to change their views to accept that it is advantageous to promote the common good. *Africae Munus* recognizes this and urges a committed involvement in education through the establishment of Catholic universities, for higher education is needed for social transformation. Reflecting on the Second African Synod, Odomaro Mubangizi articulates this viewpoint as well:

> With renewed interest in higher education as a priority for the church in Africa, there is hope that the complex issues affecting Africa will be well analyzed, and appropriate pastoral strategies will be designed. If the Church is to offer credible and efficient alternatives to what the governments have offered so far, it has to invest in the academic formation of the agents of evangelization (lay, religious, and clergy) at the university level. Attention has to be paid to the pastoral areas identified: health, justice, peace, reconciliation, development, and higher education. It is not helpful to identify these areas as priorities and then fail to train competent personnel for them.[55]

54. See Paul VI, *Gaudium et Spes*, sec. 29.
55. Mubangizi, "Agent of Reconciliation," 112.

I agree with Emmanuel Katongole's analysis that "the root of the problem is that Christianity in Africa has failed to become a *way of life*, but has remained a *spiritual* affair."[56] This separation affects African Catholicism in two ways. On the one hand, it gives rise to a *fuga mundi* spirituality that makes African Catholics consider politics as a "dirty" and unwholesome endeavor for devout Catholics, as it might limit their chances of everlasting life. On the other hand, under Pentecostalism, there is no division between the spiritual and the practical, but instead a prosperity gospel wherein making money and progress is the hallmark of a devout Christian. The material and spiritual sphere are understood as parallel to each other under this construct, resulting in a lifestyle contrary to the gospel, for it considers the wealthy as righteous and blessed while the poor are seen as sinful and cursed. Catholic social teachings balance spirituality against active involvement in the social, political, economic, and cultural life of one's community.

The period after Vatican II marked significant shifts in the church's social teachings. Theological, ethical, anthropological, and ecclesiological perspectives have emerged that could be of great assistance to African Catholicism's perception of herself and her mission, especially in the quest for social justice. First, in reading the signs of the times, *Gaudium et Spes* theologically relates the gospel values of faith, fraternal love, charity, justice, and truth to daily life. It identifies the division between the faith that people profess and their daily life as a serious problem of our age. In *Gaudium et Spes*, social life is intimately connected with the dynamic of the Reign of God. It exhorts Christians to play their roles in society and not presume that the Christian vocation exonerates them from contributing to the temporal order. *Gaudium et Spes* states: "The Christian who shirks his temporal duties shirks his duties towards his neighbor, neglects God himself and endangers his eternal salvation."[57] In his address to the Diplomatic Corps on January 17, 1967, Pope Paul VI said:

56. Katongole, *Sacrifice of Africa*, loc. 1258, emphasis Katongole's.

57. Paul VI, *Gaudium et Spes*, sec. 43.

> The Church cannot remove herself from temporal affairs, because the temporal is the activity of men, and all that concerns men concerns the Church. A disembodied Church, separated from the world, would no longer be the Church of Jesus Christ, the Church of the incarnate Word. The Church, on the contrary, interests herself closely in every generous endeavor which helps to set humanity on the road to heaven, but also in the search for well-being, for justice, for peace, for happiness on earth.[58]

The church thus commits herself to the realization of a just and equitable society and sees this as constitutive to her very self and mission. In the light of this theological shift, African Catholicism is urged to preach integral salvation. Her catechesis should form people to relate their faith to daily life, to see the connection between Christian life and a commitment to the common good, and to ensure the creation of conditions that would enable Africans to realize their full potential as human beings while remaining open to the kingdom of God.[59]

Second, anthropologically, the Vatican II and post-Vatican II documents place a greater emphasis on the appreciation of the person as subject and the importance of the aspiration to human freedom, dignity, and participation in human affairs. In these documents, the church becomes more historically conscious by acknowledging the place of history in the story of salvation. Instead of the previous emphasis on a deductive method based on the eternal, immutable, and unchanging laws of human nature, the approach outlined in these documents is more inductive, based on the experiences of each group of people in the journey of faith. The post-Vatican II documents therefore offer more emphases on orthopraxis than on orthodoxy.[60] This shift in emphasis can be a

58. Quoted in Odey, *Search for Justice and Social Justice*, 44.

59. Cf. John Paul II, *Sollicitudo Rei Socialis*, sec. 47.

60. Paul VI, for one, acknowledged the effect that rapid changes have on the human person and urged that the human person be discovered anew in each social and psychological dynamism. Cf. Pius XI, *Quadragesimo Anno*, sec. 22–37. Pope John Paul II, to some extent, reversed the historical consciousness

great asset to African Catholicism. She must contextualize faith based on the social, religious, and psychological dynamisms of her people. She must pay attention to the praxis of her people's lives based on their struggles, their needs and their hopes, and be committed to the people's search for social justice. African Catholicism, like the universal church, must speak and work for the equality and freedom of Africans, irrespective of race, language, religion, or political affiliations.

Third, Vatican II provides an ecclesiological foundation for social ministry. *Lumen Gentium*'s description of the church as "like a sacrament or sign and instrument of a closely knit union with God and of the whole human race,"[61] presents the church as both a sign and a source of unity in human affairs. So it is that the church's right and competence to speak in public affairs accords with her nature. *Gaudium et Spes* affirms that the specifically religious mission of the church gave it "a function, a light and an energy which can serve to structure and consolidate the human community according to the divine law. As a matter of fact, when circumstances of time and place create the need, it can and indeed should initiate activities on behalf of all people."[62] Rightly then, its opening statements depict solidarity with humanity's present struggles.[63] Clearly, African Catholicism cannot be involved in partisan politics. However, it will always, in line with the teachings of the church, play its proper role in the state by promoting the common good and good governance through the formation of

---

of Pope Paul VI. For instance, in his encyclicals, Pope John Paul II adopts a more general approach applicable to all modern situations without regard to the signs of the times or the important role of various local communities. This is true of the encyclicals *Laborem Exercens* (1981), wherein he proposed an understanding of work applicable to all situations of modern world, as well as of *Solitudo Rei Socialis* (1987) and *Centesimus Annus* (1991), which propose a top-down rather than bottom-up method. Cf. Curran, *Catholic Social Teachings*, 55–65.

    61. Paul VI, *Lumen Gentium*, sec. 1.

    62. Ibid., *Gaudium et Spes*, sec. 42.

    63. Ibid., sec. 1.

conscience. Pope Benedict XVI clarifies the role of the church in politics thus:

> The Church cannot and must not take upon herself the political battle to bring about the most just society possible. She cannot and must not replace the State. Yet at the same time she cannot and must not remain on the sidelines in the fight for justice. She has to play her part through rational argument and she has to reawaken the spiritual energy without which justice, which always demands sacrifice, cannot prevail and prosper. A just society must be the achievement of politics, not of the Church. Yet the promotion of justice through efforts to bring about openness of mind and will to the demands of the common good is something which concerns the Church deeply.[64]

There should therefore be no doubt as to whether the church should be involved in political life. It should. What Pope Benedict XVI clarifies is how it should do this: "Clearly the church as an institution should not get involved in partisan politics, but the church has a right and a duty to take part in civic education, election monitoring, constitutional reform processes, and peaceful protests against injustices. Individual Catholics are also free to be actively involved in party politics."[65] Politicians are often afraid when the church actually takes her prophetic role seriously, when she begins to educate the citizens on their political and social rights. African Catholicism must not shirk this responsibility for any excuse whatever.

In the religiously pluralistic societies of Africa, the church's public role, articulated in her transcendence (i.e., in not being dependent upon any political authority) and freedom (i.e., her right as a religious community to speak, act, and influence society) should arm her to become socially engaged while remaining nonpartisan. She cannot be confined to the private arena, for her mission of evangelization is aptly fulfilled by her contribution to

---

64. Benedict XVI, *Deus Caritas Est*, sec. 28.

65. Mubangizi, "Agent of Reconciliation," 114.

solving the urgent problems of development. This is especially true as she proclaims the truth about Christ, about herself, and about the human person. She must apply this truth to concrete human situations. As a product of the missionary activity of the church, African Catholicism, in collaboration with other individuals and people of goodwill, must take "courageous and prophetic stands in the face of the corruption of political or economic power" in order to "serve the poorest of the poor."[66] African Catholicism must balance spirituality against human promotion. As articulated by Iheanyi M. Enwerem, "religious zeal that is not correspondingly sensitive, attentive and responsive toward the realization of the material happiness of human beings cannot qualify to be meaningful or credible. So too does a political quest lack meaning and credibility if it is not sensitive, attentive and responsive towards the ultimate destiny of human beings."[67]

Vatican II also witnessed an ecclesiological shift away from a juridical and primarily hierarchical view of the church to one of the church as the whole "People of God."[68] According to Peter J. Henriot et al., "This biblical image holds important implications not only for ecclesiology, but also for the Church's approach to the social order. The Church as 'People of God' lifts the faithful from a passive role to an active role in defining and shaping their history in the contemporary world."[69] African Catholicism should reevaluate her notion of the church in line with the shift in the nature of the church made at the Second Vatican Council. She should ask herself how far the faithful in her local churches have been lifted from a passive to an active role in the church and how they have been empowered to define and shape the history of their contemporary world by demanding social justice. This is important for two reasons. First, as noted already, African Catholicism is over-clericalized, thus leaving less room for involvement of the laity in the affairs of the church. Second, the emphasis on *fuga*

---

66. John Paul II, *Redemptoris Missio*, sec. 43.

67. Enwerem, *Crossing the Rubicon*, 3.

68. Paul VI, *Lumen Gentium*, sec. 9.

69. Henriot et al., *Catholic Social Teaching*, 19.

mundi spirituality makes Christians less active in sociopolitical affairs and hence unaware of the myriad social injustices in their societies. African Catholicism cannot be true to her mission as a post-Vatican II church concerned with justice, human promotion, and transformation of the world if it does not pay attention to the social justice situations of her people. She does this by applying the principles of Catholic social teachings to the sociopolitical and economic conditions under which her people live. In this way, African Catholicism can hope to contribute to the change in attitudes requisite for social transformation. The political Catholicism that the *AM* calls for will bring about attitudinal change and good governance in Africa. This is not participation as an institution in partisan politics. It is, on the contrary, the development of a positive attitude toward active political and social life in its particular local contexts in order to serve as salt and light. It thus avoids the extremes of complacency, of non-involvement, of what Martin Luther King describes as "do nothingism."[70] This is specifically what the *AM* calls attention to when it tasks African Catholicism to become the salt of the earth, the light of the world. It intends that political and social life be imbued with the Catholic Church's shared meanings and values. This is not just being ideological. Such a position is informed by the church's conviction of its possession of the truth that humanity needs for abundant life.

Because it reflects on culture and the role of religion within that matrix, theology is indispensable for the preservation of culture amidst promotion of the integral development in Africa. *Africae Munus*' demands of African Catholicism to ground the people of God in African culture such that they are able to participate in social and political life responsibly in the light of the Catholic social doctrine, saying: "In order to make a solid and proper contribution to African society, it is indispensable that students be taught the Church's social doctrine. This will help the Church in Africa serenely to prepare a pastoral plan which speaks to the

70. King, "Letter from Birmingham Jail," http://mlk-kppo1.stanford.edu/index.php/encyclopedia/encyclopedia/enc_letter_from_birmingham_jail_1963/.

heart of Africans and enables them to be reconciled to themselves by following Christ" (*AM*, sec. 137). It is therefore necessary, in order to promote the integral development needed to help Africans participate in governance and enjoy the fruits of economic growth, to appropriate the Catholic social teachings and adapt them to an African context. The next chapter seeks to do this by formulating a theology for development in the light of Catholic social doctrine.

6

Theology, Culture, and Sustainable Development in Africa[1]

The Church is eager to see the globalization of solidarity progress to the point where it inscribes "in commercial relationships the principle of gratuitousness and the logic of gift as an expression of fraternity," while avoiding the temptation to regard globalization as the only lens through which to view life, culture, politics and the economy, and fostering an ongoing ethical respect for the variety of human situations in the interests of effective solidarity.

—POPE BENEDICT XVI[2]

IN THE FACE OF the dangers facing cultures and peoples arising from globalization, this chapter presents theology as a tool for the preservation of cultural identity through its emphasis on human dignity. Using themes of development in Catholic social teaching to dialogue with contemporary theories of development, it cri-

1. This chapter improves on my article, "Theology, Culture and Sustainable Development in Africa," *Association of Catholic Universities and Higher Institutes of Africa and Madagascar Journal* 2 (2012) 1–30.

2. Benedict XVI, *Africae Munus*, sec. 86.

tiques the philosophical anthropological backdrop of development as mere economic growth and suggests an integral developmental structure that takes care of the human integral scale of values in order to provide schemes of recurrence for the provision of the common good and the development of the human person. It also examines the implication of this theology for integral development of Africa, as well as the role of African Catholicism in the light of *Africae Munus*.

Considering the general understanding of development as having to do with economic profit, one might wonder why and how this should be subject matter for theology, which is generally assumed to be concerned with the study of God and of God's relationship with creation. In order words, what does theology have to offer contemporary development discourse? And in what ways can theology, by humanizing globalization, stop the erosion of cultural values and its corrosive consequences for human wellbeing? With particular reference to Africa, how does theology promote holistic sustainable development?

Contemporary development discourse refers to the various complex viewpoints on how to further development in order to promote human wellbeing. As such, it is a human phenomenon, and it impacts various aspects of human life: technological, economic, social, political, cultural, personal and spiritual. Contemporary development must therefore take note of the anthropological constitution of human beings in terms of their historical consciousness as potentially open to progress, with the possibility of decline and capacity for restoration and redemption.

As a human phenomenon, development affects values, common meanings, and the institutional structures of society. Consequently, it is not solely economic, but also includes all aspects of human life. Theology proceeds from this social historical consciousness to reflect on common grounds of human existence— the meaning, truths, and values that uncover the universal in the particular and provide unity and intelligibility to life through transcendental analysis.

Theological studies, while acknowledging transcendental reality and its grounding of the human condition, pay attention to the social historical condition of human existence. Thus, theology and religion have much to say about development: its justness, impact on life, degree of helping religious ends, and spiritual fulfillment of human beings. For instance, *Africae Munus* emphasizes the moral spiritual components of human fulfillment that must not be neglected in the process of globalization:

> The truth of globalization as a process and its fundamental ethical criterion are given by the unity of the human family and its development towards what is good. Hence a sustained commitment is needed so as to promote a person-based and community-oriented cultural process of worldwide integration that is open to transcendence.[3]

Therefore, religion, as the conscience of society and theology as reflection on religions, has to critically assess contemporary development discourse to ensure that human wellbeing is achieved through various development methodologies.

The Trajectories of Development Discourse

The major trajectory of contemporary development discourse spans various historical epochs of the Western agrarian and industrial revolution. This includes the traditional period articulated in such books as Marx Weber's *The Protestant Ethic and the Spirit of Capitalism*. The mercantilist period, characterized by government control of the economy, saw to the creation of colonies and the extraction of their resources for the benefit of the mother countries. This became true of Africa when, in 1885 at the Scramble and Partition of Africa in Berlin, various European countries divided the continent among themselves and over the following decades appropriated Africa's human and natural resources for their own development. In the classical period, the idea of a free market economy, based on Adam Smith's notion of self-interest,

3. *AM*, sec. 86..

gave birth to liberal capitalism and neoliberalism characterized by privatization and reduction of government expenditure on welfare schemes.[4] The consequences of neoliberal policies since their reintroduction in the early 1970s will be discussed further shortly, but in spite of neoliberalism's achievements, it can bring about untold hardship on people, especially the poor whose wellbeing it claims to uplift.

Modernization theory, as represented in W. W. Rostow's stages of growth theory, holds that progress and development follow a similar pattern "lying within one of five categories: the traditional society, the preconditions for take-off, the take-off, the drive to maturity, and the age of high mass-consumption."[5] Modernization theory emphasizes the need for big companies, access to large amounts of capital, and modern social organization values as necessary for developing countries to catch up with the West. Dependency theorists tie world poverty, especially as it affects developing countries, to the colonial era of 1500, the period of mercantile capitalism during which the rich countries of Europe and North America exploited the natural and human resources of Africa, South America, and Asia.

Modern globalization has been facilitated by the imposition of a structural adjustment program (SAP) on developing countries by international financial institutions like the International Monetary Fund and the World Bank. This led to the devaluation of developing countries' currencies and the opening of their markets under World Trade Organization rules and treaties. These policies crammed neoliberal policies down the throats of the heavily indebted countries of the developing world. In consequence, the sovereignty of developing countries was effectively transferred to the various transnational corporations who, through privatization, now influence most contemporary government policies. Using Ghana in West Africa as a case study, Boafo-Arthur Kwame warns:

4. See Smith, *Wealth of Nations.*

5. Rostow, "Stages of Economic Growth," 47.

It is dangerous for African development if the philosophy of the current contraction of the state embedded in neoliberal orthodoxy is not reversed. It is an incontrovertible fact that active government intervention is crucial, especially in building up social capital and physical infrastructure in education, health, housing, transport, communication and other related government services . . . In essence, the central lesson that we can learn from the NICs [newly industrializing countries] is that "there is no alternative to the state."[6]

This is especially true of Africa, whose philosophy and worldview prioritizes community life and the protection of the common good. The substitution of the state in Africa by multinational corporations contributes to the marginalization of the vast majority of the population of Africa, who are denied the welfare schemes and protections enjoyed in other continents. The implementation of the economic recovery packages like the SAP also accounts for increasing social chaos as people turn against each other in the intense struggle for survival.

Appraisal of Development Discourse

It is a challenge to assess the impact of sustainable development, and even more so to appraise its effect in Africa. This is because such assessment invariably ends up straying into an analysis of the impacts of globalization. Arguments for or against globalization appear not to have solved the basic goal of reducing world poverty and establishing a world economic and political order that can produce enough food and services to improve the human condition. However, contemporary development discourse pays attention to some aspects of the human good but often neglects certain other elements. According to Pawlikowski, "To the extent that the globalization process enables us to break down cultural, ethnic, and religious barriers and brings us into increased human understanding and solidarity, it is a good thing. Insofar as

6. Boafo-Arthur, "Tackling Africa's Developmental Dilemmas," 42.

it becomes a generator of cultural and economic hegemony by rich and powerful nations over other peoples, it deserves strong condemnation."[7] In spite of its laudable achievements, unfortunately globalization becomes just that: "a generator of cultural and economic hegemony by rich and powerful nations over other peoples." According to Escobar, "Development was—and continues to be for the most part—a top-down ethnocentric and technocratic approach, which treated people and cultures as abstract concepts, statistical figures to be moved up and down in the charts of progress."[8] The "Statement on the Lisbon Meeting by Officers of the Interreligious Peace Colloquium" sums up the domineering tendencies of neoliberalism and consequent underdevelopment of peoples: "Underdevelopment, therefore, is not simply national or cultural backwardness of people . . . It comes rather from an exploitative global system and development models imposed by the North. So Southern underdevelopment is the ugly by-product of Northern industrialization for selfish nationalist goals."[9]

This kind of underdevelopment is abundantly evident in Africa, where the postcolonial political structure is characterized by statism and arbitrariness, reducing politics to an accumulation of power that favors not development but underdevelopment. As Ake recapitulates,

> At independence the form and function of the state in Africa did not change much for most countries in Africa. State power remained essentially the same: immense, arbitrary, often violent, always threatening. Except for a few countries such as Botswana, politics remained a zero-sum game; power was sought by all means and maintained by all means. Colonial rule left most of Africa a legacy of intense and lawless political competition amidst an ideological void and a rising tide of disenchantment with the expectation of a better life . . .[10]

7. Pawlikowski, "Creating an Ethical Context for Globalization," 363.

8. Escobar, *Encountering Development*, 44.

9. Rosenhaus et al, "Statement on the Lisbon Meeting," 233.

10. Ake, *Democracy and Development*, 6.

Thus, for most of Africa, *ab initio*, there was actually no development policy in place to start with. Contemporary development discourse prioritizes the basic needs of humankind only insofar as provision of these basic needs continue to promote economic growth. It does not pay sufficient attention to other values necessary for optimum human life, wellbeing, and happiness.

Impacts on Cultural Values

The desire for economic growth and quest for profit for increased production and consumption changes the patterns of societal life and values. For instance, economic globalization in defense of a free-market economy measures growth in terms of GNP, the sum total of goods produced in a given country. GNP neglects to consider unequal distribution of goods and other non-measurable activities in an economy. Such scaled measurement of growth equally disregards the other institutions of society, which together with the economy, promote human wellbeing, progress, and development. Thus, for Amartya Sen and other economists critical of globalization like Joseph E. Stiglitz or Zygmunt Bauman, "the importance of the market for any substantial development does not preclude the role of social support, public regulation, or statecraft when they can enrich—rather than impoverish—human lives."[11]

The dominant paradigm of development as economic growth disintegrates the basic structure of societal cultural values and focuses all human endeavors on the accumulation of capital, profit, and consumption, thus secularizing society. For instance, Margaret Thatcher, as the champion of neoliberalism, states: "There is no such thing as society. There is only the economy and families."[12] Such a viewpoint leads to the dehumanization of the human person who naturally lives interdependently in society. Furthermore, as Wendell Berry recounts, economic globalization fuelled by

11. Sen, *Development as Freedom*, 7.
12. Luxton, "Doing Neoliberalism," 175.

industrialization and consumerism is not sustainable.[13] It leads to greater urban migration, reduction in the cost of labor, and the denigration of human dignity as human beings become little different from objects, things to be used and discarded at will. It also lays a heavy burden on the environment, increasing depletion of the ozone layer and global warming. This neoliberal economic globalization leads to changes in lifestyle that emphasize freedom from constraint instead of freedom to be responsible for the promotion of the common good, shifting the conception of self from being to having. Thus, individual interest is pursued in the quest for increased economic growth to enable individuals to purchase and consume whatever they want.

Some philosophers and theologians engaged in x-raying contemporary society are concerned over this loss of meaning. Taylor worries over three dangers facing our society, which include "the fading of moral horizons . . . the eclipse of ends, in face of rampant instrumental reason, and a loss of meaning."[14] Visser, following Max Weber, sees this loss as confinement in an iron cage. Unfortunately, Visser argues, we conceive of ourselves as no different than automatons—as not only moving by ourselves, but also "as causeless chance," causing loss of meaning.[15] A plethora of scholarly articles and works reflecting on like-minded viewpoints, such as those of Max Weber's *The Protestant Ethic and the Spirit of Capitalism*, share Visser's view that neoliberal capitalism produces guilt, despair, and an iron cage. Sölle links the numbing of the West to the two interconnected trends of globalization and individualization. Globalization's efficiency in productivity, consumption, and profit, leads to the alienation of humankind because, as Visser says, human beings become addicted to technocracy and are made more dependent than ever before. The interdependency of the two trends produces a different kind of human being—one who is impersonal and without feeling. Thus:

13. Berry, "Inverting the Economic Order," 484–85.
14. Taylor, *Malaise of Modernity*, 10.
15. Visser, *Beyond Fate*, 86.

One of the spiritual difficulties in our situation is the inner connection between globalization and individuation. The more globally the market economy structures itself, the less interest it demonstrates in the social and ecological webs in which humans live, and the more it requires the individual who is without any relationship whatever. The partner that our market economy needs is *Homo economicus*. This is an individual fit for business and pleasure, showing no interest in the antipersonnel mines that his car manufacturer produces, no interest in the water that his grandchildren will use—not to mention interest in God.[16]

Friedman, a known propagandist of the benefits of globalization, equally warns that the major problem facing globalization is the challenge of the loss of cultural values. "The challenge in this era of globalization—for countries and individuals," Friedman says, "is to find a healthy balance between preserving a sense of identity, home and community and doing what it takes to survive within the globalization system."[17] Pope Benedict XVI and Pera's description of Europe as a society that has lost its roots also offers a concrete example of the loss of meaning and the adverse effects of globalization on human society. The consequence, they write, is that relativism, which has "become the real religion of modern men,"[18] begins "penetrating far into the realm of theology, is the most profound difficulty of our day."[19] Following Lonergan, for whom culture is common meaning, we understand that loss of meaning for a people is a loss of their culture, of the pattern of their life, of cohesion, of order, and of a system of organizing themselves, including production and distribution of goods and services.

The effects of globalization on Africa and Asia are no less different. While globalization brings untold hardship to poor people in Africa, whose standard of living and life expectancy keeps going

16. Sölle, *Silent Cry*, 191–92.
17. Friedman, *Lexus and the Olive Tree*, 42.
18. Benedict XVI and Pera, *Without Roots*, 22–23.
19. Ibid., *Truth and Tolerance*, 84.

down, it also increases incidences of domestic violence among African immigrant families and honor killings among Asian immigrants, among other ills. Henriot, who has lived many years in Africa, asserts:

> Globalization is not working for the benefit of the majority of Africans today. While globalization has increased opportunities for economic growth and development in some areas, there has been an increase in the disparities and inequalities experienced especially in Africa . . . While neoliberal economists argue that there may be "short-term pain but long-term gain" in the implementation of SAP, it is increasingly clear throughout Africa that the short-term pain, for example, of social service cuts, ecological damages and industrial base erosion will in the long-term have truly disastrous effects upon any hope for an integral and sustainable human development.[20]

Globalization tends to make human community a secondary phenomenon in its quest for self-interest, wealth and power, comfort for a few, and domination of the weak. As such, neoliberalism is unable to provide an ideal experience for human fulfillment that goes beyond mere material needs to spiritual fulfillment. It sidelines African culture and sees it as an enemy of progress. Because it conceives of development as an autonomous process that is applicable to all cultures and peoples, contemporary development discourse pursues an undeclared war on African culture that resists projects that will not come to terms with it or recognize its impact on the life of the people. As Ake observes,

> The more the resistance of African culture became evident, the more the agents of development treated it with hostility; and soon enough, they construed anything traditional, including the rural people, negatively. They castigated peasants for being irrational, un-enterprising, superstitious, and too subjective and emotional in their attitudes . . . Because the development paradigm tends to have a negative view of the people and their culture, it

20. Henriot, "Globalization: Implications for Africa," http://www.sedos .org/english/global.html.

cannot accept them on their own terms. Its point of departure is not what is, but what ought to be. The paradigm focuses on the possibility of Africa's becoming what it is not and probably can never be. Inadvertently perhaps, it discourages any belief in the integrity and validity of African societies and offers the notion that African societies can find validity only in their total transformation, that is, in their total self-alienation.[21]

Consequently, any reorientation of societal values must include an inculcation and promotion of the practice of preferring the common good over self-interest, as well as a deep respect for the cultural and personal values of divergent peoples.

Africae Munus expects African Catholic universities and higher institutes of education to take the lead in laying such a solid foundation for Africa. This is reflected in Benedict XVI's appeal: "Dear brothers and sisters in Catholic universities and academic institutions, it falls to you, on the one hand, to shape the minds and hearts of the younger generation in the light of the Gospel and, on the other, to help African societies better to understand the challenges confronting them today by providing Africa, through your research and analyses, with the light she needs" (*AM*, sec. 135). The Pontiff repeatedly emphasizes the role Catholic social doctrine will play in shaping the future of Africa: "Christians, and young people in particular, should study the educational sciences with a view to passing down knowledge full of truth: not mere know-how but genuine knowledge of life, inspired by a Christian consciousness shaped by the Church's social doctrine" (*AM*, sec. 134). One wonders why Benedict XVI insists on education in the Catholic social doctrine and its relevance for African development, one of the tasks set out for African Catholicism.

Towards Theology of Sustainable Development

The reason is not far-fetched. Catholic social teaching emphasizes integral human development that respects the dignity of human

---

21. Ake, *Democracy and Development*, 16.

beings as created in the likeness of God.[22] It teaches each person's human right to optimum development from the resources of the earth.[23] It critiques development in terms of mere economic growth for promoting a dehumanized form of development.[24] It points to a hierarchy of values upon which human life should be organized.[25] Its theological anthropology is holistic without neglecting the socio-economic as well as political, cultural, and spiritual dimensions of human existence.[26] These principles of Catholic social teaching include the principle of the common good, of the universal destination of the earth's goods, of solidarity, and of subsidiarity, etc.

The principle of the common good insists on the promotion not only of one's own good, but also of the good of other members of one's community and of the good of humanity as a whole.[27] The principle of the universal destination of the earth's good states that the resources of the earth belong to everybody and therefore should nourish every human being.[28] It restates the right of every human being to benefit from the resources of the earth. The principle of solidarity emphasizes the fact of human interdependence and the need for mutual support for the realization of the common good, happiness, and wellbeing.[29] The principle of subsidiarity states that it is not respectful of human dignity to prevent people from expressing their community membership or prevent them from participating fruitfully at any level of community life. The principle of subsidiarity opposes the two extremes of social-

22. Paul VI, *Populorum Progressio*, sec. 14; Benedict XVI, *Caritas in Veritate*, sec. 30.

23. Pontifical Council for Justice and Peace, *Compendium of the Social Doctrine of the Church*, sec. 172.

24. John Paul II, *Sollicitudo Rei Socialis*, sec. 46.

25. Paul VI, *Populorum Progressio*, sec. 18.

26. Benedict XVI, *Caritas in Veritate*, sec. 11.

27. John XXIII, *Mater et Magistra*, sec. 65; John Paul II, *Centesimus Annus*, sec. 58.

28. John Paul II, *Centesimus Annus*, sec. 31.

29. John Paul II, *Sollicitudo Rei Socialis*, sec. 39.

ism and neoliberal capitalism in government. In socialist regimes, government takes the provision of people's needs unto itself and thus robs people of creativity, denigrating their human dignity by taking away responsibility for their lives. On the other hand, in its defense of the free-market economy, neoliberal democracy reduces government involvement in the provision of social services. The principle of subsidiarity states that the role of government should be *subsidium*, or helping people realize themselves without taking over the running of their lives.[30] At the same time, there is no alternative to the state in the provision of social services.

These principles are based on a theological anthropology that emphasizes the dignity of the human person. It insists on integral human development that benefits humanity as a whole—personally, socially, economically, politically, and religiously—and help the individual realize his or her potential to promote social wellbeing. In his encyclical *Populorum Progressio*, Pope Paul VI states: "The development We speak of here cannot be restricted to economic growth alone. To be authentic, it must be well rounded; it must foster the development of each man and of the whole man."[31] Benedict XVI agrees with Paul VI and writes, "Authentic development must be integral; that is, it has to promote the good of every man and of the whole man." Furthermore, "The truth of development consists in its completeness: If it does not involve the whole man and every man, it is not true development."[32]

Pope Benedict XVI's 2009 encyclical on the topic of *Caritas in Veritate*—Charity in Truth—is the latest articulation of the Catholic social position on integral human development. The encyclical, written within the context of the changes arising from globalization, urges adherence to transcendent values such as respect for human dignity, justice, and the common good as "not merely useful but essential for building a good human society and for true integral human development." This vocation to promote

30. Pius XI, *Quadragesimo Anno*, sec. 79.

31. Paul VI, *Populorum Progressio*, sec. 14.

32. Benedict XVI, *Caritas in Veritate*, sec. 18.

authentic development requires responsible freedom of individuals and respect for the truth of our common humanity in love, which effects a transition from neighborhood to brotherhood. He further writes:

> As society becomes ever more globalized, it makes us neighbors but does not make us brothers. Reason, by itself, is capable of grasping the equality between men and of giving stability to their civic coexistence, but it cannot establish fraternity. Fraternity, brotherly love, originates in a transcendent vocation from God the Father, who loved us first, teaching us through the Son what fraternal charity is.[33]

The powerful force of globalization the Pontiff cites needs the guidance of charity in truth without which the human family will face unprecedented damage and division.[34] Hence charity and truth confront us with an altogether new and creative challenge, one that is vast and certainly complex. "It is about broadening the scope of reason and making it capable of knowing and directing these powerful new forces, animating them within the perspective of that 'civilization of love' whose seed God has planted in every people, in every culture."[35]

Applying the principles of gratuity, solidarity, and justice (commutative, distributive, and social) to the free-market capitalist enterprise, the encyclical advocates a new way of doing business that takes note not only of the interest of the proprietors, but also of all the stakeholders who promote business enterprise: the workers, the customers, the suppliers, and the community as well. Since business is built on trust, the principle of solidarity and of the interdependence of peoples is a *sine qua non* in the new world order and business enterprise. Furthermore, "A reformed market is one that permits the free operation, in conditions of equal opportunity, of enterprises in pursuit of different institutional ends: profit-oriented private enterprise, public enterprise, and commercial

33. Ibid., sec. 19.
34. Ibid., sec. 33.
35. Ibid.

entities based on mutualist principles and pursuing social ends."[36] Businesses should also promote the common good and ensure that the interests of individual proprietors do not override the common interest. Thus, while the state should allow every citizen to participate in the process of development, it must intervene in the process to set rules that protect citizens from various forms of abuse from forces of globalization like transnational corporations (TNCs). When integral development is implemented, it becomes clear that globalization in itself is not deterministic, but instead promotes the networking needed for development and progress towards cultural, social, personal, and religious fulfillment in its provision of the basic needs of life.

The success of globalization lies not only in acknowledging the interdependence of humanity in the promotion of a free-market economy, but also in appropriating the interdependence embedded in the principle of solidarity. This means the promotion of integral human development is in the overall common interest of humanity for the simple reason that whatever happens in one part of the globe affects other parts as well.

In order to establish a truly Christian humanism founded on charity and truth, theology must promote the conversions of minds and hearts, triggering a turnaround from a development founded on materialist principles to one that is founded on God as the foundation of development. Psychic, intellectual, moral, and religious conversion is needed to balance the experience of development. For instance, where intellectual conversion is lacking, there arise controversies like those between naïve realists, empiricists, idealists, and critical realists. A flawed anthropology that views development as mere economic growth and conceives of human beings as *homo economicus* fails to comprehensively account for the cultural, personal, and religious implications of development. Absence of moral and spiritual conversion leaves the distinction between satisfaction and values unclear. It leaves contemporary development discourse stuck in the immediate need to satisfy hunger and maintain socio-economic and political

36. Ibid., sec. 38.

structures while ignoring the broader aspects of human meaning and values, leaving the human spirit yearning for dignified living.

The situation becomes more difficult when religious conversion is lacking such that people not grasped by ultimate concern become steeped in shortsighted practicality. Such people are left in the dark concerning the meaning of otherworldly love. Lacking total and permanent self-surrender without conditions, qualifications, or reservations, such individuals are incapable of self-transcendence. Little wonder then that Adam Smith's proposition that "it is not from the benevolence of the butcher, the brewer, or the baker, that we can get our dinner, but from their regard to their own interest"[37] still prevails and continues to influence public policy and shape the world political economy under the World Trade Organization rules and strategies.

Implications for Sustainable Development in Africa

The principles of Catholic social teaching, which is in consonance with the communitarian societal structure of African cultural values, address the loss of meaning confronting African peoples as they face various forms of decay in their institutional structures. African liberation theologies must emphasize conversion—intellectual, moral, psychic, and religious—for African peoples and leaders of government so as to guard against the group bias that leads to the privatization of the state, endemic corruption, ethnocentrism, violence, and wars that plague Africa and rob the content of opportunities for integral development. Such theologies must speak up against exploitative power relations in international relations and trade that deny Africa the benefits of globalization. Here, the principle of the universal destination of the earth's good, of solidarity and subsidiarity, and the common good must be brought to bear to remind the rich countries of North America and Europe and their collaborators in Africa that we are all brothers and sisters, helping them recognize that promoting integral

37. Smith, *Wealth of Nations*, 14.

development is to our common interest as human beings. At the same time, the principle of the common good must be used to emphasize, especially to the inefficient leadership of Africa, that their countries' resources belong to the people and must not be used as a private property but for the common good of all Africans.

Little wonder, then, that *Africae Munus* exhorts African Catholicism to educate the people in the Catholic social doctrine. It states: "In order to make a solid and proper contribution to African society, it is indispensable that students be taught the Church's social doctrine. This will help the Church in Africa serenely to prepare a pastoral plan which speaks to the heart of Africans and enables them to be reconciled to themselves by following Christ."[38] This education is increasingly important if the civic society in Africa is to become better organized in demanding their rights and overcoming the petty divisions by which the political class weaken their ability to effect advantageous changes. The majority of Africans are made to demean themselves, to consider themselves second-class citizens under the hierarchical societal structure set up by the few elites who benefit at the expense of the masses. But through education in Catholic social doctrine, knowledge of the inherent dignity of every human being will help Africans hold their leaders accountable. This is so important because unless Africans begin to demand changes, their condition will never improve. While it is true, as Orobator observes, that most of the Catholic social doctrine is written against a backdrop of Western socio-economic, cultural, and political contexts that often do not reflect African historical contexts,[39] the Catholic social doctrine remains relevant for the African realization of integral development, albeit in an inculturated form.

African Catholicism must re-appropriate the communitarian societal structure that respects and promotes the common good embedded in traditional African cultural values. The privatization of the state must give way to a transparent democracy whereby the people are respected and government is made accountable to

38. Ibid., 137.

39. Orobator, "Africa's Burden of (Under)Development," 320–34.

the people. Here the principles of the common good, of solidarity, and of subsidiarity become meaningful in promoting true integral development. In order to achieve this shift, a reorientation of state-craft and public institutions toward the provision of the human good will be necessary. This turnaround must be accompanied by education of civil society on citizens' power and role in democratic government. This is important because people in sub-Saharan Africa often view the state as distant and with little or no connection to or concern for their wellbeing, and therefore as an institution to be exploited for self-enrichment. Catholic universities must prioritize this education to achieve a holistic sustainable development in Africa. Catholic social teaching will surely have a positive impact not only on Africa's socio-political challenges, but also on the ongoing anthropological crisis plaguing the continent. As firmly articulated by Odozor:

> At the root of Africa's economic crisis is an anthropological crisis that has left the entire continent in search of its soul and its place under the sun for the past four hundred years. This anthropological impoverishment began around the time of the transatlantic slave trade and continues today through the brutalization of the African psyche as a result of internal and external factors. Any African renewal must first address this anthropological impoverishment of Africa. In other words, Africans must somehow be helped to believe in themselves again. The greatest contribution of CST [Catholic social teaching] is that it provides a framework for African renewal . . . Its [CST] focus has been on the human person, adequately considered, in all the dimensions of human life. African economic planners need to read these texts not just as religious opinion, but as resource materials to aid them in their appreciation of the human person who is the subject of all economic planning.[40]

May African countries begin the second part of their journey into the celebration of political independence in a manner beneficial to their citizens and to humanity by working for sustainable

40. Odozor, "Truly Africa, and Wealthy!" 284.

and integral development through the implementation of Catholic social doctrine. However, this doctrine cannot be meaningful and relevant to Africans unless African cultural values are appreciated.

7

Appreciating African Cultural Values

*Towards a More Indigenous
African Christianity*

> Beyond differences of origin or culture, the great challenge facing us all
> is to discern in the human person, loved by God, the basis of a com-
> munion that respects and integrates the particular contributions of
> different cultures.
>
> —POPE BENEDICT XVI[1]

SUBSEQUENT TO THE VATICAN Council II, Pope Paul VI declared
and charged Christians in Africa to have an African Christianity.
This statement is as profound as it is new to sub-Saharan Africans,
who at that time were in various stages of transition from colonialism to political independence as well as from expatriate to
indigenous African church leadership. However, the continent
has always been home to an African Christianity whose leaders contributed immensely to the formulation of Christian faith
and doctrines. Such fathers of the church, such as Cyprian of
Carthage, Tertullian, Montanus, and Augustine of Hippo, as well

1. Benedict XVI, *Africae Munus*, sec. 39.

133

as martyrs like "the martyrs of Massa Candida, of Theogenes of Hippo, Agapius and Secundus at Cirta, of James, Marianus, and others; of Lucian, Montanus, and their companions, showed that there were still brave and sincere Christians to be found in her [African] fold."[2] However, Paul VI's declaration "You may, and you must, have an African Christianity"[3] is a renewed wakeup call to new African Christians to appropriate the Christian faith in light of their cultural values and to uphold a Christianity not built on foreign cultural forms but founded on the rich soil of African values. It is a call for originality and genius in formulating a truly and realistically African Christianity.

Paul VI's 1969 address to the Pan-African meeting of Roman Catholic Bishops in Gaba, Uganda, proclaimed the nature of this appropriation: "the expression, that is, the language and mode of manifesting this one faith may be manifold, hence it may be original, suited to the tongue, the style, the character, the genius and the culture of the one who professes this one Faith."[4] This directive gave rise to many questions as to whether African Christianity is truly free to express the Christian faith in a way suited to the African tongue, culture, habits, and identity. This question is informed by the challenges posed by the African church's dependence on external links that fund and therefore determine the form and structure of African Christianity.[5] Furthermore, there is the challenge posed by some African Christians for whom Christian orthodoxy means sticking to the finest details of the Eurocentric cultural form of Christianity imposed on Africa by missionary enterprises in Africa. The consequence of this highly skewed missionary endeavor is a split in the African personality. It has confused Christianity with civilization based on European cultural value systems and other socio-cultural phenomena presented in chapter 3. According to Ihemalol I. Egbujie:

2. Leclercq, "Early African Church," http://www.newadvent.org/cathen/01191a.htm.

3. Paul VI, "Eucharistic Celebration," 50–51.

4. Ibid.

5. Allen, *Spontaneous Expansion of the Church*, loc. 708.

It is a fact of living history that African culture has had destructive forces brought to bear on her. The European colonialists, imperialists, mercantile men and the often not-well-informed missionaries imported their own cultures and rigorously imposed them on Africans. But since a culture does not transform itself, nor can it emerge from the non-self being of a people, a good percentage of Africans today oscillate between two cultures. Their personality has been so truncated that the performance of authentic inner-action tends to be no longer available to them. There is an inner-self tension therefore.[6]

Africae Munus identifies this "inner-self tension" as a crisis of identity for Africans. In the Second African Synod, African Catholicism is charged with the responsibility of articulating a concept of personhood attuned to reality as the fruit of authentic spiritual renewal. This chapter argues that the pathway to this African personhood is through appreciation of African cultural values. This is important because the "inner-self tension" Africans suffer arises from a conglomeration of factors in their social history, primarily the forces of imperialism (some of which has been mentioned in earlier chapters) that led to the depreciation of African cultures and hence of Africans as individuals. This chapter concentrates on the effect of early European missionary enterprises on African cultures as well as the prevailing negative attitude of African Catholicism towards African culture and religion. It reiterates an appreciation of African cultures as a path towards a more indigenous African Christianity. In this way, African Catholicism will be better disposed to enter into genuine dialogue with African traditional religions that will be of mutual benefit.

Early European Missionary Enterprises and African Cultures

Assessment of the methods of missionary enterprises in Africa has posed difficulties for theologians and for historians. Its complexity

6. Egbujie, *African Traditional Culture*, 2.

comes to the forefront when one considers the positive impact of missionary engagements, such as abolition of such practices as the killing of twins, the founding of mission schools that trained African elites and exposed them to concepts of literacy, and the translation of the Bible to local languages (which contributed in no small way to the growth of Christianity) coupled with the sacrifices of missionaries who ventured into strange lands for the sake of the good news. This success is instantiated in the work of Bishop Joseph Shanahan of southern Nigeria. According to Vincent Donovan, Bishop Joseph Shanahan "not only affected the destiny of a tribe, the Ibos; he helped to change the missionary history of all of Africa. A new era began in the African missions with Bishop Shanahan."[7] Luke Mbefo offers similar testimony about Christian missionaries in Africa. Mbefo has this to say about Bishop Joseph Shanahan:

> Shanahan's missionary endeavors cannot be restricted to the spread of Christianity among the Igbos. He has also contributed to the education of humanity by transforming the face of Nigeria and Africa. The Christianity he preached advocated a new image of God as the Provident Father of all peoples and a new human self-understanding where men and women of all races, through Christ, have equal opportunity as children of God. He banished our superstitions and desacralized nature. His schools prepared Nigerians to move quickly from mythological thought forms into scientific analysis, thereby enabling them to deal with modernity.[8]

However, in spite of the efforts of some European and North American missionaries committed to the evangelization of Africa (celebrated in the *AM*, sec. 113), Western missionary enterprises in Africa fell short in many ways. History is littered with stories of abuse of Africa's natives and of priests' infidelity to their vows. Some were involved in atrocious commercial ventures, including

7. Donovan, *Christianity Rediscovered*, loc. 374.

8. Mbefo, "Bishop Joseph Shanahan," 346.

participating in the slave trade.[9] The missionaries entrenched imperialism not only by collaborating with the Western colonial masters in their various missions, but also by depending on them for security and establishing their authority over local administrations. Lamin Sanneh's 2008 book, *Disciples of All Nations: Pillars of World Christianity*, chronicles quite a few misadventures of Western missionaries in Africa. For example, King Afonso of Congo, who accepted the faith wholeheartedly and began a full-scale process of genuine inculturation, "establishing a Christian monarchy, creating a new Christian capital—called São Salvador—learning Portuguese, building churches, promoting missions, and indeed sending his son, Henry, to Portugal to be educated and commissioned for missionary service in the Congo,"[10] was disappointed at the infidelity of the missionaries in the Congo. According to Sanneh:

> When they arrived, the priests led anything but exemplary lives. Abandoning their vows, they broke away from their religious communities and lived in separate houses that they filled with slave girls as pleasure objects, to the scandal of new believers and to the disdain of local skeptics. The people mocked the king, saying the priests showed Christianity to be a lie. Stung by the remarks, the king pleaded with Portugal: "In this kingdom the faith is still as fragile as glass on account of the bad examples of those who came to teach it. Today our Lord is crucified anew by the very ministers of his body and blood. We would have preferred not to be born than to see how our innocent children run to perdition on account of these bad examples."[11]

However, over and above these setbacks, the most devastating effect of the colonial missionary enterprise in Africa was the denigration of African cultures as pagan. Armed with the hegemonic

---

9. Sanneh recounts that Father Pedro de S. S. Trinidade, a Catholic missionary "who lived in Zumbo on the Zambezi between 1710 and 1754, owned 1600 slaves and worked a gold mine" (Sanneh, *Disciples of All Nations*, 106).

10. Ibid., 99.

11. Ibid.

construct of European Christianity as civilization (Christendom), Western missionaries embarked with zeal on the implantation of their culture into Africa as Christian culture. They established Christian villages in order to segregate converts from their kith and kin, since the missionaries considered these unconverted relatives damned because they had not accepted the Christian faith. At the same time, the missionaries were not generous or Christian enough to treat the converts well as fellow Christians, but instead regarded them as primitive, uncultured people unworthy of equal relationships with civilized Europeans. As reflected in the way Albert Schweitzer (1875–1965) lived in Africa, many European missionaries, although living in Africa, remained aloof, having little to do with the Africans.[12]

Missionaries' disregard for Africans was even more insidious. Notions of white superiority justified the slave trade, and together with the influence of later colonialism, became entrenched in Christianity as well. African names that had held important cultural meanings were rejected for baptism. African music and instruments, dance and festivities, religion and arts, titles and awards, social and political institutions, personality traits and character, etc., were condemned in favor of Eurocentric "saint names," classical solemn music, and cultured dances and festivities "befitting" Christians. The missionaries doubted Africans' intelligence and hence their ability to comprehend Christian doctrines. For most of them, "it was a strange idea that Africans could become Christian without being European, or without possessing the European capacity for universal rationalization."[13] Christian missionaries thought it their duty to evangelize Africans to at least save their souls from damnation. The missionaries also thought it their duty to "civilize" Africans, bring them "culture," and teach them how to behave.

This superiority complex pervaded the attitude of Christian missionaries. As already noted, the impact of the condemnation

12. Ibid., 140.
13. Ibid.

of African culture was its denigration by African Christians. As articulated by socio-cultural anthropologist Sabine Jell-Bahlsen,

> The conceptual devaluation of Africa and her peoples, the derision of African religious beliefs, the dismantling of African cultures, and the simultaneous organization of knowledge and values along a scale favoring the conqueror's culture at the expense of those conquered, has long buttressed both slavery and colonialism. Religious colonialism, a twin to political and economic imperialism, imposes the conqueror's religion, such as Christianity or Islam, on the colonized people. This type of spiritual colonialism is a highly supportive and effective partner of imperialistic politics through its own compound strategy of derision and reduction of what it denounces as "pagan," paired with a claim to spiritual supremacy of the conqueror's religious views.[14]

The African crisis of identity is therefore not merely political, economic, and psychological, but also religious and spiritual. From a Catholic perspective, the consequence is a mixture of Catholicism with the practices of African traditional religious spirituality. This amounts to syncretism, for it leads Christians to worship both as Christians and according to African traditional religions. Whether syncretism is interpreted positively or negatively, the fact remains that Africans cannot be Christians outside of their religious cultural value system. To think otherwise is not to think of these Christians as Africans, or as distinctly unique people guided by the common meanings they uphold as human beings. Vincent Donovan discovered the intrinsic connection between culture and the Christian faith in the course of his missionary work among the Masai people in Africa and asserts:

> The gospel must be brought to the nations in which already resides the possibility of salvation. As I began to ponder the evangelization of the Masai, I had to realize that God enables a people, any people, to reach salvation through their culture and tribal, racial customs

14. Jell-Bahlsen, *Water Goddess in Igbo Cosmology*, 6.

and traditions. In this realization would have to rest my whole approach to the evangelization of the Masai. I had no right to disrupt this body of customs, of traditions. It was the way of salvation for these people, their way to God. It was one of the nations to whom we had to bring the gospel—bring the gospel to it as it was. In those customs lay their possibility of salvation.[15]

Just as the Christian Jews adapted Christianity to their culture (Acts 15) and the Greeks Hellenized Christianity and the Europeans inculturated Christianity into their cultural form and spread it wherever they were sent as missionaries, so too Africans are Africanizing Christianity and imbuing it with their own distinct cultural forms. As Ikenga R. Ozigbo notes: "Any attempt to build a strong and healthy local church that plays down the local cultural heritage cannot be germane. The very concept of the local church implies an admission of cultural diversity and the need of the Christian Church to adapt itself to the various cultures of mankind. Therein lies the crucial problem of Christian inculturation and indigenization."[16]

Inculturation and Liberation Hermeneutics

The emphasis on the need for religio-cultural praxis among African theologians was the initial response to the harm done to African cultures by missionary enterprises in Africa. Following Pope Paul VI's challenge to the African church to foster an African Christianity, African theology has almost always been contextual theology, defending, explicating, and laying out the parameters of inculturation.[17] At some point, the issue was overemphasized

15. Donovan, *Christianity Rediscovered*, loc. 757.

16. Ozigbo, *Igbo Catholicism*, 63.

17. See Arbuckle, *Culture, Inculturation, and Theologians*, 171–74. It is good to note the progress from *Adaptation* (which Paul VI encouraged but rejected as inadequate) to *Incarnation* (which Paul VI rejected as implying plurality of Catholicity) to *Inculturation* (generally accepted from the late 1970s), which has been in use to mean Christian faith expressed in African cultural, thought, and forms.

with little practice beyond the acceptance of indigenous names for baptism and the use of traditional vestments for liturgy, in addition to the celebration of the sacraments in local languages and translation of the Bible into various indigenous languages. The psychological impact of inculturation in leading to political and economic liberation, and subsequently, to the formulation of African liberation theologies was overlooked. As Emmanuel Martey observes: "Instead of envisioning both religio-cultural and politico-socio-economic factors as mutually interpenetrating elements which must shape African societal life and experience, both African and black theologians have used much energy fighting a battle over a false dilemma—a battle which, doubtlessly, has obstructed rather than facilitated more effective development in theological and transformative praxis."[18]

The dichotomy between inculturation theology and liberation theology accounts for the often-complacent attitude African Catholicism exhibits towards issues of socio-political and economic concern. While it publicly endorses the preferential option for the poor, in practice, African Catholicism does little towards realizing this goal because it fails to initiate the cultural revolution that will help Africans appreciate themselves enough to reject all forms of injustice. Yet African *anthropological poverty*, referred to in *Africae Munus* as "anthropological crisis" (*AM*, sec. 11), impoverishes Africans on a socio-political and economic as well as a religio-cultural level. The African crisis affects not only what Africans "have," but also who Africans "are."[19] Africa is beset not only with the cultural challenges that arise from ethnic, religious, and linguistic pluralism, but also from structural injustices arising from national and international socio-political and economic structures that militate against good governance and equitable distribution of resources for the common good of Africans. Africanization of the church must go hand in hand with liberation as a theological hermeneutic for African Catholicism in order to enable Africans to have abundant life. The theological trends in Africa must be

18. Martey, *African Theology*, 2.
19. Ibid., 38.

harmonized to relate the African condition to the practice of the Christian faith. Thus Emmanuel Marty reiterates his thesis about the unity of theology in Africa:

> Presently there are two major theological directions in Africa: inculturation, which stresses Africa's religio-cultural realities and finds expression in the narrowly defined "African theology" (now inculturation theology); and liberation, with its emphasis on the continent's politico-socio-economic realities, which finds expression not only in Black theology in South Africa, but also in African liberation theology and African women's theology. The future task of theologians in Africa is to develop a synthesis between these seemingly conflicting approaches, since the African theological reality cannot be reduced exclusively to the politico-socio-economic or to the religio-cultural existence of African life.[20]

The trust placed in African Catholicism by Africans who come to God through the church for solutions to virtually all their problems must be sustained. African Catholicism must neither feign ignorance of Africans' deep yearnings for their traditional cultures, nor pretend not to connect to the quest for abundant life inherent in African culture. Insofar as African life is an integrated whole, African culture is coterminous with politico-social and economic life. Naturally, therefore, religio-cultural life is intrinsically connected with politico-social and economic life in African thought. To remain relevant, African Catholicism must lead Africans to an appreciation of African cultures and become actively involved in a social transformation aimed at good governance, social justice, and equitable economic distribution for the common good of all.

African Catholicism, Evangelization, and Culture

Ecclesiastically, the special assembly of the Synod of Bishops is set up primarily to spread the good news in the light of the signs of

20. Ibid., 69–70.

the times. With his 1965 *Motu Proprio: Apostolica Solicitudo* apostolic letter, Paul VI established the Synod of Bishops, assigning its institutional task thus:

> The Apostolic concern leading Us to carefully survey the signs of the times and to make every effort to adapt the means and methods of the holy apostolate to the changing circumstances and need of our day, impels Us to establish even closer ties with the bishops in order to strengthen Our union with them "whom the Holy Spirit has placed . . . to rule the Church of God" (Acts 20:28).[21]

The "signs of the times" for Christian evangelization are the change from a strictly Eurocentric form of Christianity and understanding of Christendom to a world Christianity characterized by a plurality of cultural forms expressing the Christian faith. The first special assembly of the Synod of Bishops for Africa, with its elements of African culture on the theme of "The Church in Africa and Her Evangelizing Mission towards the Year 2000: 'You will be my witnesses' (Acts 1:8)" was held in 1994. Its major themes—evangelization, inculturation, dialogue, family, and means of social communication—defined the African church as a "Family of God" on mission. It incorporated the theology of inculturation with liberation theology's quest for social justice. Moreover, the second special assembly of the Synod of Bishops for Africa dwelt on the public relevance of the church in Africa. The Synod emphasized the need for good governance and education in Catholic social teachings as a tool for grassroots mobilization, emphasizing civic education on the rights and responsibilities of citizens for the common good.

These special assemblies' emphasis on native culture and liberation implies that when Africans appreciate their culture, they come to terms with who they are and can become empowered to take their destiny into their own hands to liberate themselves from politico-social and economic oppression. Since the mistake of years of African oppression has been to crush the African

---

21. Paul VI, preface to *Motu Proprio*.

personality to the point of anthropological crisis, the liberation of Africans and their prospect for progress lies in appreciation of their own culture. African Catholicism must begin to undo the mistake of the missionaries by recognizing the human dignity of all Africans, irrespective of differences in creed, code, and cult. The missionaries' mistake was in treating mature Africans as children unable to grasp the complexities of Christian doctrine. These missionary attitudes stemmed more from the fear of losing of control and an inner desire for power than from love of Christ and the gospel. Instead of establishing self-expressing, self-propagating, and self-reliant churches, the missionaries instituted the culture of dependence that continues to haunt African Catholicism to this day. Reflecting on Henry Venn's idea of a self-reliant, self-propagating church based upon his experience of mission in China, Ronald Allen recommends that missionary enterprises in India, Africa, and other places build truly indigenous churches that will *ab initio* self-propagate the good news and overcome the fears and controlling impulses responsible for stultifying the progress of Christian faith.[22]

Accepting the validity of African cultures and the African capability to manage their affairs, especially in establishing and maintaining an indigenous Christianity, is extremely important for the universal church, if the special assemblies for Africa truly aim at self-reliant, self-propagating, and self-governing churches in Africa. Both *Ecclesiae in Africa* and *Africae Munus'* emphasis on the importance of African traditional religions for African Catholicism are steps in the right direction in this regard. However, one wonders what Pope Benedict XVI meant by cautioning African bishops in *Africae Munus* against absolutizing the African culture:

> Be one with the Successor of Peter, together with your priests and all the faithful. Do not waste your human and pastoral energies in the vain search for answers to questions which are not of your direct competence, or in the twists and turns of a nationalism that can easily blind. It is easier to follow this idol, or to *absolutize African*

22. Allen, *Spontaneous Expansion of the Church*, loc. 209.

culture, than to follow the demands of Christ. Such idols are illusions. Even more, they are a temptation, that believing that human efforts alone can bring the kingdom of eternal happiness to earth.[23]

If this means setting limits to our appreciation of African culture, then it is unfortunate. If it means setting conditions for inculturation in line with his earlier position as Secretary of the Congregation for the Doctrine of the Faith, when he dismissed African theology as "more a project than a reality,"[24] then the bishops and African Catholicism must take note of his possible Eurocentric bias and not be bound by it. However, if it is, as it seems to be, a distinction of the possible extremes of the two poles of inculturation and liberation, then African Catholicism must heed it. The statement must be seen as emphasizing the intrinsic connection between appreciation of African cultures and liberation of African peoples, not only from religio-cultural oppression, but also from the politico-social and economic suppression responsible for African anthropological crisis. Accepting and appreciating African cultures as equal creates an enabling environment for mutual coexistence, especially for the religiously, culturally, ethnically, and linguistically diverse communities in Africa.

Africae Munus calls for interreligious dialogue not only with African traditional religions, but also with Islam. This call is particularly germane in light of the increasing religious conflicts afflicting Africa as Christians and Muslims clash in many African countries. Interreligious dialogue, therefore, is a challenge African Catholicism must not take for granted, but must tackle in order to ensure not only the continuous growth of the church in Africa, but also to secure lives and property, as well as to promote the integral development of Africa. Thus, the next chapter focuses on interreligious dialogue from the perspective of religious exclusivism, which African Catholicism has to find a way of extricating itself from and benefit from the riches of African religio-cultural pluralism.

23. Benedict XVI, *Africae Munus*, sec. 102, emphasis mine.

24. Ratzinger, *Ratzinger Report*, 193.

8

Religious Exclusivism

Challenge to Interreligious Dialogue

As many social movements indicate, peace in Africa, as elsewhere, is conditioned by interreligious relations. Hence it is important for the Church to promote dialogue as a spiritual disposition, so that believers may learn to work together, for example in associations for justice and peace, in a spirit of trust and mutual help.

—POPE BENEDICT XVI[1]

ONE OF THE FEATURES of the modern world is the recognition of the plurality of human societies— differences in social order and political institutions, multiplicity of cultures and peoples, complexities of personality types, diversity of religious affiliation and expression, pluralism in theology, etc. These differences often pose various challenges as individuals struggle to come to grips with the reality of pluralism. According to Roger Haight, "We live in a world of wild pluralism which calls into question every tradition and the notion of truth itself."[2] These differences could be poten-

1. Benedict XVI, *Africae Munus*, sec. 88.
2. Haight, *Dynamics of Theology*, 17.

tially rich in themselves when they are recognized and mutually respected. Or they could be destructive when misinterpreted or ignored. As Abdulaziz Sachedina observes:

> The term pluralism is one of the catchwords of a new world order whose diversity of cultures, belief systems, and values inspires both exhilaration at the endless shadings of human expression and dread of irreconcilable conflict. The invocation of pluralism has become as much a summons as a celebration, an urgent exhortation to the citizens of the world to come to terms with their dizzying diversity. The endless conflicts between Christians and Muslims, Hindus and Sikhs, Tamils and Buddhists, and the attendant atrocities committed against innocent civilians, have imparted a direct urgency to the moral imperative of recognizing the human dignity of the other, regardless of his or her religious, ethnic, and cultural affiliations.[3]

This call to respect the human dignity of all must be heeded by all and sundry. It is important, urgent, and necessary, especially in places where minority groups are persecuted on account of differences in creed, code, and cult. It must be a clarion call to all parts of the world, especially where people are denied their human rights just because they are different from the orthodox mainstream. This is particularly important not only in the Christian-dominated West, but also for Asia's Hindu and Buddhist religious majority, as well as in the Arabic world dominated by Islam, and in Africa's increasing Christian and Muslim conflict. In any place where people are regarded as less than human because of their religious faith, Sachedina's call to concentrate on the human dignity of all peoples as a response to religious pluralism is an imperative. The challenge in responding to this call lies in religious exclusivism as well as in the halfhearted inclusivism of various religious traditions which, though conscious of religious pluralism, hold to traditional conceptions of salvation that exclude people of other faiths.

3. Sachedina, *Islamic Roots*, 22.

Because it deals with ultimate value, the wealth of religious pluralism, if properly harnessed, could contribute to world peace and help promote human progress and development. Thomas Banchoff brings this out clearly in his definition of religious pluralism as "the interaction of religious actors with one another and with the society and the state around concrete cultural, social, economic, and political agendas."[4] Since people of faith find meaning in life, form their conscience, develop their personality, and strive to be responsible members of society from their grounding in religion, it is not only important, but essential for various religions to interface with each other for mutual understanding. In order to collaborate in social action to improve human wellbeing, ongoing dialogue between world religions at all levels is indispensable.

By examining the religious exclusivism of the major world religions, this chapter argues that recognition of religious pluralism is a step in the right direction towards promoting religious dialogue. Further, it urges, through appropriation of historical consciousness, a theological anthropology that accords dignity to every human being irrespective of differences. Contrary to a rejection of religious truth, it points to various religious traditions' truth claims as constituting an important component of religious dialogue. This has become necessary as religious leaders begin to recognize, through historical consciousness, the inadequacy of human language to state clearly the transcendent object of religious faith. With particular reference to Africa's religious pluralism, this chapter offers recommendations that will hopefully be helpful to African Catholicism as it implements the *Africae Munus* task of promoting interreligious dialogue in Africa.

Recognizing Religious Pluralism

This chapter will survey the growing consensus among leading religions that religious pluralism offers opportunities for mutual growth in dialogue. It begins with Catholicism, the major focus of

4. Banchoff, *Religious Pluralism, Globalization*, 5.

this book. The Conciliar document, *Nostra Aetate*, on the relationship of the church to non-Christians, recognizes religious pluralism and declares:

> From ancient times down to the present, there has existed among diverse peoples a certain perception of that hidden power which hovers over the course of things and over the events of life . . . The Catholic Church rejects nothing which is true and holy in these religions. She looks with sincere respect upon those ways of conduct and of life, those rules and teachings which, though differing in many particulars from what she holds and sets forth, nevertheless often reflect a ray of that Truth which enlightens all men . . . The Church therefore has this exhortation for her sons: prudently and lovingly, through dialogue and collaboration with the followers of other religions, and in witness of Christian faith and life, acknowledge, preserve, and promote the spiritual and moral goods found among these men, as well as the values in their society and culture.[5]

This document, which acknowledges the tenets of major world religions, including Hinduism, Buddhism, Islam, Judaism, and "other religions to be found elsewhere,"[6] marks a significant shift from the church's earlier position on people of other faiths. From the times of the apostles up until the Vatican Council II, the position of Christianity towards other religions was one of intolerance, because of the conviction of Christianity as the one true religion. As aptly described by H. Richard Neibuhr: "Christians were members of Roman society, and in the midst of that society explicitly and implicitly expressed their scorn for the religions of the people."[7] Although there is no specific official document condemning other religions, past pronouncements of leading officials of the Catholic Church show hesitancy to accept other religions as other paths to God. Although Thomas Aquinas was not writing directly about Islam, he classifies it as a natural religion and calls

5. Abbott, "Relationship of the Church to Non-Christians," 661–63.

6. Ibid., 662.

7. Neibuhr, *Christ and Culture*, 7–8.

only Christians believers. According to Archbishop Michael L. Fitzgerald, M. Afr., "The categorisation of Muslims as unbelievers is to be found in the writings of Saint Thomas Aquinas. He was naturally inclined to reserve the term 'believer' to one who shared the Christian faith. Thomas is not treating Islam as a corrupt version of Christianity but, implicitly at least, as a separate religion. In fact his writings could be considered the foundation for the position which classifies Islam as a natural religion."[8] However, in the new dispensation after Vatican Council II, Pope Paul VI set up a secretariat for the development of relations with non-Christian religions on May 17, 1964, in order to promote the work of inter-religious dialogue.

In a similar vein, recognizing religious pluralism as early as 1971, the World Council of Churches Central Committee recommended dialogue as a way of approaching people of other faiths. It set up a subunit called "Dialogue with People of Living Faiths and Ideologies" (DFI), which went on to publish "Guidelines on Dialogue with People of Living Faiths and Ideologies." The document aims at correcting distorted images Christians may have of their neighbors and at encouraging Christians to learn about people of other faiths.[9] In 1986 DFI also published the study guide, "My Neighbor's Faith—and Mine: Theological Discoveries through Interfaith Dialogue," which called upon churches to reflect on the implication of being Christian in a religiously plural world by studying the themes of creation, Scripture, Jesus Christ, salvation,

8. Fitzgerald, "From Heresy to Religion." See the beginning of *Summa Contra Gentiles*, where Aquinas offers reasons why Muhammad should not be accepted as a prophet. In *De rationibus fidei contra Saracenos, Graecos et Armenos ad Cantorem Antiochenum*, Aquinas devotes several chapters to refuting Islamic arguments against the Christian faith. Cf. Kenney, "Thomas Aquinas, Islam and the Arab Philosophers," http://www.catholicapologetics.info/apologetics/islam/thomas.htm.

9. World Council of Churches, "My Neighbor's Faith—and Mine: Theological Discoveries through Interfaith Dialogue," http://www.oikoumene.org/en/resources/documents/wcc-programmes/interreligious-dialogue-and-cooperation/christian-identity-in-pluralistic-societies/study-guide-my-neighbours-faith-and-mine/index.

witness, spirituality, community, hope, and vision.[10] DFI moved from theory to practice by organizing the Multicultural Dialogue Meeting in New Delhi in 1987. This meeting aimed at bringing religious leaders together to consult on the practice of dialogue. The formal report of the meeting states, "it will be necessary to find out new ways of enabling both ourselves and our own communities to learn to see the world from the point of view of our neighbor," and goes on to recommend the institution of study centers within world religions to study faith in light of religious pluralism.[11]

Judaism, which is generally tolerant of other faith traditions in spite of the avowed religious particularism in its claim to be the chosen people of God, has been moving towards an inclusivism that incorporates all peoples under God. Judaic scholars approach religious pluralism in many ways by acknowledging the limitations of human knowledge of God. According to Rose Or N, "If I accept the reality of God's mystery and the limits of human knowledge, then I must also acknowledge that Judaism, like all other religions, is an imperfect attempt by my forebears at translating their religious experiences, ideals, and values into a communal culture with specific religious symbols, rituals, spaces, and times."[12] This approach offers a groundbreaking attempt at sustainable interreligious dialogue, for even as it highlights the religious exclusivism of Judaism, it accords other religions such exclusivism and commits not only to mutual respect of other religious values and beliefs, but also to learning from one another for shared enrichment.[13]

10. Ibid., "Guidelines on Dialogue with People of Living Faiths and Ideologies," http://www.oikoumene.org/en/resources/documents/wcc-programmes/interreligious-dialogue-and-cooperation/interreligious-trust-and-respect/guidelines-on-dialogue-with-people-of-living-faiths-and-ideologies.

11. Davison, "Church of England's Response to Religious Pluralism," 5. I am indebted to Davison's work for resources on the World Council of Churches' recognition of religious pluralism.

12. Rose, "Footsteps of Hillel," 63.

13. See especially Irving Greenberg's call on followers of various religions to partner with one another not only in social justice action, but also intellectually, treating interfaith dialogue as an opportunity to learn from one another. He writes, "Thus, a follower of Islam marveling at the perfect submission that Islam teaches would affirm the relevance of another path (Christianity), in

Islamic scholars are divided on whether the Qur'an favors religious pluralism. Afraid of losing the purity of revelation to the secularizing forces of modernization, especially by relativizing religious truth, many Islamic scholars are hesitant to recognize the plurality of religious expression. According to Abdulaziz Sachedina, "Muslim religious discourse on the subject of pluralism indicates that there is a vehement rejection of any such notion that would take away the unique claim of Islam as the only religion that is acceptable to God. In fact, both the Arabic *ta'addudiya* and the Persian *takththur-garayi* for pluralism are treated as foreign imposition on Muslim religious thought, and hence, are treated as lacking internal cultural legitimacy."[14] However, in the face of increasing religious pluralism, Islamic scholars are increasingly urging Muslims into dialogue with people of other faiths, citing those passages of the Qu'ran that promote interreligious dialogue and teach that people of other faiths will also attain salvation. Particularly relevant is the section of the Qu'ran (Sura 2:62, 5:69) that makes a clear statement on religious pluralism: "Surely those who have faith, the Jews, the Christians and the Sabaeans, whoever accepts faith in God and the last day and performs good deeds, those shall have their reward with their lord; no fear shall come upon them nor will they grieve."[15] However, according to Mahmoud M. Ayoub, this passage is interpreted with different hermeneutic keys, the most widespread of which limits its applicability only to Muslims and as referring to Islam as an organized religion.[16]

---

which God intervenes to suffer with and lift up humans, and a Judaism that places tremendous emphasis on human action and responsibility in the world" (Greenberg, *Heaven and Earth*, 211).

14. Sachedina, "Religious Pluralism in Islam," 222.

15. Quoted in Ayoub, "Challenge of Religious Pluralism," 61. See also ibid., *Muslim View of Christianity*, 2.

16. Ibid., "Challenge of Religious Pluralism," 61.

Challenges of Interreligious Dialogue

The challenge of interreligious dialogue is various religions' inability to go beyond their provisional inclusivism to embrace pluralism. On account of this, various religions find it difficult to accept other religions as equal and alternate ways to salvation akin to their own religious faith. So often what appears as interreligious dialogue ends up as an inadequate response to the challenge of religious pluralism. Increasingly, one notices an avoidance of encounters with other religions because it remains much more comfortable to hold on to one's own faith tradition or to comparatively analyze other religions from the familiar perspective of one's own. The truth claims of one religion are regarded as higher in absolutistic fashion than the truth claims of other religions. There is a subtle fear of relativizing truth, when what should be relativized is one's interpretation of one's own truth claims.[17]

This is true of Judaism's position that although ultimately all religions are ways to God, humanity will eventually learn that Judaism is the most direct path to God.[18] Its tolerance of people of other faiths on the condition that they worship one God as "anonymous Monotheists"[19] limits people of other faiths' full right of credibility for their creeds, rites, and rituals. Similar criticism equally applies to the position of Christianity, for while granting status to other religious faiths as containing ways toward salvation, it holds that ultimately these others benefit in God's own way from the salvific mystery of Christ. The Congregation for the Doctrine of Faith states this clearly in response to Father Jacques Dupuis' book, *Religious Pluralism and the Uniqueness of Christ*, which the congregation thinks endorses outright religious pluralism: "It is consistent with Catholic doctrine to hold that the seeds of truth and goodness that exist in other religions are a certain participation in truths contained in the revelation of or in Jesus Christ. However, it is erroneous to hold that such elements of truth and goodness, or

17. Samartha, "People of Other Faiths," 253.
18. Cohn-Sherbok, "Jewish Religious Pluralism," 327.
19. Ibid.

some of them, do not derive ultimately from the source mediation of Jesus Christ."[20] The Congregation's words offer a clear example of the struggle with pluralism that the Vatican tolerance of people of other faiths, as expressed in *Nostra Aetate*, does not solve. As Prefect of the Congregation for the Doctrine of Faith, Cardinal Joseph Ratzinger (later Pope Benedict XVI) explained, "The Congregation for the Doctrine of the Faith also concerned itself with his [Dupuis'] work, since the average reader—in all loyalty to the uniqueness of Jesus Christ—would nevertheless get an impression of a leaning toward pluralist positions. The dialogue with the author led to a 'Notification,' in which all the theological points important to Fr. Dupuis were clarified by mutual agreement and the boundary in the direction of pluralism was thus also clearly marked out."[21]

This type of magisterial teaching and statement, clearly marking out the boundaries of pluralism, is similar to Karl Rahner's hypothesis of the "anonymous Christian" in reference to people of other religious faiths: "The 'anonymous Christian' in our sense of the term is the pagan after the beginning of the Christian mission, who *lives in the state of Christ's grace* through faith, hope and love, *yet who has no explicit knowledge* of the fact that his life is orientated in grace-given salvation to Jesus Christ."[22] Although Christian theologians are divided on Karl Rahner's theology of the "anonymous Christian," Christians generally express the uniqueness of their faith in the light of the salvific role of the death and resurrection of Jesus Christ for humankind. The apostolic church teaches salvation as coming only in the name of Jesus Christ: "There is no salvation through anyone else, nor is there any other name under heaven given to the human race by which we are to be saved" (Acts 4:12).

---

20. Congregation for the Doctrine of the Faith, "Notification," sec. 4.

21. Benedict XVI, *Truth and Tolerance*, 52–53.

22. Rahner, *Ecclesiology, Questions*, 283, emphasis mine. See also Benedict XVI, *Truth and Tolerance*, 16–17.

Islam's inclusivism, which struggles with pluralism, arises from exclusive Islamic religious claims. As Abdulaziz Sachedina explains:

> Traditionally, Muslims had developed a theory about Islam's self-sufficiency in relation to other religions, and had regarded Islam in possession of the religious and moral truth required by all humanity until the end of time. The Qur'an spoke of Muhammad as "the seal of the prophets," who confirmed the revelations to previous prophets where they were sound, and corrected them if they had been corrupted. This doctrine also implied that there would be no other prophet after Muhammad, so that he was God's final word to humanity. This theology was the foundation of Muslim exclusiveness. The finality of Islamic revelation, in addition to the corporate solidarity founded upon the sacred Shari'a and Muslim rule, formed the resilient self-assurance with which Muslims considered the exclusive truth they possess, over against the abrogation or supersession of other traditions like Christianity and Judaism.[23]

Islam's religious exclusivism makes it reluctant to embrace religious pluralism, which it at times equates with globalization as another form of Western imperialism.[24] In light of this, Jane Smith recalls an incident in a forum on religious pluralism: "'If you believe your religion to be true,' a Pakistani cleric asked at a post 9–11 Fulbright conference on pluralism, 'and you believe it is your duty to share this truth with others, then why would you think that religious pluralism is a good thing?'"[25]

Although ancient Eastern religions like Hinduism and Buddhism may appear to be more tolerant than the monotheistic religions by relativizing other religions as many alternate manifestations of the one Divine, they ultimately see other religions within the periscope of their own faith. According to Daniel Cohn-Sherbok:

23. Sachedina, "Religious Pluralism in Islam," 226.

24. Ayoub, "Challenge of Religious Pluralism," 57.

25. Smith, "American Muslims," 192.

> Although Hindus are tolerant of other faiths, it is as-
> sumed that in this life or in the life to come all will come
> to the fullness of Vedic understanding. Further, in ad-
> vaitic philosophy it is maintained that the theistic forms
> of religion embody an inferior conception of ultimate
> Reality. Thus Hindus believe that their faith is uniquely
> superior to other religious conceptions. Likewise, in
> the Buddhist tradition it is assumed that the true un-
> derstanding of the human condition is presented in the
> teachings of Gautama Buddha. The Dharma, Buddhists
> stress, contains the full and saving truth for all humanity.
> Each of these religious traditions, then, affirms its own
> superiority; all rival claims are regarded as misapprehen-
> sions of ultimate Reality.[26]

Aylward Shorter confirms this possibility of religious exclusivism in pluralistic religions like Hinduism by remarking on the
subtle forms through which it writes off other religions: "The Hindu for example, belongs to a diffuse and pluralistic religion and
may be tempted to absorb other faiths on his own terms, forcing
them against their will into his own syncretic mould."[27]

There is obviously nothing wrong with upholding the religious exclusivism of one's religion, provided one recognizes that
other religions offer other forms of religious truth which are
equally as exclusive for their adherents. In fact, there is no other
way of being religious apart from believing in one's religious truth.
What becomes problematic is the religious zeal to universalize
these truth claims as applicable to all humanity, along with the
misconception that one's own religion is the only way to salvation,
perhaps due to interpretations of one's religious history or historic
past as unique. I cannot accept a Muslim's claim that I am assured
of salvation as a non-Muslim based on the Qu'ran any more than
I will expect a Muslim to accept my position that he or she is assured of salvation as an anonymous Christian. A Hindu does not
need my approval to validate his or her religious truth any more
than a Muslim needs to accept the Hindu position that theistic

26. Cohn-Sherbok, "Jewish Religious Pluralism," 334.
27. Shorter, *Toward a Theology of Inculturation*, 101.

religions will on the last day realize that salvation comes by participation in Hindu religious practice. Expecting any of these or related statements to be true is only a recipe for misunderstanding and a stumbling block to accepting the reality of religious pluralism. The outcome is unending religious conflict, making religion appear to be a problem rather than as a means to build peace and end to violence. The consequence is a tendency to throw out the baby with the bath water, prompting the reductionist question of whether religion is a force for good or for evil. The ensuing debate over the role of religion in society thus results in diametrically opposing viewpoints. As R. Scott Appleby observes:

> Recent debates about the roles of religion in deadly conflict find analysts gravitating toward one of two extremes. Some follow in the tradition of religion's cultured despisers, pointing to incidents of religious terrorism or to the religiously inspired atrocities in conflict settings like the Balkans as evidence that religion is inherently opposed to progress, threatening a return of the Dark Ages. Others, including secularists who are friendlier to organized religion, as well as many religious officials themselves, expect it to uphold the humanist credo, including the proposition that human life is the highest good, the one inviolable reality.[28]

It is the credibility of religion that is at stake in such debates, when instead of promoting peace, religions antagonize and instill hatred for one another in the quest to universalize their exclusive religious claims, threatening world peace. As Hans Küng argues, "peace among the religions is the prerequisite for peace among the nations."[29]

While attempts to universalize exclusivist religious claims could potentially harm the reputation of any religion, it is equally erroneous in interreligious dialogue to champion the view that seems to presume a melting pot, of not bringing one's views into engaged dialogue and of focusing only on what unites. As Ayoub

28. Appleby, *Ambivalence of the Sacred*, 10.
29. Küng, *Theology for the Third Millennium*, 209.

remarks, "Pluralism does not necessarily mean a tower of Babel, where everyone speaks a different language with no possibility of communicating with or understanding one another. Rather, underlying religious pluralism must be a unity of purpose and open dialogue."[30] Although emphasis on the commonalities is important, it is necessary in true dialogue to bring one's own religious position into real conversation with people of other faiths. While this approach may initially seem to bring conflict, it enables people to appreciate one another's faith and could possibly bring about changing positions in those areas of doctrine that appear intolerant of other faiths. According to Colin Grant, religious groups must be able to confront each other "in their own distinctive particularities."[31] While the search for what each religion holds in common must not be neglected, their unique essence as a distinct religion must not be trivialized or humanized, disrobed of transcendence. As Grant warns, "A genuine recognition of a plurality of world religions must accept these traditions in their own right, and resist reducing them to the status of manifestations of some common essence such as human rationality or human experience."[32]

Some people think that recognizing other religion's claims to the Absolute brings about relativism. While this may at first appear to be the case, it actually does correct claims to certain knowledge of God understood in almost all religions as the Absolute, which itself is a limitation of the Absolute. For an absolute or transcendent being that can be known with certainty is no longer absolute. Such a God or gods, previously limited to human knowability, would now be human and not absolute anymore. As articulated by Greenberg Irving, "The pluralist has not lost the encounter with and the experience of the absolute. But, if you will, out of the encounter with others' equally powerful experiences of the absolute, the pluralists come to know the limits of their own absolutism. Pluralism is an absolutism that knows its limits. Therefore it leaves room for other absolute claims and for other faith systems to

30. Ayoub, "Challenge of Religious Pluralism," 57.
31. Grant, "Prospect of Religious Pluralism," 51.
32. Ibid., 53.

express themselves in all their power and validity."[33] Actually, such openness in dialogue that does not shy away from speaking from the perspective of one's religious truth becomes a journey of faith that offers opportunities for mutual spiritual growth. As DFI notes, dialogue implies openness to one's faith expression. For Christianity, this means recognition of the salvation in Christ. However, at the same time, this conviction must not be presented in a way that denies the distinctive particularities of various religions.

Dialogue through Witness of Life

However, beyond the recognition of one another's exclusive religious claims, and actually on account of it, interreligious dialogue bears much fruit by genuine witness to religious belief through a life of love characterized by hospitality and kindness, participation in promoting peace in a social order, and contributing to the common good. For instance, the hospitality Louis Massignon (1883–1962) encountered under the care of his Muslim hosts during an illness inspired him to study and pen a four-volume work restoring the prestige of Mansur al-Hallaj (ca. 858–922), a Persian pantheist Sufi who was burned as a heretic during the Abbasid inquisition.[34] Such recognition, appreciation, and publication of exemplary religious life in other religious traditions points to the wealth of potential for good life and mutual collaboration that can be tapped by an open mind ready to love unreservedly. In fact, emphasis on exclusivist religious claims without a witness to the good of religious faith that promotes peace and mutual coexistence in respect to equality and human dignity could have negative consequences for civil society. As Wade Clark Roof notes, this is especially true in situations "when it is so rich and complex that it dilutes the larger polity, undercuts the common good, and leaves bewilderment or chaos."[35]

33. Greenberg, "Religious Roots of Pluralism," 385–93.
34. Sanneh, *Disciples of All Nations*, 149.
35. Roof, *Religious Pluralism and Civil Society*, 18.

While what matters in religion is the human person who practices religion, religious leaders, teachings, and doctrines have often, in the exercise of power, reversed the order and placed religion above the person. Karl Barth equates a religion that displaces the human being with death.[36] As Kosuke Koyama notes, "Religion is embodied in people... Religion migrates as people migrate. Religions pick up and discard local languages and symbols as they travel. Any particular religious situation is inter-religious"[37] It is people who engage in interreligious dialogue, not religions—not Hinduism in discussion with Christianity in the abstract, but rather a Hindu person engaged in real conversation with a Christian.

Although the specific role of interreligious dialogue is not pragmatic but religious, when religions are able to mutually respect and understand one another's differences, the end result is good news for religion and the promotion of conditions conducive to integral development and peace. As Wade Clark Roof observes, "Through discussion and active involvement with people of other faiths, and with those of no faith, believers also become more self-conscious of who they are, affirm common values, and build social capital."[38] Such social capital is built when religious leaders, aware of one another's exclusive religious claims, jointly build unity through a dialogue of life—not merely through academic discussions and roundtable conferences, but through concrete actions for peace, justice, defense of moral values, and promotion of true human freedom. Muslim Christian Action for Advocacy Relief and Development (MUCAARD) is an example of an organization committed to such dialogue of life. Aimed at promoting sustainable development through joint action between Christians and Muslims, MUCAARD works for peace, justice, and human freedom in many parts of the world in the hope of helping people to live qualitative, fulfilled lives worthy of human dignity.

Religious leaders have shown they can work together for social justice once they build trust among themselves. For example,

36. Barth, *On Religion*, 9.

37. Koyama, "Religious Pluralism," 165.

38. Roof, *Religious Pluralism and Civil Society*, 6–12.

during the food and energy crisis of the 1970s, religious leaders intervened at the 1975 Interreligious Peace Colloquium on Food and Energy to declare food and energy to be a basic human right. They issued a statement urging structural changes in world societies in order to alleviate hunger and malnutrition across the globe.[39]

Overcoming the Challenges

The challenge of religious exclusivism could be overcome by a paradigmatic shift akin to a Copernican Revolution if various religions would move from the provisional inclusivism of religious tolerance to an acceptance of religious pluralism. This change is paradigmatic because it will demand openness to other religions in a way that has not been the historical norm. It will not imply a change in individuals' religious beliefs as such. But it will demand recognition of the religious exclusivism of other religions in just such a way as understanding that loving one's own wife and children does not preclude acknowledging the beauty of other people and families. It will involve a humble acknowledgement of the limitation of one's knowledge of the transcendent object of faith—God, whose essence surpasses the capability of human knowledge even after revelation. As finely articulated in Pope Francis' urge for a new balance in the Catholic Church's approach to truth: "If a person says that he met God with total certainty and is not touched by a margin of uncertainty, then this is not good. For me, this is an important key. If one has the answers to all the questions—that is the proof that God is not with him."[40] This approach goes beyond the reluctant acceptance of other religions as participating in one's own salvific plan. It advances to a full acknowledgement of other religions' salvific plans without diminishing one's own faith or traditional belief systems.

39. Gremillion, *Food/Energy*, 4, 7.

40. Spadaro, "Big Heart Open to God," http://www.americamagazine.org/pope-interview. See also "A New Balance," https://www.commonwealmagazine.org/new-balance.

However, while one would wish one's own religious exclusivism to apply to all human beings, this approach prefixes one's belief to one's faith tradition and refrains from statements that diminish other faith traditions. In actual fact, accepting the validity of other religions' truth claims does not diminish the validity of my own truth claims. If anything, it validates them as a shared expression of faith in God. It manifests an acknowledgement of the limitations of human language and truth claims about God. According to Cohn-Sherbok, "This new pluralistic model further reflects our current understanding of the world in which no truth is viewed as unchanging. Rather, truth-claims by their very nature must be open to other insights. They prove themselves not by triumphing over other belief systems, but by testing their compatibility with other truths. Such a conception of relational truth affords a new orientation to our understanding of truth in religion; in this view religious truth is not static but instead undergoes continual interaction and development."[41]

I do not see any other way of approaching the reality of religious pluralism other than an acknowledgment of each other's truth claims. One of the things we cannot change is the religious truth claims themselves—the religious traditions that define one another's faith traditions. We cannot hope to convert other people to our own religious faith traditions, either. And even if we were, that is no guarantee that our own truth claims are best, final, or absolute. Hence the need for this paradigmatic shift from religious inclusivism to acceptance of religious pluralism. As Raficq Abdullah articulates:

> I believe that until we really take not only our own contingency but that of our collective beliefs seriously, until we learn that we are truly naked notwithstanding the doctrinal, liturgical and even the transformative power of our religions, we will not be capable of talking to each other from the heart and from a position of abiding and acknowledged ignorance. Then can we strive to know each other within our limited understanding and act

41. Cohn-Sherbok, "Jewish Religious Pluralism," 330.

towards each other with goodwill; in this way we may learn to see each other in another more enabling perspective that reduces the pretensions and enhances the possibility for a degree of agreement.[42]

Frederick Crowe presents this clearly in the light of the universal mission of the Holy Spirit. He urges Christians, while thanking God for the gift of Jesus Christ, to also acknowledge the Spirit as gifted to humankind as a whole. Just as Paul agonized over the loss of the privilege of Israel as the "chosen people of God" because they refused to abide by the divine conditions of the gift (Rom 11:19–22), Christians should also beware lest they find themselves in similar position by excluding other peoples, for:

> It is not enough to thank God daily for the blessings bestowed on us in Christ the Lord, blessings that seem to make us a people set apart, unless we acknowledge also that the infinite generosity and kindness of God our savior has included all the peoples of the world in the divine family, has made them all vessels of the divine election, and has blessed all with the first and foundational gift of God, the divine love in the person of the Holy Spirit. We too have to beware lest, by refusing to acknowledge the breath and depth and height of the divine mercy, we become unfaithful stewards of the very privilege that we do in fact possess, and turn into avatars of the people so broken-heartedly lamented in Romans 9–11.[43]

Abdullah and Crowe's positions suggest a radical change in various religions' attitudes to one another's truth claims. They demand, as Doran asserts, a new language to express ourselves in relation to other religions, a language "in which to communicate across the borders of the religions."[44] The starting point in the formulation of such language may be found in the language of love expressive of authentic religion; that is, of God's love for each human being and the obligation to love not only God, but fellow

42. Abdullah, "Islamic View on Pluralism," 117.

43. Crowe, "Son of God," 334.

44. Doran, *Trinity in History*, 74.

human beings in return. Doran expresses this beautifully, writing, "I would suggest instead that we employ the twofold relation suggested here: the memory of being on the receiving end of an unqualified love and the invitation to love in an unqualified fashion in return."[45] Of course, this will not be an easy position to accept. But this appears to be the only option in light of the religious pluralism of our time. Perhaps it will help if we look beyond claims to religious supremacy to consider one another as fellow human beings. We need to reconsider our religious anthropologies.

The theological anthropology requisite for religious pluralism is to be drawn from a faith that is open to the truth claims of other religious traditions and understands humankind as children of one transcendent God. Such a theological anthropology relates people to one another as fellow human beings who are not categorized based on their religious beliefs, but rather united in the dignity they all share as human beings deserving of respect and love. Under this theological anthropology, nobody is regarded as a pagan, an infidel, heretic, gentile, etc. It accepts that people of different cultures and religions acknowledge the presence of God in many ways. They worship and articulate their creeds, codes, and cults using a limited human language to express their appreciation of the reality of the sacred. Each path to the divine reality or transcendent being leads to a salvation that converges in the presence of God conceived in divergent ways. Thus, belonging to a society, nation, and community of nations is not dependent on one's expression of faith. This attitudinal change must happen mentally if there is to be a transition from religious inclusivism to religious pluralism. And it is a task that must be accomplished in the light of the religiously pluralistic society and globalized reality human beings inhabit.

45. Ibid., 75.

The Task ahead for African Catholicism

As noted in a previous chapter, the mixture of political, ethnic, and individual biases account for increasing religious tensions, clashes, and violent conflicts resulting in the meaningless loss of lives and property in sub-Saharan Africa. With the population of Christians and Muslims rising exponentially in Africa, struggles for supremacy often lead to strained relationships that can result in hateful intolerance of one another's religious doctrines and practices. According to the Pew Forum on Religion and Public Life, "the number of Muslims living between the Sahara Desert and the Cape of Good Hope has increased more than twenty-fold, rising from an estimated eleven million in 1900 to approximately 234 million in 2010. The number of Christians has grown even faster, soaring almost seventy-fold from about seven million to 470 million. Sub-Saharan Africa now is home to about one-in-five of all the Christians in the world (21 percent) and more than one-in-seven of the world's Muslims."[46] This growth in Christian and in Muslim adherents in Africa makes efforts to ensure mutual coexistence an increasingly pressing imperative.

Since religion plays an important role in every aspect of African life, attention must be paid to religious exclusivism in Africa. Although religiously devout and morally conservative, Africans are not ordinarily fundamentalist or religiously militant, but rather syncretistic. Because of the continuing impact of traditional African religion, Africans could be considered religiously liberal in a certain sense, not being given to taking an ideological "all-or-nothing" position on religion. Unlike the impression recent bloody religious conflicts might present, Africans tend to be tolerant of one another's faith, since ordinarily they do not go to war in defense of religious beliefs. Although this position may sound contradictory to the increasing intolerance awash in media coverage about Africa, it is important to find out why Africa is now engaged in bloody religious conflicts. The Pew Forum on Religion and Public Life's 2010 poll confirms Africa's tolerance of

46. Pew Forum on Religion and Public Life, "Tolerance and Tension," i.

other religions, explaining that "Africans have long been seen as devout and morally conservative, and the survey largely confirms this. But insofar as the conventional wisdom has been that Africans are lacking in tolerance for people of other faiths, it may need rethinking."[47]

While Africans are naturally tolerant on account of the acceptance imbued by traditional African religions, the religious exclusivism of Christianity and Islam poses a challenge that stretches this tolerance beyond all limits. The exclusivist theological anthropologies arising from Christianity and Islam's claims to certainty in their religious truths about God leads them to demonize one another as infidels unless converted to each other's religion. This religious position is oblivious to the fact that religious pluralism breeds hatred and creates situations of mutual suspicion between Christians and Muslims. This tense situation is exacerbated by the African communitarian societal structure which, as noted earlier, while emphasizing the common good and the sacredness of life, is limited to one's kith and kin to the exclusion of "outsiders" who are not members of one's immediate community. The group bias of this African ethnocentrism now takes a religious undertone whereby "the other" includes even one's kith and kin if they do not belong to one's religious faith. Since, following Christian and Islamic practice in history, heretics are burned at the stake and infidels are killed unless they convert, Christianity and Islam seem a force not for good but for evil as they stoke violence and bloodshed in Africa. Thus compromised, both religions become tools at the hands of politicians and ideologues who aim at dividing the masses by inciting religious and ethnic tension to cover their incompetence as rulers.

Furthermore, and perhaps due to exclusivist theological anthropologies, Christians and Muslims in Africa often have little knowledge of one another's faiths. A 2010 poll by the Pew Forum on Religion and Public Life on Christian-Muslim relations in Africa found that:

47. Ibid., iii.

> By their own reckoning, neither Christians nor Muslims in the region know very much about each other's faith. In most countries, fewer than half of Christians say they know either some or a great deal about Islam, and fewer than half of Muslims say they know either some or a great deal about Christianity. Moreover, people in most countries surveyed, especially Christians, tend to view the two faiths as very different rather than as having a lot in common. And many people say they are not comfortable with the idea of their children marrying a spouse from outside their religion.[48]

Because of this, Christians and Muslims in Africa easily accept almost any story formulated by ideologues of Christianity or Islam against one another. Political and ethnic differences easily take on religious overtones and lead to suspicion of dominance, real or imagined, by either religion. Thus, *Africae Munus* rightly describes the Christian-Muslim relationship in Africa as complex:

> The Synod Fathers highlighted the complexity of the Muslim presence on the African continent. In some countries, good relations exist between Christians and Muslims; in others, the local Christians are merely second-class citizens, and Catholics from abroad, religious and lay, have difficulty obtaining visas and residence permits; in some, there is insufficient distinction between the religious and political spheres, while in others, finally, there is a climate of hostility.[49]

In spite of or on account of this checkered relationship, *Africae Munus* calls on the church to live in respect for Muslims with the aim of ensuring reconciliation, justice, and peace in Africa: "I call upon the Church, in every situation, to persist in esteem for Muslims, who 'worship God who is one, living and subsistent; merciful and almighty, the creator of heaven and earth, who has also spoken to humanity.'"[50] Christians and Muslims are to work

48. Ibid., 8.

49. Benedict XVI, *Africae Munus*, sec. 94.

50. Ibid.

together to promote charity and peace, for "If all of us who believe in God desire to promote reconciliation, justice, and peace, we must work together to banish every form of discrimination, intolerance and religious fundamentalism."

Interreligious dialogue is an imperative for African Catholicism. *Africae Munus* asks "the whole Church, through patient dialogue with Muslims, to seek juridical and practical recognition of religious freedom, so that every citizen in Africa may enjoy not only the right to choose his religion freely and to engage in worship, but also the right to freedom of conscience. Religious freedom is the road to peace."[51] Meaningful interreligious dialogue, if it is to promote religious freedom, must presuppose acceptance of religious pluralism. Here African Catholicism must learn from the tolerant disposition of the traditional African religions, which, though they predated Christianity and Islam, are nevertheless tolerant of their influence in Africa. Catechesis in Africa must be presented in such a way that African Catholics will appreciate Islam and traditional African religions as equally containing the seeds of God's salvation. The old practice of demonizing each other must come to an end. This ought to be the case even in predominantly Christian regions of Africa. Catholicism must acquaint Christians with knowledge of other faiths by teaching the value of religions other than Christianity in her schools. In this way, the same inspiring tolerance and interculturation that led Massignon to recover the work of an Islamic mystic will be inculcated between Islam and Christianity to the benefit of all.

51. Ibid.

9

The Ministry of the Church in Africa

The Lord has entrusted us with a specific mission, and he has not left us without the means of accomplishing it. Not only has he granted each of us personal gifts for the building up of his Body which is the Church, but he has also granted the whole ecclesial community particular gifts which enable it to carry out its mission. His supreme gift is the Holy Spirit.

—BENEDICT XVI[1]

ONE OF THE CHALLENGES to human development in Africa, especially sub-Saharan Africa, where more people are becoming Christians, is the distortion of the scale of values: vital (caring for the poor), social (influencing the social structures with the good news), cultural (reexamining the meaning underlying human communities), personal (ensuring integrity of personal lives), and religious (mediating the grace of God active in society). Such distortion affects this scale from below and from above. Politics have become the concrete determinant of economics and culture.

---

1. Benedict XVI, *Africae Munus*, sec. 139.

Thus, money, power, and political influence have come to dominate the social order and the executive, judiciary, and legislative arms of government. The consequence has been massive corruption of all aspects of African life, constitutive meaning, and reality. The prevalent materialistic culture, under cover of faith in God, perpetuates oppression and destroys not only the social order, but also the human spirit of Africans, deadening popular conscience in such a way that the social system is controlled by greed. *Africae Munus'* call to African Catholicism is to think through another way of being church that enables her to operate at the level of her times, bearing in mind the changing realities of the African continent. As the number of Christian and especially Catholic converts continues to increase in Africa, it becomes necessary to set road maps for African Catholicism to improve its public relevance.

The *lineamenta* for the Synod is clear on reading the signs of the times as the reason for the convocation of the Second African Synod. It states: "Since the last synodal meeting, however, the situation in Africa has changed considerably. This new reality requires a thorough study in view of a renewed evangelization effort, which calls for a more in-depth analysis of specific topics important for the present and future of the Catholic Church on the great African continent."[2] *Ecclesia in Africa*, the post-synodal document of the First African Synod in 1994, formulated the communion ecclesiology of African Catholicism as "the Church-Family of God in Africa."[3] In continuity with *Ecclesia in Africa*, the Second African Synod sought answers to these questions: "What has *Ecclesia in Africa* accomplished? What has the Church in Africa done with *Ecclesia in Africa*? What remains to be done, using its guidelines in response to the evolving situations on the African continent?"[4] And so *Africae Munus* aims at formulating an ecclesiology for African Catholicism drawing on and in continuity with *Ecclesia in Africa*. The premise underlying the holistic mission of the church in Africa is the Catholic Church's integral understanding of mis-

2. Synod of Bishops, preface to *Lineamenta*.

3. Ibid., sec. 4.

4. Ibid., sec. 1.

sion. As Neil Ormerod and Clifton Shan explain, this integrated understanding of mission "acknowledges that the church exists to minister to the vital needs of the poor, to influence the social structures that frame communities, to prophetically challenge the cultural values that guide and sustain society, and to seek the transformation and wholeness of persons in all walks of life. Within this holistic framework, however, it remains the case that the church's primary responsibility is to proclaim and embody the religious values that are constitutive of Christian faith."[5]

Reading *Africae Munus*, one draws the conclusion that its ecclesiology is foundationally theological anthropology. In *Africae Munus*, African Catholicism is "called, in the name of Jesus, to live reconciliation between individuals and communities and to promote peace and justice in truth for all."[6] It emphasizes the promotion of Africans' human dignity and seeks healing from the anthropological crisis inflicted on Africans by centuries of historical subjugation. It calls for civic education through Catholic social teachings to uphold the human dignity and rights of Africans in their native countries. Its pointed quest for good governance, justice, and peace teaches that, as humans created in the image of God, Africans must not be denied opportunities to realize their full potential. The Synod's themes of reconciliation, justice, and peace make this theological anthropology not just orthodoxy, but also praxis aimed at promoting the human dignity of Africans, which must remain inviolable.

The ministry of the church in Africa, as elsewhere, is bearing witness to Christ through the continuation of his prophetic, pastoral, and kingly offices. This consists not only in the promotion of spirituality through sacramental worship, but also the promotion of social transformation through the implementation of the integral scale of values. Applying Lonergan's scale of values, the anthropological foundation of the ecclesiology of *Africae Munus* that seeks to address the anthropological crisis of Africa, lies in personal value, which is at the base of the three dialectics

5. Ormerod and Clifton, *Globalization and the Mission*, loc. 4341.

6. Benedict XVI, *Africae Munus*, sec. 1.

underlying the integral scale of values: the dialectic of the subject, the dialectic of community, and the dialectic of culture. The person whose integrity is dependent on the grace of religious value generates authentic cultural values at the superstructural and infrastructural levels that make possible the recurrence of schemes for the production and distribution of the human good without which the vital values of life will not be possible. This means that individuals' personal religious values make up (and therefore influence) collective cultural values at the superstructural and infrastructural levels. Hence when social structures are imbued with individuals' good values, the result will be a good society. The generation of such a person of integrity will only be possible through the instillation of authentic religious values. Here the ministry of the church in Africa is called forth. This ministry, charged with making the reign of God visible in the world, demands that African Catholicism seriously consider the faith-formation process. This should no longer consist only of the catechetical process that prepares candidates for the sacraments, but also the wholesome formation of Christians in terms of personal values; that is, the generation of people of integrity ready and able to act as agents of social transformation through the integral scale of values. In order to achieve this, the spirituality, ecclesial praxis, and theology[7] of African Catholicism must be overhauled.

Orthodox ecclesial praxis approximates the reign of God by its prophetic ministry and promotion of the integral scale of values. The church's ecclesial ministry as the bride of Christ is Christological; that is, doing as Jesus did. This consists of fashioning an alternative to the prevailing way of being church and the order of life in African societies. The aim is to establish the reign of God on earth by evoking an alternative to the prevailing order by creatively imagining the rule of God in human affairs and history.[8]

Of course, this involves the church's reexamination of its ministry in the light of the kenosis of Jesus, who sacrificed himself for sinful humanity. African Catholicism must be prepared to do

7. Ibid., 110.
8. Doran, *Theology and the Dialectics*, 119.

as Jesus does in this regard. The clergy and the hierarchy's readiness to self-sacrifice remains a recipe for the church's ministry in Africa. The result will be not only ecclesial praxis founded on the witness to the paschal mystery, but also the practical formation of people led by a willingness to sacrifice for the common good instead of the greed and self-interest. On this witnessing to the law of the cross, on the kenosis exemplified in Jesus, lies the integrity of African Catholicism. Related to this, then, is the question of how African Catholicism is perceived in various African cultural milieus. In the light of Africans' pastoral and sacramental worship, one must not fail to ask: When people want to worship God, do they go to the church as a place of spiritual nourishment or do they perceive the church only as an institution that offers them charitable social services like hospitals, schools, or loans?

Ecclesial praxis for African Catholicism must balance spirituality with involvement in human promotion. The interrelatedness of spirituality, social order, and the personal transformation needed for social change and the promotion of human development and progress in Africa, makes the necessity of attending to the integral scale of values an immediate imperative. People of integrity who will be able to take responsibility for pursuing the human good in Africa cannot emerge if the religious values forming the African mind are inauthentic. Cultural integrity will remain a mirage without the emergence of people of integrity able to critique the cultural forms inherited from past traditions and integrate current cultural changes with the noble aspects of Africa's cultural past. How can African societies expect to progress and develop if the meaning constitutive of their attitudes and values is not genuine? That is, if the superstructure of culture fails to inform the infrastructure of culture critical standards of value to guide the everyday life in the arts, the economy, politics, technology, etc. Of course, a peaceful and harmonious social order cannot exist in Africa in the face of cultural values that are no longer meaningful for the people. Violence, chaos, revenge, and warfare awaits African countries with an inadequate social order, leaving them incapable of establishing viable institutions that enable society to participate in the harmonious production and distribution of goods and services. A social order that fails to care for the masses, leaving both young people and adults unemployed and uncared for, sows the seeds not only of poverty, destitution, and wretchedness, but also opens the way for a degrading dependence on the foreign committee of nations for survival. No one can fully survive or wish to live in a society that lacks the basic infrastructures of existence: affordable healthcare, constant electricity, well-paved roads, food, clothing, and shelter. The mission of the church in Africa, as *Africae Munus* envisions it, will be achieved if the integral scale of values is maintained and not distorted.

The ministry of the church in Africa, in line with the mission of her Lord Jesus, is to actively convert Africans in order to heal the anthropological crisis. There must be less talk and more action to advance social transformation, development, and improvement in the general wellbeing of Africans. The conversion being referred to here is nothing short of a radical about-face—a deep turnaround characterized by the conscientious choice of values instead of mere satisfaction, an overcoming of all forms of bias that impede progress, a readiness to collaborate in bringing about schemes for the human good. This conversion should be intellectual, for it consists of changing the materialistic outlook of life. It must also be moral: facilitating choice of good over evil, of progress over decline, of values over mere satisfaction, of common good over individual or group self-interest. Moral conversion lies not in the shallow shells of superficiality characteristic of a hypocrisy by which inauthenticity deceives only itself. Conversion must, of course, be religious. The challenge is that in Africa, where an increasing number of people are becoming Christian and a reputation for religiosity prevails, this conversion is taken for granted and then neglected. The consequence is inauthentic religiosity whereby religion is not only commercialized, but also spawns negative religious forms. In African Catholicism, when conversion is not religious, magic and superstition are confused with spirituality. Then charlatans reign, and their stock-in-trade is trickery used to swindle the sweat of their fellow Christians through various forms of abracadabra.

The religious and spiritual landscape of African Catholicism swings between the two poles of shallowness in the grounding of faith and superficiality in the expression of faith. Both poles affect the theory and practice of Christian faith and thus necessitate, as *Africae Munus* demands, not just rote memorization of catechism, but a deepening of Christian faith critically, so that it is allowed not only to permeate Africans' intellectual, moral, and spiritual consciousness, but also to reorient Africans as agents of the moral transformation and development of Africa. The challenge of religion in Africa—nay, Catholicism—is not that people have yet to be converted to Christian faith. African Christians number in the millions, as the statistics in the introduction to this book indicates. On the contrary, the challenge is in Christianity's inability to fashion a critical approach that not only incarnates the Christian faith, but also allows Christianity to be transformative of African society and its values. The spirituality that rises up to this challenge must be the result of the intellectual ministry of the church, and be conscious not only of God as the transcendent being, but of God as bringing about changes through faith conversion in the individual, social, and cultural values of Africans. Unfortunately for African Catholicism, as well as for the universal church, the distorted dialectics of community affects the church and makes it difficult for such spirituality and authentic religion to bring about the transformation requisite for social change.

Theology, as the intellectual ministry of the church, struggles to bring about an alternative situation. The battle for survival in much of Africa affects this intellectual ministry of the church. It is all too easy to cave in to the pressure to seek one's own wellbeing, or that of one's family, relations, clan, or tribe, instead of facing the hardship and difficulties associated with seeking an alternative situation that will make the social system work better through the integral scale of values. For this reason, the praxis of theology must begin with the Christian faith's transformation of theologians themselves, who will then be committed to bringing about an alternative situation instead of being gripped by inaction because of the difficulties, suffering, and hardship engendered by poverty.

Many of the institutions of African Catholicism compromise their prophetic role by not "walking the talk" of their preferential option for the poor. Because it seems more comfortable and materially rewarding to protect the status quo, African Catholicism often hides under the cover of the Catholic Church's purported noninvolvement in politics. This leads to a lack of action beyond the work that faith-based organizations are doing in their various dioceses. Thus, instead of being engaged in bringing about changes in African societies, African Catholicism dwells exclusively on individual salvation achieved by reconciling sinners with God. The paradox, which has already been highlighted, is the hybrid of materialism and *fuga mundi* spirituality by which Christians are made to concentrate on achieving the kingdom of God in the next life instead of the present. By so doing, African Catholicism fails to evaluate the ideological role religion could play in furthering social change within Africa's cultural matrix.

Using Doran's appropriation of Lonergan's scale of values, I suggest the intellectual collaboration and ministry of theology in Africa be based not so much upon a social or cultural context, but on human valuation grounded in genuine African cultural values. As noted earlier, African culture is critical of all forms of despotism, totalitarianism, materialism, dehumanization, dishonesty, and desacralization that disorganize the communitarian structure of the African social order. The appreciation of the good and the beautiful, the constant quest for wisdom and knowledge, the promotion of the common good fostered by social responsibility, the deeply-rooted religiosity characterized by a balance of belief in the transcendence as well as the immanence of God as the beginning and end of all actions, are embedded in African cultural values and remain—as eminent scholars have noted—the way out of Africa's quagmire. African Catholicism has an important role to play in integrating the scale of values that will reorient the distorted dialectics of African communities.

In accordance with the theological anthropological foundation of the ecclesiology of *Africae Munus*, African theology should be neither inculturation nor liberation theology. On the contrary, the ecclesiology of *Africae Munus*, respectful and appreciative of African cultures as it is, promotes both inculturation theology and liberation theology in an integral way. Inculturation leads to liberation. Liberation is for the purpose of appreciating Africa's cultural values. For this reason, *Africae Munus* tasks African Catholicism to single out "knowledgeable individual converts, who could provide the Church with guidance in gaining a deeper and more accurate knowledge of the traditions, the culture and the traditional religions. This would make it easier to identify points of real divergence. It would also help to clarify the vital distinction between culture and cult and to discard those magical elements which cause division and ruin for families and societies" (*AM*, sec. 92). At the same time it should, with the assistance of men and women of goodwill, promote good governance in their various countries. The principal task of African Catholicism is bearing witness to the good news through the promotion of the human dignity of Africans by enabling Africans to appreciate their cultures and serving as the voice of the Africans masses who desire good governance, reconciliation, justice, and peace.

The spirituality to be engendered by such theology takes seriously elements of African culture and spirituality that are often misunderstood in orthodox Catholic spirituality. African Christian spirituality cannot begin to impact the lives of Africans if it is not incarnated according to African lifestyles and religious worldviews. However, African Catholicism must not cave in to religious gullibility, for such gullibility takes advantage of the piety of Africans to exploit and deceive them by not criticizing elements of African spirituality that border on superstition. A balance must be struck between faith in Jesus and the life of the suffering servant, whose example of suffering on the cross must be emulated by his followers.

In order to effect cultural change, African Catholic spirituality must not distort the dialectic of culture. It must not tilt either to the side of cosmological constitutive meanings dominated by myth and magic or to the anthropological constitutive meanings of culture that are devoid of mystery and cancel out the transcendent nature of human existence. Christian spirituality appropriate for African ecclesial praxis must recognize both the transcendent and the worldly aspects of human existence. Human beings must not usurp the place of God as if the ultimate reality were nonexistent; at the same time, a critical approach must be encouraged towards religion so that fear and ignorance do not displace authentic religion such that everything is reduced to magic. Genuine cultural values must integrate the cosmological and anthropological constitutive meaning of communities, as this is itself a function of the genuine religious value of God's grace.

The intellectual ministry of theology in African Catholicism must evoke authentic cultural values. The major question here is whether African cultural values are adequate for the changing circumstances of an Africa that has undergone multiple social transformations over the centuries. For example, are these cultural values able to meet the dynamics of modern statehood in Africa? Do they meet the requirements for good social order in modern Africa, a continent now constituted of heterogeneous communities woven together as independent countries? The global scope of contemporary social dialectic is also an important consideration, for it equally impacts Africa. How can African cultural values be developed to respond to the changing realities of modern African socio-cultural, political, and economic realities?

These questions are important because African Catholicism cannot hope to be the catalytic agent of social transformation in addressing the anthropological crisis Africans suffer if African cultural values are not brought up to the level of the times. Since cultural values cannot effectively address contemporary issues arising from the global social dialectic, the rest of the levels of value must be involved: vital, social, cultural, personal, and religious. While Africans as a whole recognize the need for vital values of food, clothing, shelter, healthcare infrastructure, etc., African Catholicism cannot be merely religious, or presume to be catering to the spiritual needs rather than schemes for the constant provision of these vital values. Unfortunately, what has often happened is that African Catholicism has demand of these vital values for the church hierarchy at the expense of the laity, thus neglecting a good percentage of the laity who lack access to these vital values. When African Catholicism fails to promote peace or even becomes an agent of religious crisis in communities, the social order that should promote harmonious existence for the provision of vital values is disrupted. Before the advent of Christianity, African cultural values formed Africans to the social existence at the level of those times. Christianity brings different sets of meaning into these cultural values, which can disrupt the social order. This disruption at times accounts for the civil unrest that wreaks violence within African societies. According to Elisée Rutagambwa, who lost loved ones in the 1994 Rwandan genocide,

> Catholic missionaries fractured Rwandan civil society by prohibiting native religious and cultural traditions and by forcing people to renounce their secular beliefs. Specifically, by introducing a dualistic Manichean worldview in which people were either "saved" or "damned," the missionaries created significant cleavages in the Rwandan civil society. New converts were separated from their unconverted family members, thereby abolishing the role of their ancestors, who traditionally served as intergenerational "glue," that is, as mediators between the living and the dead. Thus the Judeo-Christian bipolar vision, divided between the Bakristu (Christians) and Bapagani-Bashenzi (pagans), replaced the traditional tripolar view . . . This new identity schema served as the foundation of the new collective memory of Rwandans, to the detriment of their national identity . . . When the powerful new ethnic ideology emerged following the colonial rule, it was transformed into a new dual identity schema of the Hutus and Tutsis.[9]

African Catholicism cannot impose different sets of cultural values without inculturating the Christian faith into the African cultural values. African religiosity is attuned to African cultural values. Conversion to Christianity implies change at the deepest level of individuals' consciousness. How will African Catholicism

9. Rutagambwa, "Rwandan Church," 175.

respond to the impact of this change? Is African Catholicism able to provide sufficient spiritual nourishment to this African religiosity? In other words, African theology, in service to African Catholicism, must pay attention to the full scale of values and their relationship to one another.

Because cultural values are important to the entire process of human good, development institutions must pay attention to the meaning constitutive of a communities' existence. African Catholicism must pay attention to Africa's cultural values and aim at bringing it up to the level of its time through the integral scale of values. The link cultural values have to the rest of the scale of values is in the formation of authentic human subjects—people of integrity who, by the grace of religious values, become active agents for the human good in bringing about social order for the provision of vital values. For instance, the narrow scope of African cultural values, which limits generosity to one's kith and kin, must be broadened by the Christian agapic love that promotes human dignity and extends love, hospitality, sacredness of life, and fraternity to every human being. Broadening African cultural values in this way could transform the African social order to be inclusive of people of other ethnic backgrounds, which is expected of modern African statehood. It could go a long way towards healing the evil of ethnocentrism, which as we have seen, has bedeviled the continent with nepotism, hatred, violence, and even ethnic cleansing.

To give another example, reconfiguring the African cultural value of brotherhood and sisterhood—which implies the responsibility of Africans to care for members of their family as well as extended relations—will stem the tide of corruption. This is because corruption often arises from Africans in positions of authority (including ecclesial positions like pastors and bishops) trying to use their positions to benefit family members and cronies at the expense of the common good. African Catholicism reconfigures such African cultural values pastorally through the pulpit, as well as through its curriculum in colleges and universities. African Catholicism also has to change the African concept of distributive justice, which emphasizes revenge, with an understanding of

Christian charity that emphasizes forgiveness. In this way, African Catholicism can hope to stem the tide of violence that has so often disrupted the social order.

The intrinsic African religiosity by which religion is brought into all aspects of African life is an essential ingredient for African Catholicism to help emphasize the implication of God's presence manifest in the incarnation. This has the potential to overcome the fearful belief in malevolent forces unleashed to destroy progress and development that surround African religious life. The religious value of the God's love for each person must be emphasized, because African religiosity is not sufficiently cognizant of this dimension of religious values. God is traditionally feared and respected. For this reason, African Catholicism's development of an alternative to *fuga mundi* spirituality is important. The soteriological principles of the law of the cross and of the paschal mystery must be incarnated in African Catholicism in such a way that God's love for each person in Africa is noted. In the spiritual warfare that preoccupies most African Catholics, the fear of the evil one, of witches, wizards, and other evil forces often distracts from the power of salvation in Christ. I suggest the development of an African theology of grace in the light of the African worldview.

Furthermore, African Catholicism must confront and seek to transform aspects of African cultural values that are hierarchically structured in such a way that unjustly limits individuals' contributions to society on the basis of age, gender, affluence, family background, etc. Such conceptions limit the potential of human dignity, human intelligence, ability, and so on, to the exclusion of some and the unfair advantage of others. It is basically a limitation of the human good in aristocratic form. But on the contrary, following the soteriological principle of the law of the cross, the normative criteria for human dignity is common to humanity, male and female, young and old, rich and poor alike. For this reason, when African Catholicism insists on hierarchy that favors the clergy, it endorses an aristocratic model that negates the gospel values of love and human dignity based on our status as beings created in the image of God. Such an unjust structure disrupts the social order as it rewards some people more than others in the distribution of goods.

Closely related to African religious values, or perhaps because of it, African Catholicism must attend to globalization and the impact of international financial institutions on African economies. This is important because multinational corporations' influence on national economies indirectly affect African religiosity. National indebtedness to international financial institutions results in economic policies like the structural adjustment program (SAP), which results in widespread privatization and the collapse of government welfare schemes. The attendant increase in unemployment, poverty, disease, and violence leads many African Catholics to prayer centers, spiritual healing houses, and other forms of spiritual activities in search for solutions. Because the cause of this social malaise is not spiritual, Africans' faith in God is affected. On the surface, it would seem a good thing that more African's are seeking spiritual succor. However, critical examination reveals that at times, it is economic problems that drive Africans to seek religion for the wrong reasons. In such situations, God the Father of our Lord Jesus Christ appears powerless to confront the problems afflicting Christians in Africa. This increases syncretism and lends credibility to spiritual charlatans who further deceive the people into questing after spiritual problems, which are often the least of their problems. To combat this difficulty, African Catholicism should partner with economists to champion the cause of the common good and contribute to good governance not only by warning against bad economic policies, but also by educating the people on government policies that militate against national economic interests and the wellbeing of the people.

Equally important here is configuring African cultural values to the global social order. By this I mean that considering the interdependence of the globalized world order, African Catholicism must participate in forging a new cultural matrix with meanings and values drawn from African cultural values yet attuned to the contemporary global situation in the light of Christian revelation. The new sets of meanings and values that will emerge from such an integration of African cultural values with the global situation in terms of Christian revelation will equip African Catholics to choose wisely when confronted with values—often foreign—that run counter to the Christian faith. Here it is important to recognize the respect African cultural values accord to nature, some elements of which are seen as sacred. However, in the light of Christian faith, care is taken not to subordinate human dignity and society to these cosmological principles. For instance, some African cultures regard the birth of twins as taboo, an evil omen against the mother earth. While respecting the sacredness accorded to nature, Christian faith upholds the value of human life as gift from God, and thus abrogates such practice. This contribution of Christianity to an aspect of African culture should continue in African Catholicism, promoting African cultural values in such a way that a new cultural matrix arises in accordance with ever-recurring contemporary situations. New insights must always be introduced into African cultural values so as to prevent domination by forces intent on new forms of cultural imperialism. Thus, while respectful of African cultural values, African Catholicism must evoke, through critical analysis of African religiosity in the light of Christian revelation, the human capacity to bring about changes in society. This will balance out African religiosity's tendency towards fear surrounding magic. In this way, theology mediates faith and culture by helping to bring about a new cultural order that will promote progress and development in Africa.

Theology transforms the subject, bringing about authentic cultural values by reorienting the meanings and values constitutive of society. As ecclesial ministry, theology aims at the praxis of the rule of God on earth. This begins with a transformation of the theologian and his or her willingness to overcome the moral impotence of human fallibility. Theology as praxis in this sense begins with the psychic conversion underlying, as Doran says, a theology of history.[10] The transformative dynamics of theology then evokes an alternative situation by transforming the superstructure of culture, which by evolving an authentic culture, transforms the

---

10. Doran, *What Is Systematic Theology?* 195–97.

constituents of society to generate good social order. African theology must develop different ways of understanding the mysteries of the Christian faith and communicating these to the common meaning of the people. African Catholicism, founded merely on general categories of human promotion without a sufficient grounding in a systematic understanding of the doctrine of God, distorts the scale of values and will end up promoting inauthentic religiosity lacking in Christian spirituality. Conversely, African Catholicism that ignores an integrated and holistic understanding of the mission of the church and excludes or is less concerned with human promotion equally distorts the scale of values and therefore is not ministering according to the dialectics of history. The task ahead for African Catholicism must be to continuously challenge the common meaning of African societies so as to mutually self-mediate faith and culture in Africa.

10

Proposals towards Reconciliation, Justice, and Peace

The three principal elements of the theme chosen for the Synod, namely reconciliation, justice, and peace, brought it face to face with its "theological and social responsibility," and made it possible also to reflect on the Church's public role and her place in Africa today.

—Pope Benedict XVI[1]

Attention to Religious Values

In the face of conflict and violence ravaging Africa, how can the African Church serve as medium for reconciliation, justice, and peace, the three major themes of *Africae Munus*? In attempting to answer this question, it will be beneficial to examine models already in place vis-à-vis the recommendations of the Second African Synod. One of the most widely read books on religious violence, R. Scott Appleby's *The Ambivalence of the Sacred*, offers such a model.

---

1. Benedict XVI, *Africae Munus*, sec. 17.

Appleby argues that violence is in some sense fundamental to the religious imagination. He concerns himself with three questions about the ambivalence of religion: Why and under what conditions do religious actors choose to become violent? Conversely, under what conditions do religious actors justify violence as a sacred duty or privilege? Finally, under what conditions do non-violent religious actors become agents of peacebuilding? The book, through a case-by-case articulation, responds, "*Religious violence* occurs when religious leaders, in reaction to perceived injustices in the structural environment of the society, successfully employ religious arguments designed to mobilize religious (or ethno religious) actors to retaliate against their enemies."[2]

Appleby's first chapter takes a phenomenological approach based on theories of religion that anchors Appleby's ambivalence to the sacred—an ambivalence that is the inevitable result of the limits of human understanding. We can see this ambivalence, Appleby explains, in the two kinds of religious activists, or "militants," on the scene today: extremists, on the one hand, and peacemakers, on the other.[3] In subsequent chapters, Appleby presents contrasting case studies of militants who use violence as well as those who work for peace:

> *Religious resistance to forces of extremism* becomes possible when religious leaders succeed in inculcating nonviolent militancy as both a religious norm and a strategy to oppose and redress injustices in the structural environment. *Religious peacebuilding* occurs when religious militants dedicated to nonviolence acquire technical and professional skills in prevention and early warning, mediation and conciliation, and other elements of conflict transformation.[4]

Appleby describes, for example, the work of Samdech Preah Maha Ghosananda, Buddhist primate of Cambodia, Liz Bernstein, Jewish human rights activist, and Bob Maat, a Jesuit priest who led

2. Appleby, *Ambivalence of the Sacred*, 282, emphasis Appleby's.

3. Ibid., 10, 283.

4. Ibid., emphasis Appleby's.

efforts to train Cambodian Buddhists in conflict resolution.[5] In 1993, Maha Ghosananda led hundreds of Buddhist monks, nuns, and laity on a dramatic month-long march from Siem Reap in the country's northwestern region all the way to the capital in Phnom Penh.

Rejecting what he calls the "minimalist" approach to religion's participation in public life, an approach by which religion is kept separate and privatized, Appleby offers the view that the right kind of religious zeal, rather than religious restraint, is the answer to global violence. To the critical questions: "Why and under what conditions do some religious actors choose the path of violence while others seek justice through nonviolent means and work for reconciliation among combatants?" and "What might be gained from involving such actors more directly in peace-building?" Appleby suggests that the remedy is education.[6] In order for this solution to be realistic, religious actors must be integrated into conflict-resolution and peacebuiliding teams. He asserts that in order to achieve this goal, religious leaders—spiritual leaders, governing officials of religious bodies or organizations, institutional administrators, and the like—must make three significant commitments to religious peacebuilding:

> First, they must give priority to the religious education and spiritual and moral formation of the largest possible pool of believers in addition to the disciples or novices in their charge; to be effective, religious leaders must draw on symbols, concepts, values, and norms shared by the wider community. Second, religious authorities must also dedicate precious resources, including the time and energy of many of their most gifted coreligionists, to conferences and dialogues designed to develop culturally nuanced methods of conflict transformation. Finally, religious authorities must agree to collaborate, as necessary, with trainers, educators, and facilitators who come from outside the religious community.[7]

5. Ibid., 282.
6. Ibid., ix–8, 19–21.
7. Ibid., 285.

Such religious education, in accordance with the Scripture and traditions of various religions, must prioritize inculcating nonviolence and promoting interpretations of the sacred that give priority to reconciliation, restraint, forgiveness, and analogous peace-related values. As Appleby prognosticates, "Armed not with weapons of destruction but with technical skills, material resources, and transnational networks of support, such believers stand the chance of becoming formidable militants for peace."[8]

Of course, Appleby's book contains far more riches than can be articulated in these few paragraphs. However, his contribution is not without its limitations. Appleby's penchant for definition of religion is one difficulty, while his reliance on Rudolf Otto's dated book, *The Idea of the Holy*, is another. However, Appleby's excellent contribution to peacebuilding through religion is significant. There is no doubt that religion could be a force either for good or for evil, depending on its use. The role of religion is ambiguous. At a given time and under particular circumstances, it can be misused to incite violence. Yet, under different circumstances, religion has the potential to prevent violence and promote peace. Because of the complexity of the social, cultural, economic, and political factors that can either give rise to religious conflict or promote peace, religion's ambivalent role in human conflict ought to be carefully studied in the light of social progress or decline. For this reason, it is important to pay attention not only to religious values, but also to the personal, cultural, social, and vital values of each community. The German Institute of Global and Area Studies (GIGA)-sponsored report on the role of religion in conflict in sub-Saharan Africa asserts: "In sum, one may conclude that the abusive use of religion in conflict typically takes place in settings where overlapping religious and other boundaries as well as organizational connections between religion and politics offer the opportunity for the mobilization of religion."[9] In other words, because of the interconnections of human historical process, the

---

8. Ibid., 286.

9. Basedau and De Juan, "'Ambivalence of the Sacred' in Africa," 22.

scale of values are related and could either promote social progress or decline.

Ecclesia in Africa[10] also mentions the interrelatedness of the various sectors of the state as responsible for one of the challenges facing the African church, pointing to "the various forms of division which need to be healed through honest dialogue" (*EIA*, sec. 55). It traces the source of these divisions to external and internal factors, including "the borders left behind by the colonial powers, the coexistence of ethnic groups with different traditions, languages," and "tribalism, nepotism, racism, religious intolerance and the thirst for power taken to extremes by totalitarian regimes which trample with impunity the rights and dignity of the person" (*EIA*, sec. 55, 117). These wars and conflicts, *Ecclesia in Africa* says, are fueled by the arms trade, which it describes as "a scandal since it sows the seed of death" (*EIA*, sec. 118). While appealing to countries that sell arms to Africa to stop supplying weapons, *Ecclesia in Africa* asks African governments to spend more on education, health, and the wellbeing of their citizens instead of making huge military expenditures, and also calls on national, regional, and international organizations to find equitable and long-lasting solutions to the problems of refugees and displaced persons (*EIA*, sec. 119).

The *lineamenta* for the Second African Synod dwells more on the problem of violence, conflict, and war in Africa. While acknowledging some positive developments in Africa since the *EIA*, it laments deplorable socio-political, socio-economical, and socio-cultural conditions in Africa. It observes that "in some African countries, persistent social tensions impede progress and give rise to political disturbances and armed conflicts. Tribalism, border disputes and attempts at expansion lead to armed struggles which take a heavy toll in human life and deplete financial resources."[11] In other words, the *lineamenta* advocates a praxis-oriented approach towards Africa's religious, political, cultural, and social issues in order to provide not only the vital values needed to uplift Afri-

10. Cited hereafter as *EIA*.

11. Synod of Bishops, *Lineamenta*, sec. 11.

ca's standard of living, but also to heal the anthropological crisis arising from centuries of subjugation and oppression. According to Raymond Olusesan Aina, "this praxis has concrete relevance for Africa (with its wars and 'low density violence') because of the ineluctable connection between sustainable justice and the peace process and issues of social justice. This is what traumatized persons and peoples in Africa [as elsewhere] need to regain control over their destiny. The loss of control is not usually micro-based. It flows from their collective traumatization."[12] Although the *lineamenta* fails to directly mention religion as a source of conflict, it admits tension and difficulty in establishing dialogue with Islam. This is important for Africa, considering the degree to which Christian-Muslim conflicts fuel violence in Africa.

EIA and the *lineamenta* both seek reconciliation, justice, and peace by teaching Christians that they are brothers and sisters. The *EIA* adopts the church as a "Family of God" in Africa as its image of the church in Africa in the hope of bringing an end to conflict, violence, and war. If Africans see each other as brothers and sisters, the thinking goes, they will not go to war against each other. The *lineamenta* surmises, "Since the same Blood of Christ circulates in each of us, and since we are all members of the Church-Family of God in the Body and Blood of Christ, it stands to reason that to shed a brother's or sister's blood, the Blood of Christ; this is killing his life in us."[13]

Surely the concept of the church as "Family of God" can help bring about reconciliation if Africans could accept the image of themselves as brothers and sisters by virtue of their priesthood in Christ. But as Archbishop Obiefuna rightly remarked during the first Special Assembly for Africa, the blood of tribes tends to run thicker than the blood of the waters of baptism.[14] As has been elaborately treated in a previous chapter, even among the church hierarchy, ethnic alliances have continued to be obstacles to church administration. While the church promotes reconciliation, it must

12. Aina, "*Lineamenta* for the Second African Synod," 1.

13. Synod of Bishops, *Lineamenta*, sec. 39.

14. Quoted in Shorter, "Curse of Ethnocentrism," 29.

bear in mind the words of Pope John Paul II that there is "no peace without justice, no justice without forgiveness."[15] The church in Africa must be involved in the quest for human promotion. In this regard, it should sensitize its flock by educating them on their civic responsibilities and the importance of their involvement in politics and the economic development of their nations. Unless poverty is eradicated, the poor will always turn against each other in the quest for scarce resources. Unless the healthcare system is improved upon, people will always accuse each other of witchcraft and other crimes, and conflict will inevitably continue. The church in Africa must take up and put into practice its prophetic image of itself from the First Special Assembly for Africa as "the voice of the voiceless" (*EIA*, sec. 70).

The importance of the integral scale of values in relation to the mission of the church is evident in the multifaceted topics covered in the Second African Synod. It likewise portrays the public role of the church in Africa. As explained in *Africae Munus*, "The three principal elements of the theme chosen for the Synod, namely reconciliation, justice, and peace, brought it face to face with its 'theological and social responsibility,' and made it possible also to reflect on the Church's public role and her place in Africa today" (*AM*, sec. 17). These concerns are reflected in Orobator's *Reconciliation, Justice, and Peace: The Second African Synod*. The convocation of a Second Synod for Africa in less than two decades of the First African Synod shows the Catholic Church's commitment to peace, good governance, and development of Africa. The contributors whose works make up the five parts of this book reflect on the various ecclesiological dimensions of the Second African Synod's themes of reconciliation, justice, and peace, highlighting the ambivalent role religion plays in politics and the social order. On the one hand, religion is capable of inciting violence; on the other hand, it could serve as agent for peace. John S. Mbiti clearly articulates this ambivalence by highlighting the potential for peacemaking by the three dominant religions in Africa:

---

15. John Paul II, "Celebration of the World Day of Peace," sec. 15.

> Neither African Religion nor Christianity nor Islam is innocent of engaging, aggravating, or promoting conflicts and wars. But their teachings can challenge people to make and practice peace at all levels: peace among people, peace between people and nature, and peace between people and God. As long as there are religious insights, they should continue to inspire and challenge society to move in the direction of peace. This is not to overlook the many forces that cause conflicts and make it so difficult to put peace into practice in the family, at work, in the community, in the nation, in the world, and with nature at large.[16]

In spite of its weaknesses, Appleby's widely read, reviewed, and quoted book emphasizes the need for authentic religiosity whereby organized religion is made to become a force for good in the social order. The themes of both the First and the Second African Synod showcase the multifaceted nature of Christianity's involvement in public policy. In communicating the good news, Christianity is involved in administering to the religious, personal, cultural, social, and vital needs of people in any society. If it is to be a force for good and not for evil, if it is to promote peace and not violence, then religion's negative tendencies and the abuse of its institutional authority must be curtailed. Particularly important for African Catholicism in this regard is the transformation of African psyche and broadening of African cultural values with regard to tolerance and mutual coexistence. Because the African sense of fraternity is often ethnic, Christian love—even of one's enemies—must permeate African Christian consciousness. This is important because of the often-negative attitude towards the other, which tends towards mistrust. As Eugene Uzukwu observes, "It is a common practice among Africans to stigmatize peoples outside their area of social relationship as tricky, deceitful, and cannibalistic."[17] Christian love, which is a participation in the Trinitarian love of the Father, Son, and Holy Spirit, has the potential to overcome this tendency toward hate and revenge. It imbues the highest sense

16. Mbiti, "Never Break the Pot," 20.

17. Uzukwu, "God of our Ancestors," 347.

of justice and reconciliation because of its respect for the human dignity of all beings created in the image of God. The scandal of the genocide in Rwanda, where African Catholics were killed in the very churches where they sought refuge, must never be allowed to repeat itself. African Catholicism must always and in all circumstances emphasize the self-emptying love of Jesus Christ, who died for the love of humanity. As Appleby suggests and as the First and Second African Synods emphasize, religious education must inculcate love and promote peace, justice, and reconciliation for all Africans.

In spite of advances in ecumenism, much still needs to be done to further mutual relationships between churches and Christians. The hierarchy in African Catholicism has a lot to learn from the grassroots experience of Christians who generally relate harmoniously with one another across denominational lines. Differences in faith not withstanding, Africans are reputed to be pious, bringing religion into all aspects of their lives. Perhaps the African idea of God, which integrates all aspects of life as a symbol of unity, could be of help in promoting not only ecumenical relationships among Christians and advancing interreligious encounters, but also in bringing about an integral wholeness capable of healing the African crisis of identity. It also has the potential of pastorally contributing to a distinctly African Christian spirituality.

From the perspective of traditional West African religions, marked as they are by openness to duality or plurality and expressed in the practice of "looking at everything twice," Elochukwu Uzukwu proposes a "perception of and approach to the divine [that is] characterized by flexibility and tolerance" based on the African love for flexibility.[18] "Religion that focuses on people," Uzukwu asserts, "might align itself with the humanist project."[19] In this way, traditional African religions eschew violence, promote tolerance, and remove God from wars on account of the duality or plurality of African religious thought. This, Uzukwu argues, could be the contribution of African traditional religion to world religion and

18. Ibid., *God, Spirit and Human Wholeness*, 13.

19. Ibid., "Re-Evaluating God-Talk," 55.

to interreligious dialogue: "West African traditional religions that remove inter-communal violence from the purview of the Supreme God, that ensure equal distance of God from each human and each community, incline one to the provisional conclusion that ethnic religions focus on the realisation of the destiny of communities and individuals. They do not generate violence as such in the name of God. They challenge us to reexamine the claims of jihads and crusades in the name of God."[20] God's transcendence in such a construct does not negate the existence or interfere with the role of divinities or deities. In other words, religions are multiple and they harmonize pluralistic relationships between the transcendent being and human person.[21]

African Catholicism stands to benefit by appropriating the duality and flexibility inherent in the traditional religion of her people. This approach has three advantages: First, it promotes dialogue, conversation, and prayer fundamental to the human divine encounter. Second, it respects the human dignity at the core of Christian values. Third, it is communitarian, a virtue important not only for African cultural values, but also for Christianity.[22] Africans often have little difficulty converting to Christianity because Christian values resonate with African socio-cultural and religious ethics, a fact that speaks volumes and makes this appropriation not only important, but urgent and necessary as a model for authentic African Catholicism. Since Africans cannot be Catholics without at the same time being Africans, Uzukwu's proposal above could serve as one way of being both Christian and authentically African. Emphasizing the role of the Holy Spirit in mission and faith community as manifested in the African practice of Christian faith and life, Uzukwu's proposal—while acknowledging the value of Western Trinitarian theology—anchors African faith experience of the revealing God of the crucified and risen Jesus on the manifestation of the Holy Spirit in African communities. Within Uzukwu's theological construct, the spirituality of African Christianity and Ca-

20. Ibid., 71.

21. Ibid., *God, Spirit and Human Wholeness*, 13–19.

22. Ibid., "Re-Evaluating God-Talk," 67.

tholicism as the lived faith of the community under the direction of the Holy Spirit becomes meaningful, for "In the final analysis the pre-eminence of the Holy Spirit is not only informed by the desire to transform 'the spirits around us.' The intentionality of the spirit-focused, spirit-directing and spirit-embedding Christian life is holistic liberation: the Spirit bestows gifts, material and spiritual, and frees individuals and the community from satanic or spiritual powers."[23] Approaching the experience of Christian faith from this experience of relationship with the divine opens Africans up to diverse forms of communication with God in Christ. Such an approach deepens the African Christian experience and cements the faith under the lead of the Holy Spirit.

Although some people advocate a hermeneutic of discontinuity between African traditional religions and Christian faith, what is clear is that Africans cannot abandon their traditional spiritual heritage in order to become Christian. Patrick A. Kalilombe corroborates this understanding in writing, "the most obvious place to search for spirituality is in the context of traditional religious practice: in worship, ritual, and prayer. Here the shape of a people's spirituality becomes easier to grasp, for their deepest aspirations are made manifest and their underlying outlook on the world of realities is revealed, not in theories or formulas, but in practical attitudes."[24] Because memory and identity are profoundly linked, attempts by the hermeneutic of discontinuity to make Africans forget their story and their culture are attempts at making them forget who they are. This erasure has been partly responsible for the crisis of identity traumatizing Africans. Uzukwu's proposal, in spite of its inadequacies, clearly indicates an African way of being church and being Christian modeled after other peoples who have been Christians from ages past—through continuity with their traditional heritages. Grace builds on nature and on the attentiveness, intelligence, reasonableness, and responsibility that are transcendental precepts for the authenticity of any human being, irrespective of differences of culture and context. Such religious

23. Ibid., *God, Spirit, and Human Wholeness*, 224.
24. Kalilombe, "African Perspective," 119.

values, in continuity with the spirituality native to Africans, will be the springboard for an African Catholicism capable of standing for reconciliation, justice, and peace.

Reconciliation

The urgent need for reconciliation in Africa cannot be overemphasized. The "anthropological crisis" *Africae Munus* details as traumatic for Africans pushed Africans' naturally imbued virtue of tolerance to the limit. Psychologically, Africans turned against themselves and against one another in the quest for survival in situations where might became right. The colonial policy of divide and rule that structured the nation-state in Africa intensified ethnic tensions and rivalries.[25] The result has been hatred, violence, civil wars, and even genocide. At times, African Catholicism has been complicit in these conflicts, as in Rwanda, where together the church and state fanned the embers of ethnic hatred between Hutus and Tutsis. In order to maintain order and a false sense of stability, reconciliation has been pursued without seeking justice or love to forestall future reoccurrence of wrongs. Reconciliation is vital for peace and for maintaining a social order able to provide the basic necessities of life. In other words, reconciliation is the precondition for stable political, social, legal, economic, and technological infrastructures requisite for progress and development in human society. When the social order is disrupted by violence or war, not only is society destroyed, but the scale of human values is also distorted. The consequence can be unimaginable crimes against humanity.

The relationship between reconciliation, justice, and peace is well noted in *Africae Munus*, which states:

> Human peace obtained without justice is illusory and ephemeral. Human justice which is not the fruit of reconciliation in the "truth of love" (*Eph* 4:15) remains incomplete; it is not authentic justice. Love of truth—

---

25. See Rutagambwa, "Rwandan Church," 175.

"the whole truth," to which the Spirit alone can lead us (cf. *Jn* 16:13)—is what marks out the path that all human justice must follow if it is to succeed in restoring the bonds of fraternity within the "human family, a community of peace," reconciled with God through Christ. Justice is never disembodied. It needs to be anchored in consistent human decisions. A charity which fails to respect justice and the rights of all is false.[26]

Acknowledging that reconciliation is a pre-political concept and a necessary condition for peace, *Africae Munus* approaches reconciliation pastorally, first by convincing people of the power of reconciliation made possible through the power of God's love, and second, by promoting reconciliation between people through seeking forgiveness. And third, by ensuring that justice is done by punishing criminals and bringing them to repentance.[27]

However, *Africae Munus'* pastoral approach falls short in its recommendations for reconciliation by shifting the responsibility to government authorities, local chiefs, and the citizens without explicitly acknowledging its own responsibility as an institution besides impressing on people the power of reconciliation. It fails to admit its role when atrocities are committed in church institutions or when church officials incite crimes like genocide, and it evades its responsibility to seek and receive forgiveness. And so even in spite of the Rwandan genocide, African Catholicism has not seen the need to change its posture towards reconciliation. It maintains its traditional approach, an approach aptly summarized by Emmanuel Katangole as the pious, political, and the pastoral postures by which the church fails to ask necessary questions, take necessary steps to stop the perpetuation of heinous crimes like genocide, and finally, out of the church's charity and compassion, ends up as cleaning up after the violence has been committed.[28] The church's pastoral posture arises from a wrong biblical notion

---

26. Benedict XVI, *Africae Munus*, sec. 18.

27. Ibid., sec. 21.

28. Katongole and Wilson-Hartgrove, "Postures of Social Engagement," 71–75.

of reconciliation as "solely about reconciling God with humanity with no reference to social realities."[29]

Reconciliation must be deep down, rigorous but not obstructive, complicated but hope-oriented, aimed at resolving conflict but gradual and not rushed. It must not be aimed at serving the interests of people in power, for that is just another way of making the poor sheath their swords and accept a top-down approach to allow for "peace" to reign. The church must always be clear whose justice is being sought in reconciliation. The justice that must precede reconciliation must be to the interest of the aggrieved, marginalized, and oppressed. This question must be asked and answered: "Reconciliation *toward what*?"[30]

In answering this question, which is important in any process of reconciliation and especially between church and society, Katongole and Rice step back to formulate measures towards a successful and fruitful Christian reconciliation that offers a vision of hope leading to forgiveness, transformation, communion, and peace. Katongole and Rice's book offers a different category of reconciliation as a transformation from "outside in" to "inside out."[31] Reconciliation, they say, is a journey rather than an achievement. It is a movement of interiority that anchors reconciliation to self-transformation in a personal conversion that recognizes oneself as part of the brokenness of the world. Hence, this is a conversion of recognizing oneself as being in need of healing, from seeing oneself as a fixer to the one needing fixing, of understanding oneself as a beneficiary of reconciliation through interior reconciliation, and of reconciliation as "quiet revolution."[32] Reconciliation is a movement from the old kind of life to a new life in Christ, always keeping in mind the vital skill of memory that prevents us from forgetting the past too quickly and recalling the example of God who reconciles humanity with himself in Christ.

29. Katongole and Rice, *Reconciling All Things*, loc. 189.

30. Ibid., loc. 256.

31. Ibid., loc. 48.

32. Ibid., loc. 347.

Within this category, it makes sense that the language of reconciliation is lament. This is a kind of prayer to God in the face of atrocities. Lament is abandonment of self in prayer to God preceded by an acknowledgment of evil and crying to the heavens not for vengeance, but for God's mercy and love. Lament does not rush for the easy fix, the soothing balm that asks the rhetorical question: Why can't human beings simply get along? It neither provokes rage that will only end up inflaming the raging fire of violence nor does it wish away evil as if it never existed. On the contrary, it protests the wound and rupture of the human world, objecting to the pain and suffering of wronged people, for "Lament calls us into a fundamental journey of transformation. If we are to follow the path this practice lays out for us, we have to unlearn three things: speed, distance and innocence."[33] Lament shows reconciliation to be a slow, gradual process that begins at the margins, at the bottom, in our homes, among relatives, friends, in work places, villages, etc. Reconciliation demands compassion in the sense of suffering with the suffering, soaking oneself in the cry of the oppressed and recognizing our own brokenness as individuals, as groups, and as institutions.

Katongole and Rice's use of lament is groundbreaking. Not only is lament shattering, it is transformative in unimaginable ways, especially as it relates human suffering to one's inmost being. It transformed Archbishop Oscar Romero from an academic supporter of the status quo to a champion of social justice speaking out against repressive government in his country.[34] It provokes the deep sacrifice and commitment that leaves one prepared to lay down one's life for the course of justice and peace. Lament evokes a hope of a better future of peace and nonviolence, of forgiveness and love even in the face of suffering and pain. It sustains the process of reconciliation in faithful trust in God, without whom reconciliation would not be possible.

The year 1994 is a memorable one for African Catholicism. It was a happy moment that marked the opening of the

33. Ibid., loc. 656.
34. Brockman, *Romero: A Life*, 4–7, 82–84.

much-anticipated First African Synod. At the same time, it was a sad year, for the political situation in Rwanda—the most evangelized country that could be said to be truly Christian—imploded between April 6 and the end of July 1994 in a genocide that left over 800,000 Tutsis and moderate Hutus dead.[35] The aftermath of the killings raises the question of what will happen to the faith in Rwanda after the genocide. *Africae Munus* states, "only authentic reconciliation can achieve lasting peace in society" (*AM*, sec. 21). Such reconciliation can bring people together after crimes, war, and even genocide when people grant and receive forgiveness from one another. But *Africae Munus* fails to say how this authentic reconciliation is brought about.

Emmanuel Katongole, whose parents were Tutsi and Hutu and who lost family to the genocide, offers suggestions on how to resurrect faith after the Rwandan genocide. Katongole traces the genocide to the body politic in Rwanda, which was heavily connected to the church. Since most of the killings took place in churches and as the handiwork of Christians against their fellow Christians, finding out how to resurrect the church after the genocide is paramount. Katongole's fine book, *Mirror to the Church: Resurrecting Faith after Genocide in Rwanda*, not only gives a detailed account of the genocide, but also notes the complicit negligence of the international community in abandoning Rwandans to their fate when they could have prevented the genocide. Katongole's position is that the church has to be involved in forming a Christian identity that will go beyond tribal divisions by recognizing how far a role politics plays in shaping human identities. His position is worth repeating: "If Christian identity has any chance of subverting or at least resisting the tribal loyalties of our time, Christians will have to recognize the ways in which politics shapes not only our view of the world and ourselves, but also the tribal patterns that we so often overlook."[36] Katongole is suggesting a

35. See Safari, "Church, State and Rwandan Genocide," 876–80 for an account of the events leading up to the genocide, as well as efforts or lack thereof from the church to avert or fuel the genocide.

36. Katongole and Wilson-Hartgrove, *Mirror to the Church*, loc. 444.

major change in the church's image and vision of itself. First, the church should not see itself as perfect and therefore as providing solutions, but as equally broken and fractured. Second, the church should reexamine its role and fundamentally question its own identity, as well as the faithful's perception of who they are and what makes them act the way they do, especially in such a situation as in the fixed categories of Hutu/Tutsi identity in Rwanda.

Katongole's position is true not only of Rwanda, but of many African countries whose identities have been formulated by their erstwhile colonial masters. My mind goes to Nigeria, with its so-called isolation of three groups of people: the Hausa, the Yoruba, and the Igbo, despite Nigeria's over 250 different ethnic groups and languages.[37] The subdivision of roles among these ethnic groups precipitated the first civil war in independent Africa, the Nigeria-Biafra war (1967–1970), and is still responsible for political turmoil that hampers progress and national development. Once such stories of historic divisions and ethnic identities have formed, a shared religion often makes no difference to people. Being fellow Christians, Muslims, or traditional religionists does not matter anymore. Katongole concludes that the solution lies not in multiplicity of suggestions, but in imagining new possibilities, "renewing the Christian mind" to think differently, outside the false identities we have been made to make our own.[38]

Christianity, Katongole is convinced, "is meant to shape a new identity within us by creating a new sense of we—a new community . . . offering a fresh lens through which to see ourselves, others, and the world."[39] The Christian prophetic witness is resistance against those false identities that divide the Christian identity of love in Christ. And the time for this witnessing cannot be put off, just as Martin Luther King Jr. could not put off the march that eventually led to repeal of laws against racial segregation. Any fruitful resurrection of the church after the genocide must begin with lament, as Katongole emphasizes. The church must be differ-

37. Amba, *My Beautiful Nigeria*, 1–2.
38. Katongole and Wilson-Hartgrove, *Mirror to the Church*, loc. 661.
39. Ibid.

ent, with an alternate mindset that goes beyond the categories of division:

> The denominational church that is so grounded in racial, tribal, ethnic, and national identities is dead. Any church that thinks Hutu and Tutsi or black and white are natural does not have the life of Christ in it. The Church that believes it is interesting or somehow advantageous to be American is the church of yesterday. That is the church that lies at the ruins at Nyange, with all the saints buried underneath crying, "How long?" The resurrected church—the church of the future—must look and be different . . . The resurrected church is drawn from different nations, black and white, African and Western, Hutu and Tutsi, Catholic, Protestant, and evangelical. It is a people on pilgrimage together—a mixed (and hopefully mixed-up) group, bearing witness to a new identity made possible by the gospel.[40]

According to Katongole, a new social imaginary is needed for a new African Christianity to emerge. Such social imaginary will answer the question of why, in spite of increases in the number of Christians in Africa, war, poverty, and disease still plagues the continent. Christianity should not be defining itself within the social imaginary of the state, which is self-serving and marginalizing of its African citizens. An alternative paradigm should guide the church's definition of itself as not only an intervention force or mere charitable institution like other non-governmental organizations. Instead, this calls for new ecclesiological category of the church's involvement in politics not as an external agent, but as a political influence capable of forming alternative social imaginary. African Catholicism, Katongole argues, *"will have to reposition itself as a form of politics that is based on distinct stories, and that is capable of forming alternative imaginations and patterns of social existence."*[41]

40. Ibid., loc. 1625–32.

41. Katongole, "Violence and Social Imagination," 147, emphasis Katongole's.

Through carefully crafted stories of simple but charismatic Christians, Katongole 's famous book, *The Sacrifice of Africa: A Political Theology for Africa*, gives examples of how Christianity could engage in this task of the social reimagination of Africa. As an alternative to the state social imaginary, which has failed the nation-states in Africa, Katongole presents the Christian imaginary of salvation in Christ, a salvation that is not merely spiritual but holistic, integrating the concrete social, political, cultural, economic, technological, legal, and everyday lives of Africans. In this way, Christianity can hope to influence African self-identity by challenging people to make a difference through its strong commitment to this new vision, going beyond the fixed categories that divide people to easily turn them to violence, killing, war, and genocide.

Katongole is proposing a theology of engagement, a theology of involvement and commitment to socio-political, economic, cultural, and religious change. His theology envisions another way of being church for the Catholic Church in Africa. This theology is expected to have a different engagement with the social history prevalent in Africa. It is meant to interpret Africa's social history in a way that deemphasizes the binary divisions that differentiate people into tribes. It is expected to reconcile aggrieved peoples through new engagement with their shared social history. Thus, Katongole's theology of reconciliation has the potential to correct and advance *Africae Munus'* theology of reconciliation. It anticipates Pope Francis' call for a humble church that is conscious of its brokenness and ready to be reconciled with itself and with society. Katongole is right on-target; the church must stop defining itself and its role according to the nation-states in Africa. Such self-identity makes the church lose its vision and role in social transformation. It does not exist merely to engage in charitable works in the sense of a firefighter putting out the flames caused by the rot of the nation-states of Africa. It does not exist to offer definitions, thereby defining itself outside of the society in which it exists. When it does so, its suggestions at best end up being merely utopian ideals—and the nation-state in Africa knows it and therefore does not take them seriously. Katongole's insistence on the church formulating a new social imaginary for Africa is akin to Elias Kifon Bongomba's charging Christian theology in Africa to incarnate their suggestions for social transformation in Africa based on the sufferings and pain of Africans and on the structures of sin responsible for them:

> Christian theology in Africa has a new imperative to bring new reflection to bear on political power in Africa today. Churches in Africa now have the opportunity to engage with political leaders, empower the weak, and take a stand against the abuse of power, which has led to crisis and to the neglect of the state and of its most vulnerable members. In cultivating such an understanding of power, Christian churches will have to provide models of empowerment as alternative to the abuse of power by post-colonial politicians. Christian churches ought to work toward a new *kairos*, where political power and authority are a gift and blessing to the political community, not a curse and tool of domination and marginalization.[42]

Katongole and Bongomba's proposals raise the issue of what the role of the church is or should be in politics and in public policy. Does the new social engagement Katongole proposes for the church in Africa imply the church's involvement in partisan politics, and if so, does this not contradict the neutral role the church should play in society? If it does not imply such involvement, how can the church reconstruct the social imaginary of Africans in such a way as to combat the divisive social history imposed on them by the colonial Eurocentric categorizations that continue to polarize them into bitter tribes? It doesn't appear that Katongole's proposal is political in the sense of pushing the church into partisan politics. He seems rather to suggest healing through the reconstruction of African social imaginary. Such a reconstruction of social history is equally aimed at healing the African psyche. Thus, there is a great relationship between Katongole's proposal and Robert M. Doran's

42. Bongmba, *Dialectics of Transformation*, 197.

psychic conversion. Healing the African mind must go deep down to the undertow of the African psyche, where repressed insights hide to the self-destruction of the African personality.

On an individual level, psychic conversion is the healing that occurs in the inner experiences that define personal life at the deepest level—often reaching the blind spots that show themselves to others are hidden from us in the inattentiveness and inauthenticity we are embedded in for as long as we fail to attend to them. Inattentiveness to these distortions of the psyche accounts for the double-standard characteristic of inauthentic living. Joseph Flanagan's description of dramatic bias captures this problem all too well: "If you do not successfully integrate these neurophysiological changes into your higher conscious, psychic, and intellectual schemes, but suppresses them instead, the result may be a variety of abnormal patterns of behaviors. Such abnormalities may remain within the field of your own inner consciousness, resulting in a split between the outer persona you disclose to others in playing social roles and the inner ego that behaves in quite different ways on the private stage of your own awareness."[43] The liberation of such repressed insights demands a conversion made possible by the grace of God, the universal willingness as operator that capacitates the psyche to integrate through a dialectic of contraries between the psyche and experience. Through psychic conversion, the healing of memories of Africa's past are thrown up and acknowledged, and once they are no longer repressed, Africans can heal their history of dehumanization through the grace of God and hopefully walk beyond the destructive Hamitic legacy of colonial imaginary towards a new history.

Education in Catholic social teaching can also help African Catholicism construct a new social imaginary to reconstruct African social history. Catholic social teaching, while not an alternative to the government of any nation-state, connects the word of God to social justice issues. Through its preferential option for the poor and its principles centered on the dignity of human beings created in the image of God, Catholic social teachings aim at creating

43. Flanagan, *Quest for Self-Knowledge*, 81–82.

conditions for optimum fulfillment of human potential. Catholic social teachings provide answers to often-unexpressed questions surrounding the church's involvement in social justice, questions about the social and spiritual mission of the church, and questions on the dualism of the church and the natural and the supernatural or sacred and profane divisions of the world. These questions leave many people thinking the sole mission of the church is to prepare people for heaven and not to wade into the muddy waters of the social order, which basically is the concern of the state. These persistent questions are articulated by Thomas Hughson:

> Why does a just society, and contribution toward it, matter to a Christianity whose gospel many have received as directing believers beyond earthly structures and institutions to a spiritual salvation begun in the present and fulfilled in heavenly glory, whose liturgical worship takes participants into public prayer beyond social utility? What links faith and charity with concern for justice? Is that link intrinsic or extrinsic to Jesus the Christ in his totality of identity, mission, public ministry, death, resurrection, and risen Lordship? Which theological principles invite Christian commitment to promoting a just society? Are there reasons of faith and charity besides those that biblical exegesis and social ethics have gained clarity about, that they have brought into personal and ecclesial deliberations?[44]

The tension between contemplation and action, between kerygma and the Jesus-event, between revelation and social justice—coupled with the Eurocentric backdrop of most of the documents of the Catholic social teachings—obstruct reception of Catholic social teachings in most of Africa. Perhaps for this reason, theologians do not look towards Catholic social teachings for guidance in constructing Africa's social imaginary. Katongole's vision of the church in Africa as integrating politics and other structures of society—culture, social order, personal integrity, legal and administrative structures, etc.—will be realized through a Catholic social

44. Hughson, *Connecting Jesus to Social Justice*, xxii.

teaching situated within the context of lived Christian faith amidst the challenges arising from dysfunctional institutional structures. As Hughson emphasizes, "In Catholic social teaching social justice responds to actual problems suffered by people enmeshed in distorted structures of social, economic, political, and cultural life."[45] While doing this, however, African Catholicism must retell the story of Africa in ways that do not rely on colonial socio-cultural anthropological studies that distort Africa's story by imposing binary visions onto many African tribes—visions that continue to cause and intensify ethnic conflicts. African Catholicism retells Africa's stories by going back before colonial and Western missionary enterprises to find stories that contain sources of unity among different tribes in Africa to base structures that reconcile instead of divide the people. This is important because involvement in social injustice that fails to reconstruct Africa's self-identity might result in taking the wrong side in conflict situations. One element to be emphasized here is that redemption after social decline is actually not so much the work of human beings as it is the result of social structures filled by the grace of God, which Robert M. Doran calls "grace-filled social structures,"[46] or social grace.

Whether the emphasis is education in Catholic social teaching or change in catechesis, *Africae Munus* points to Catholic universities as having the responsibility of healing Africans of the anthropological crisis traumatizing them. Education is therefore important for the reconstruction of the social imaginary and for forging the new *kairos* for African Catholicism.

Education

The education linked to social change that will enable Africans to reconstruct their social history and critique the false identity they have been forced to adopt must follow a problem-posing approach that enables people to critically question the way they

---

45. Ibid., xxii.

46. Doran, *What Is Systematic Theology?* 188.

live. By questioning their identity as well as the rationale for their anthropological poverty, critical education questions the forms of education that marginalize Africans and resign them to the various forms of oppression and destitution under which they live. Paulo Freire's widely read book addressed to his native South America, *Pedagogy of the Oppressed*, critiques the "banking concept of education." [47] Unfortunately, most of African education system is based on similar concept. Hence his book could provide a blueprint for correcting the miseducation of Africans in hopes of reconstructing an African identity.

Freire's *Pedagogy of the Oppressed* aims at the liberation of the oppressed and the oppressor both. Authentic liberation, Freire writes, is awakening the oppressed to critical consciousness of the dehumanizing actions of the oppressor in such a way that the oppressed engages in action towards not only their own humanization and freedom, but their oppressors' as well. [48] Authentic liberation settles for nothing short of total liberation whereby people exercise their right to actualize themselves and to be fully human without mere concessions from their oppressors. In living so long under the clutches of the oppressor, the oppressed become afraid of freedom and begin to think that consciousness of their deplorable living conditions will lead to anarchy. They internalize oppression and give in to self-depreciation, considering themselves as good for nothing beyond subservience to their oppressors. When they become compliant, or give up hope of the possibility of change, or even worse, religiously sublimate their oppression as the fatalistic will of God, liberation becomes extremely difficult, if not impossible. The oppressed have played into the hands of the oppressors; they have become compliant, the "law-abiding citizens," the nice guys of the nation-state, appreciative of the "generosity" of the rich and powerful, ready to take orders, always asking for what to do and readily doing it for the "common good" of the oppressors. The oppressor turns everybody into an object for their satisfaction. They want to remain the dominant class who enjoy being among

47. Freire, *Pedagogy of the Oppressed*, 72.
48. Ibid., 79–86.

the "haves" in a sea of the "have-nots." Thus, the oppressors are also dehumanized in the process. On the other hand, because the oppressed internalize the exercise of power by the oppressor as a way of being human, they are likely to become oppressors themselves in turn at the slightest opportunity. As such, it is necessary to liberate the oppressed from the dehumanizing trappings of power as exercised by the oppressor. In their powerlessness, the oppressed turn against themselves, seeking to make up for their wounded egos from fellow oppressed people by violence at the least provocation.

It falls on the oppressed themselves to resist the dominating power of the oppressor, to stop the oppressor from dehumanizing both the oppressed and themselves as well. And this can only be achieved by the process of "concientización,"[49] by which the oppressed become conscious of their fear of freedom and then to liberate themselves through a process of resistance that can liberate their oppressors as well. The purpose of concientización is not to create further dependence on the part of the oppressed; neither is it another way of dehumanizing them by attempting to take over and run their lives for them. Concientización presupposes trust in the capability of the oppressed to run their own affairs. What concientización does is to bring the oppressed to an awareness of their power to transform their lives and that of their societies and to encourage them to do so. Freire asserts:

> The oppressed, who have been shaped by the death-affirming climate of oppression, must find through their struggle the way of life-affirming humanization, which does not lie *simply* in having more to eat (although it does involve having more to eat and cannot fail to include this aspect). The oppressed have been destroyed precisely because their situation has reduced them to things. In order to regain their humanity they must cease to be things and fight as men and women. This is a radical requirement. They cannot enter the struggle as objects in order *later* to become human beings.[50]

49. Ibid., 35.
50. Ibid., 68, emphasis Freire's.

Freire asserts that the oppressed attain this knowledge through common reflection and action—reflection that makes them consciously aware of their oppression and action that disposes them to bring about change to put an end to their oppression, to resist the oppressors' domination, and to create a new society and new personality by which they are free to be fully human.

Freire's analysis of the dialectic of the oppressed and the oppressor is true of the nation-states of Africa, whose citizens are oppressed by the elite few and denied opportunities to live fully as human beings. Not only have the oppressed of Africa given up hope, they self-deprecate themselves into thinking they are good for nothing beyond the role designed for them by the elite and international community of oppressors bent on lucrative schemes to extract their natural resources. Education in Africa is not far different from the "banking concept of education" critiqued by Freire. Such education denies African people the critical thinking that would liberate them from their enslavement and oppression. From the period of colonialism to the post-independent Africa, formal education has been aimed at producing people who will serve the government and comply with directives without question.

This form of education is designed to make the colonized people adapt, submit, and cooperate within the dominating environment without realizing their desperate, dehumanizing situation. It aims at producing automatons unfit for critical thinking and therefore incapable of challenging the status quo. This "banking concept of education" creates students and citizens who are not creative and who do not dream of something else, "an empty 'mind' passively open to the reception of deposits of reality from the world outside."[51] *Africae Munus* condemns this form of education when it rejects mere memorization of the catechisms or rote repetition of the doctrines of Christian faith without understanding what they mean. Freire opts instead for "problem-posing" education that focuses on human intentionality, or "consciousness as consciousness of consciousness."[52] Comparing the banking with

51. Ibid., 75.
52. Ibid., 79.

the problem-posing approach to education reveals a world of difference: One submerges consciousness, stifles creativity, and is aimed at perpetuating oppression by stifling awareness among the oppressed. The other creates awareness, promotes creativity, and is aimed at social transformation. In the words of Freire, "Whereas banking education anesthetizes and inhibits creative power, problem-posing education involves a constant unveiling of reality. The former attempts to maintain the *submersion* of consciousness; the latter strives for the *emergence* of consciousness and *critical intervention* in reality."[53] I knew I was a recipient of a banking system of education when I found it difficult to avert to intentionality when I was introduced to Lonergan in my graduate studies. I had no idea what understanding of understanding meant. My relationship with my teachers exactly matched Freire's description of the teacher as a depositor of knowledge into the "empty" mind. As long as education in Africa continues to operate under the banking concept of education, the contradiction between the oppressor and the oppressed will continue to go unchallenged. Naïve thinking will continue to replace critical thinking; dialogue will always give way to monologue; hate, pride, and hopelessness will displace love, humility and faith as people live unreflexively; empty rhetoric will take the place of reflection and action.

Africae Munus classifies education as one of the major areas of the apostolate of African Catholicism (*AM*, sec. 134–38). It is confident that Catholic education will be able to strengthen the bonds of peace and reconciliation. It is convinced that education is extremely important for the future of Africa. It recommends teaching Catholic social doctrine as indispensable tool for reconciliation. Although *Africae Munus* takes for granted efficient methodologies for teaching, it clearly rejects a banking concept of education as critiqued by Freire. Instead, *Africae Munus* seeks to foster education that promotes the kind of authenticity that could enable African crosscultural dialogue and the emergence of a truly African theology through the inculturation of Christian faith. It therefore urges the establishment of new Catholic universities in

53. Ibid., 81, emphasis Freire's.

places where they do not exist and advocated for strengthening the functional efficiency of the existing ones.

Africae Munus presumes the existence of a Catholic intellectual tradition upon which Catholic universities are founded. However, it fails to note how far modernity has impacted this tradition, casting doubt in some quarters about its true existence and relevance.[54] Perhaps *Africae Munus* underrates the impact of modernity on Africa, where the Christian faith is expanding by leaps and bounds. Although their circumstances are different from the Western world, modernity has impacted African universities as well, with a good number of these universities and colleges offering more secular courses and preferring religious studies to theology. African universities are practical enough to realize many students have little use of theology in the job market. One of the major challenges facing African universities—apart from paucity of resources to finance research and commensurate remuneration, appointments, and promotions—is the persistence of the banking concept of education. Here Freire's problem-solving education, which respects students and fosters humanizing student-teacher relationships that prepare students for liberation, must be encouraged in African universities.

54. See Orji, *Catholic University and the Search for Truth*, 79–107 for the contemporary challenges to Catholic universities.

Bibliography

Abbott, Walter M. Ed. "Declaration on the Relationship of the Church to Non-Christians." *The Documents of Vatican II*. New York: America Press, 1966.

Abdullah, Raficq. "Islamic View on Pluralism." *European Judaism* 39 (2006) 116–22.

Aborisade, Sunday. "JDPC Trains Police, Prison Officers." *Punch Newspaper*, June 7, 2012, http://www.punchng.com/news/jdpc-trains-police-prison-officers/.

Achebe, Chinua. *The African Trilogy: Things Fall Apart; No Longer at Ease; Arrow of God*. With an introduction by Chimamanda Ngozi Adichie. Everyman's Library. New York: Knopf, 2010.

Afigbo, A. E. "The Age of Innocence: The Igbo and Their Neighbours in Pre-colonial Times." *1981 Ahajioku Lecture*, http://ahiajoku.igbonet.com/1981/.

African Studies Center and MATRIX Digital Humanities Center. "Exploring Africa: Unit Two: Studying Africa through the Social Studies: Module Ten: African Politics and Government; Activity Two: Explore (Pre-Colonial Political Systems)." Michigan State University, http://exploringafrica.matrix.msu.edu/students/curriculum/m10/activity2.php.

Aguigwo, Geoffery M. *The Problem of Poverty in Nigeria and the Role of the Church: A Socio-Pastoral Approach*. Theologische Studien. Aachen, Germany: Shaker, 2002.

Aina, Raymond Olusesan. "The Lineamenta for the Second African Synod: A Foundation for Promoting Economic Justice and Building Sustainable Peace?" Presentation at the annual member's forum of *Africa-Europe Faith and Justice Network*, Rome, November 7, 2008, http://www.sedosmission.org/web/fr/sedos-bulletin/doc_view/1535-the-lineamenta-for-the-second-african-synod-a-foundation-for-promoting.

Ake, Claude. *Democracy and Development in Africa*. Washington, DC: Brookings Institution, 1996.

Allen, John L., Jr. "Pope Addresses Corruption, Conflict in Africa," *National Catholic Reporter*, March 17, 2009, http://ncronline.org/node/12630.

Allen, Roland. *The Spontaneous Expansion of the Church: And the Causes That Hinder It*. 1927. Reprint, n.p.: Jawbone Digital, 2011. Kindle edition.

Bibliography

Amin, Samir. "The Challenge of Globalization: Delinking." In *Facing the Challenge: Responses to the Report of the South Commission*, edited by the South Centre, 132–38. London: Zed, 1993.

Appiah, Kwame Anthony. *Cosmopolitanism: Ethics in a World of Strangers*. Issues of Our Time. New York: Norton, 2007.

Appleby, R. Scott. *The Ambivalence of the Sacred: Religion, Violence, and Reconciliation*. Carnegie Commission on Preventing Deadly Conflict Series. Lanham, MD: Rowman & Littlefield, 2000.

Arbuckle, Gerald A. *Culture, Inculturation, and Theologians: A Postmodern Critique*, Collegeville, MN: Liturgical, 2010.

Asue, Daniel Ude. "Muslim Youth in Search of Identity in Nigeria: The Case of Boko Haram Violence." *The International Journal of African Catholicism* 3 (2012) 22–38.

August, Oliver. "Special Report: Emerging Africa: A Hopeful Continent." *The Economist*, March 2, 2013, http://www.economist.com/news/special-report/21572377-african-lives-have-already-greatly-improved-over-past-decade-says-oliver-august.

Ayoub, Mahmoud M. "Islam and the Challenge of Religious Pluralism." *Global Dialogue* 2 (2000) 53–64.

———. *A Muslim View of Christianity: Essays on Dialogue*. Edited by Irfan A. Omar. Faith Meets Faith. Maryknoll, NY: Orbis, 2007.

Banchoff, Thomas F., ed. *Religious Pluralism, Globalization, and World Politics*. Oxford: Oxford University Press, 2008.

Barth, Karl. *On Religion: The Revelation of God as the Sublimation of Religion*. Edited and translated by Garrett Green. London: T. & T. Clark, 2006.

Basedau, Matthias, and De Juan, Alexander. "The 'Ambivalence of the Sacred' in Africa: The Impact of Religion on Peace and Conflict in Sub-Saharan Africa." *GIGA Working Papers 70*. Hamburg: German Institute of Global and Area Studies, 2008.

Bauman, Zygmut. *Liquid Modernity*. Cambridge, UK: Polity, 2000.

Bellah, R. "Faith Communities Challenge—and Are Challenged by—the Changing World Order." In *World Faiths and the New World Order: A Muslim-Jewish-Christian Search Begins*, edited by J. Gremillion and William F. Ryan, 148–70. Washington, DC: Interreligious Peace Colloquium, 1978.

Belshaw, Deryke. Et Al. Ed. *Faith in Development: Partnership between the World Bank and the Churches of Africa*. Oxford: Regnum, 2001.

Benedict, Ruth. *Patterns of Culture*. Boston: Houghton Mifflin, 1934.

Benedict XVI, Pope. "Caritas in Veritate: On Integral Human Development in Charity and Truth." London: Catholic Truth Society, 2009, http://www.vatican.va/holy_father/benedict_xvi/encyclicals/documents/hf_ben-xvi_enc_20090629_caritas-in-veritate_en.html.

———. "Deus Caritas Est: Encyclical Letter of the Supreme Pontiff Benedict XVI to the Bishops, Priests, and Deacons, Men and Women Religious, and All the Lay Faithful on Christian Love." Vatican City: Libreria

Editorice Vaticana, 2005. http://www.vatican.va/holy_father/benedict_ xvi/encyclicals/documents/hf_ben-xvi_enc_20051225_deus-caritas-est_ en.html.

———. "The Post-Synodal Apostolic Exhortation: Africae Munus." Nairobi, Kenya: Paulines Africa, 2011, http://www.vatican.va/holy_ father/benedict_xvi/apost_exhortations/documents/hf_ben-xvi_ exh_20111119_africae-munus_en.html.

———. *Truth and Tolerance: Christian Belief and World Religions.* Translated by Henry Taylor. San Francisco: Ignatius, 2004.

Benedict XVI, Pope, and Marcello Pera. *Without Roots: The West, Relativism, Christianity, Islam.* Translated by Michael F. Moore. New York: Basic, 2006.

Berry, Wendell. "Inverting the Economic Order." *Communio: International Catholic Review* 36 (2009) 475–86.

Boafo-Arthur, Kwame. "Tackling Africa's Developmental Dilemmas: Is Globalization the Answer?" *Journal of Third World Studies* 20 (2003) 27–54.

Bongmba, Elias Kifon. *The Dialectics of Transformation in Africa.* New York: Palgrave Macmillan, 2006.

Bujo, Benez. *African Theology in its Social Context.* Translated by John O'Donohue. Maryknoll, NY: Orbis, 1992.

Carpenter, Lindsay. "Malawians Bring Down 30-year Dictator, 1992– 1993." *Global Nonviolent Action Database,* February 8, 2011, http:// nvdatabase.swarthmore.edu/content/malawians-bring-down-30-year- dictator-1992-1993.

Chinweizu. *Decolonizing the African Mind.* Lagos, Nigeria: Pero, 1987.

———. *The West and the Rest of Us: White Predators, Black Slavers, and the African Elite.* Toronto: Random House, 1975

Cohn-Sherbok, Daniel. "Jewish Religious Pluralism." *Cross Currents* 46 (1996) 326–42.

Comeliau, Christian. "The South: Global Challenges." In *Facing the Challenge: Responses to the Report of the South Commission,* edited by the South Centre, 67–74. London: Zed, 1993.

Commission for Africa. *Our Common Interest: Report of the Commission for Africa.* London: Penguin, 2005.

Cone, James H. *The Cross and the Lynching Tree.* Maryknoll, NY: Orbis, 2011.

Congregation for the Doctrine of the Faith. "Notification on the Book, *Toward a Christian Theology of Religious Pluralism,* by Father Jacques Dupuis, S.J." Rome, January 24, 2001, http://www.vatican.va/roman_curia/ congregations/cfaith/documents/rc_con_cfaith_doc_20010124_dupuis_ en.html.

"Congolese Have Lost Confidence in the Electoral Commission, Catholic Bishops Say," *Congo News Agency,* January 13, 2012, http://www. congoplanet.com/news/1939/congolese-have-lost-confidence-in-the- electoral-commission-catholic-bishops-say.jsp.

Bibliography

Copeland, M. Shawn. *Enfleshing Freedom: Body, Race, and Being*. Minneapolis: Fortress, 2010.

Corey-Boulet, Robbie. "With 176 Million Catholics, Africa Gains Prominence." *USA Today* March 12, 2013, http://www.usatoday.com/story/news/world/2013/03/12/catholic-church-africa/1963171/.

Cormie, L. "The Sociology of National Development and Salvation History." In *Sociology and Human Destiny: Essays on Sociology, Religion, and Society*, edited by Gregory Baum, 56–85. New York: Seabury, 1980.

Council on Foreign Relations. "Summary: A Symposium on Religious Conflict in Nigeria." May 8, 2007, http://www.cfr.org/content/meetings/nigeria_symposium_summary.pdf.

Cowell, Alan. "Slain Rwanda Bishops Had Urged Peace Talks." *New York Times*, June 10, 1994, http://www.nytimes.com/1994/06/10/world/slain-rwanda-bishops-had-urged-peace-talks.html.

Crowe, Frederick. "Son of God, Holy Spirit, and World Religions." In *Appropriating the Lonergan Idea*, edited by Michael Vertin, 297–314. Washington, DC: Catholic University of America Press, 1989.

Curran, Charles. *Catholic Social Teaching 1891—Present: A Historical, Theological and Ethical Analysis*. Washington, DC: Georgetown University Press, 2002.

Davison, Anne. "The Church of England's Response to Religious Pluralism." Rev. Phd diss., University of Surrey, 2000, http://www.anglicanism.org/admin/docs/coereligiouspluralism.pdf.

Davidson, Basil. *Africa in History: Themes and Outlines*. New York: Macmillan, 1991.

Dawson, Christopher. *The Age of the Gods: A Study in the Origins of Culture in Prehistoric Europe and the Ancient East*. New York: Sheed & Ward, 1934.

Donovan, Vincent. *Christianity Rediscovered: An Epistle from the Masai*. London: SCM, 2001. Kindle edition.

Doran, Robert M. "Education for Cosmopolis." *Method: Journal of Lonergan Studies* 1 (1983) 134–57.

———. *Theology and the Dialectics of History*. Toronto: University of Toronto Press, 1990.

———. *The Trinity in History: A Theology of the Divine Missions*. Vol. 1 of *Missions and Processions*. Lonergan Studies. Toronto: University of Toronto Press, 2012.

———. *What Is Systematic Theology?* Lonergan Studies. Toronto: University of Toronto Press, 2005.

Dupuis, Jacques. *Toward a Christian Theology of Religious Pluralism*. Maryknoll, NY: Orbis, 2002.

Economic Commission for Africa. "Popular Participation and Decentralization in Africa." http://www.uneca.org/sites/default/files/publications/popular-participation-decentralization-in-africa.pdf.

Egan, Anthony. "Governance beyond Rhetoric: The South African Challenge to the African Synod." In *Reconciliation, Justice, and Peace: The Second*

African Synod, edited by Agbonkhianmeghe E. Orobator, 193–104. Maryknoll, NY: Orbis, 2011.

Egbujie, Ihemalol I. *The Hermeneutics of the African Traditional Culture: An Interpretative Analysis of Culture.* Roxbury, MA: Omenana, 1985.

Ehusani, George. "Evangelising Ethnic Loyalty in Nigeria: The Challenge before Church Leaders." *Encounter* 6 (2003) http://www.georgeehusani.org/home/index.php/papers-and-essays/208-evangelising-ethnic-loyalty-in-nigeria-the-challenge-before-church-leaders-.

———. *A Prophetic Church.* Nigeria: Society of Saint Paul's, 2003.

Ekwunife, Anthony. "The Image of the Priest in Contemporary Africa: The Nigerian Connection." In *The Clergy in Nigeria Today,* edited by Luke Mbaefo and Ernest Ezeogu, 21–32. Enugu, Nigeria: Snaap, 1994.

Enwerem, Iheanyi M. *Crossing the Rubicon: A Socio-Political Analysis of Political Catholicism in Nigeria.* Ibadan: BookBuilders Editions Africa, 2010.

Escobar, Arturo. *Encountering Development: The Making and Unmaking of the Third World.* Princeton: Princeton University Press, 1995.

Eze, Chielozona. *Postcolonial Imagination and Moral Representation in African Literature and Culture.* Lanham, MD: Lexington, 2011.

Falk, R. "Satisfying Human Needs in a World of Sovereign States: Rhetoric, Reality and Vision." In *World Faiths and the New World Order: A Muslim-Jewish-Christian Search Begins,* edited by Joseph Gremillion and William F. Ryan, 109–39. Washington, DC: Interreligious Peace Colloquium, 1978.

Falola, Toyin. *Violence in Nigeria: The Crisis of Religious Politics and Secular Ideologies.* Rochester, NY: University of Rochester Press, 1998.

Fitzgerald, Michael L. "From Heresy to Religion: Vatican II and Islam." *The Pastoral Review,* January 2004, 21–32, http://www.thepastoralreview.org/index.php/issues/past-issues/98-january-february-2004/522-from-heresy-to-religion.

Flanagan, Joseph. *Quest for Self-Knowledge: An Essay in Lonergan's Philosophy.* 1997. Reprint, Toronto: University of Toronto Press, 2002.

Flannery, Austin, ed. *Vatican Council II: The Conciliar and Post Conciliar Documents.* Concilium Vaticanum 2 (1962–1965). Bombay: Saint Paul, 1975.

Freire, Paulo. *Pedagogy of the Oppressed.* Translated by Myra Bergman Ramos. New York: Continuum, 2000.

Friedman, Thomas L. *The Lexus and the Olive Tree.* New York: Anchor, 2000.

Geertz, Clifford. "The Impact of the Concept of Culture on the Concept of Man." In *Man in Adaptation: The Cultural Present,* edited by Yehudi A. Cohen, 19–32. Chicago: Aldine, 1968.

———. *The Interpretation of Cultures.* New York: Basic, 1973.

Gifford, Paul. *African Christianity: Its Public Role.* London: Hurst, 1998.

Goulet, Denis. *The Cruel Choice: A New Concept in the Theory of Development.* New York: Atheneum, 1973.

Grant, Colin. "The Threat and Prospect in Religious Pluralism." *The Ecumenical Review* 41 (2010) 50–63.

Greenberg, Irving. "Seeking the Religious Roots of Pluralism: In the Image of God and Covenant." *Journal of Ecumenical Studies* 34 (1997) 385–93.

———. *For the Sake of Heaven and Earth: The New Encounter Between Judaism and Christianity.* Philadelphia: Jewish Publication Society, 2004.

Gremillion, Joseph. *Food/Energy and the Major Faiths.* Maryknoll, NY: Orbis, 1978.

Gremillion, Joseph, and William Ryan. Eds. *World Faiths and the New World Order: A Muslim-Jewish-Christian Search Begins.* Washington, DC: Interreligious Peace Colloquium, 1978.

Gutema, Bekele. "Problems in the Emergence of Responsible Governance in Africa." In *Philosophy, Democracy, and Responsible Governance in Africa,* edited by J. Obi Oguejiofor, 107–20. Studies in African Philosophy 1. Münster: Lit, 2003.

Gyekye, Kwame. "Person and Community in African Thought." In *The African Philosophy Reader,* edited by P. H. Coetzee and A. P. J. Roux, 297–312. New York: Routledge, 2003.

———. *Tradition and Modernity: Philosophical Reflections on the African Experience.* Oxford: Oxford University Press, 1997.

Haight, Roger. *Dynamics of Theology.* Maryknoll, NY: Orbis, 2001.

Handley, Meg. "The Violence in Nigeria: What's behind the Conflict?" *Time Magazine,* March 10, 2010, http://www.time.com/time/world/article/0,8599,1971010,00.html.

Hegel, G. W. F. *The Philosophy of History.* Translated by John Sibree. Buffalo, NY: Prometheus, 1991.

Henriot, Peter J. "Globalization: Implications for Africa." January 12, 1998, http://sedosmission.org/old/eng/global.html.

Henriot, Peter J. Et Al. *Catholic Social Teaching: Our Best Kept Secret.* Maryknoll, NY: Orbis, 2001.

Hughson, Thomas D. *Connecting Jesus to Social Justice: Classical Christology and Public Theology.* Lanham, MD: Rowan & Littlefield, 2013.

Idowu, Bolaji. *African Traditional Religion: A Definition.* Maryknoll, NY: Orbis, 1973.

Ilo, Stan Chu. *The Church and Development in Africa: Aid and Development from the Perspective of Catholic Social Ethics.* Eugene, OR: Pickwick, 2011.

———. *The* Face of Africa: *Looking Beyond the Shadows.* Eugene, OR: Wipf & Stock, 2012.

Independent Commission of the South on Development Issues. *The Challenge to the South.* Oxford: Oxford University Press, 1990.

Isichei, Elizabeth A. *Ibo People and the Europeans: The Genesis of a Relationship to 1906.* London: Faber & Faber, 1973.

Jell-Bahlsen, Sabine. *The Water Goddess in Igbo Cosmology: Ogbuide of Oguta Lake.* Trenton, NJ: Africa World, 2008.

John Paul II, Pope. "Centesimus Annus: Encyclical Letter on the Hundredth Anniversary of Rerum Novarum." Washington, DC: United States Catholic Conference, 1991, http://www.vatican.va/holy_father/john_

paul_ii/encyclicals/documents/hf_jp-ii_enc_01051991_centesimus-
annus_en.html.

———. "Message of His Holiness Pope John Paul II for the Celebration
of the World Day of Peace, 1 January 2002." Vatican City: Libreria
EditriceVaticana, 2002, http://www.vatican.va/holy_father/john_paul_ii/
messages/peace/documents/hf_jp-ii_mes_20011211_xxxv-world-day-
for-peace_en.html.

———. "Post-Synodal Apostolic Exhortation: Ecclesia in Africa." Washington,
DC: United States Catholic Conference, 1995, http://www.vatican.va/
holy_father/john_paul_ii/apost_exhortations/documents/hf_jp-ii_
exh_14091995_ecclesia-in-africa_en.html.

———. "Redemptoris Missio: Encyclical Letter of the Supreme Pontiff John
Paul II on the Permanent Validity of the Church's Missionary Mandate."
Washington, DC: United States Catholic Conference, 1990, http://www
.vatican.va/holy_father/john_paul_ii/encyclicals/documents/hf_jp-ii_
enc_07121990_redemptoris-missio_en.html.

———. "Sollicitudo Rei Socialis: Encyclical Letter on Social Concern."
Washington, DC: United States Catholic Conference, 1987, http://www
.vatican.va/holy_father/john_paul_ii/encyclicals/documents/hf_jp-ii_
enc_30121987_sollicitudo-rei-socialis_en.html.

John XXIII, Pope. "Mater et Magistra: Encyclical Letter of Pope John XXIII on
Christianity and Social Progress." London: Catholic Truth Society, 1961,
http://www.vatican.va/holy_father/john_xxiii/encyclicals/documents/
hf_j-xxiii_enc_15051961_mater_en.html.

Jomier, Jacques. "Islam and the Dialogue." *Nigerian Dialogue* 1 (1974) 4–23.

Justice Development and Peace Commission. "About Us: Organizational
Chart." Catholic Archdiocese of Ibadan, Nigeria, http://jdpcibadan.org/
index.php?option=com_content&view=article&id=37&Itemid=153#.

Kale, Yemi, and National Bureau of Statsistics. "Nigeria Poverty Profile 2010
Report." Press briefing, National Bureau of Statistics, Abuja, Nigeria,
February 13, 2012, http://nigerdeltabudget.org/National%20Bureau%20
of%20Statistics%20Poverty%20Profile%20of%20Nigeria%202012%20(1).
pdf.

Kalilombe, Patrick A. "Spirituality in the African Perspective." In *Paths of
African Theology*, edited by Rosino Gibellini, 115–35. Maryknoll, NY:
Orbis, 1994.

Kanu, Macaulay A. "The Indispensability of the Basic Social Values in African
Tradition: A Philosophical Appraisal." *OGIRISI* 7 (2010) 149–61.

Katongole, Emmanuel. *The Sacrifice of Africa: A Political Theology for Africa.*
Eedmans Ekklesia. Grand Rapids: Eerdmans, 2010. Kindle edition.

———. "Violence and Social Imagination: Rethinking Theology and Politics in
Africa." *Religion and Theology* 12 (2005) 145–71.

Katongole, Emmanuel, and Chris Rice. *Reconciling All Things: A Christian
Vision for Justice, Peace and Healing.* Downers Grove, IL: InterVarsity,
2008. Kindle edition.

Bibliography

Katongole, Emmanuel, and Jonathan Wilson-Hartgrove. *Mirror to the Church: Resurrecting Faith after Genocide in Rwanda*. Grand Rapids: Zondervan, 2009. Kindle edition.

———. "Postures of Social Engagement: Reflections on Christianity after Rwanda's Genocide." *Review of Faith and International Affairs* 8 (2010) 71–75.

Kaulem, David. "The African Synod for Those of Us Who Stayed at Home." In *Reconciliation, Justice, and Peace: The Second African Synod*, edited by Agbonkhianmeghe E. Orobator, 143–58. Maryknoll, NY: Orbis, 2011.

Kenney, Joseph. "Thomas Aquinas, Islam and the Arab Philosophers." http://www.catholicapologetics.info/apologetics/islam/thomas.htm.

Kenya Catholic Bishops. "Kenya's Commitment to Peaceful General Elections in the Light of Justice, Forgiveness, Healing, Reconciliation, and Peace: Pastoral Letter of the Catholic Bishops of Kenya." Kenya Episcopal Conference. Nairobi, Kenya: Paulines Africa 2012, http://www.cjpckenya.org/userfiles/Pastoral%20Letter%20of%20the%20Catholic%20Bishops%20of%20Kenya(1).pdf.

"Kenya's Churches Driving Peaceful Resolution to Crisis." *Christian Today*, February 14, 2008, http://au.christiantoday.com/article/kenyas-churches-driving-peaceful-resolution-to-crisis/3863.htm.

King, Martin Luther, Jr. "Letter from Birmingham Jail." http://mlk-kpp01.stanford.edu/index.php/encyclopedia/encyclopedia/enc_letter_from_birmingham_jail_1963/.

Koyama, Kosuke. "A Theological Reflection on Religious Pluralism." *The Ecumenical Review* 51 (1999) 160–71.

Küng, Hans. *Theology for the Third Millennium: An Ecumenical View*. New York: Doubleday, 1988.

Leclercq, H. "Early African Church." In *The Catholic Encyclopedia*, edited by Kevin Knight, New Advent. New York: Appleton, http://www.newadvent.org/cathen/01191a.htm.

Le Sueur, James D., ed. *The Decolonization Reader*. New York: Routledge, 2003.

Lonergan, Bernard J. F. "Belief: Today's Issue." In *A Second Collection Papers by Bernard J. F. Lonergan*, edited by William F. Ryan and Bernard J. Tyrrell, 87–99. Toronto: University of Toronto Press, 1996.

———. *Collection*. Collected Works of Bernard Lonergan 4. Edited by Frederick E. Crowe and Robert M. Doran, 232–45. Toronto: University of Toronto Press, 1988.

———. "Healing and Creating in History." In *A Third Collection: Papers by Bernard J. F. Lonergan*, edited by Frederick E. Crowe, 100–112. New York: Paulist, 1985.

———. *Insight: A Study of Human Understanding*. Edited by Frederick E. Crowe and Robert M. Doran. Collected Works of Bernard Lonergan 3. Toronto: University of Toronto Press, 1992.

————. "Insight Revisited." In *A Second Collection: Papers by Bernard J. F. Lonergan*, edited by William F. J. Ryan and Bernard J. Tyrrell, 263–78. Toronto: University of Toronto Press, 1996.

————. *Method in Theology*. Toronto: University of Toronto Press, 1990.

————. "Natural Right and Historical Mindedness." In *A Third Collection: Papers by Bernard J. F. Lonergan*, edited by Frederick E. Crowe, 169–83. New York: Paulist, 1985.

————. "A Post-Hegelian Philosophy of Religion." In *A Third Collection: Papers by Bernard J. F. Lonergan*, edited by Frederick E. Crowe, 202–23. New York: Paulist, 1985.

López, Miguel Ángel Martín. "The Problem with the Dependence on Food Imports in Africa and Pathways to Its Solution." *African Journal of International and Comparative Law* 20 (2012) 132–40, http://www.euppublishing.com/doi/pdfplus/10.3366/ajicl.2012.0025.

Luxton, Meg. "Doing Neoliberalism: Perverse Individualism in Personal Life." In *Neoliberalism and Everyday Life*, edited by Susan Braedley and Meg Luxton, 163–83. Montreal: McGill Queen's University Press, 2010.

Makozi, A. O. "Bishop's Welcome Address." In *Ethnicity and Christian Leadership in West African Sub-region: Proceedings of the Conference of the Fifteenth CIWA Theology Week Held at the Catholic Institute of West Africa, Port Harcourt, 29 March–1 April 2004*, edited by Ferdinand Nwaigbo, 15–17. Port Harcourt, Nigeria: CIWA, 2004.

Marshall, Katherine. "Development and Faith Institutions: Gulfs and Bridges." In *Religion and Development: Ways of Transforming the World*, edited by Gerrie ter Haar, 27–53. New York: Columbia University Press, 2011.

Martey, Emmanuel. *African Theology: Inculturation and Liberation*. Eugene, OR: Wipf & Stock, 2001.

Marty, Martin E. "Pluralisms." *Annals of the American Academy of Political and Social Science* 612 (2007) 13–25.

Mazrui, Ali A. *The African Condition: A Political Diagnosis*. New York: Cambridge University Press, 1980.

————. *The Africans: A Triple Heritage*. Boston: Little, Brown, 1986.

————. *A Tale of Two Africas: Nigeria and South Africa as Contrasting Visions*. Edited by James N. Karioki. London: Adonis & Abbey, 2006.

Mbefo, "Bishop Joseph Shanahan: A Missionary Who Loved Africans." *African Ecclesiastical Review* 36 (1994) 332–49.

Mbiti, John S. *African Religions and Philosophy*. London: Heinemann, 1992.

————. "Never Break the Pot That Keeps You Together." *Dialogue and Alliance* 24 (2010) 4–21.

Meyer, Ben F. "Introduction." In *Lonergan's Hermeneutics: Its Development and Application*, Ben F. Meyer and Sean E. McEvenue, 1–18. Washington, DC: Catholic University of America Press, 1989.

Metuh, Emefie Ikenga. *African Religions in Western Conceptual Scheme: The Problem of Interpretation*. Ibadan, Nigeria: Claverianum, 1985.

Bibliography

Mubangizi, Odomaro. "Agent of Reconciliation, Justice, and Peace: The Church in Africa in an Era of Globalization." In *Reconciliation, Justice, and Peace: The Second African Synod*, edited by Agbonkhianmeghe E. Orobator, 105–116. Maryknoll, NY: Orbis, 2011.

Murphy, Laura. "The Curse of Constant Remembrance: The Belated Trauma of the Slave Trade in Ayi Kwei Armah's Fragments." *Studies in the Novel* 40 (2008) 52–71.

Murray, John Courney. *We Hold These Truths: Catholic Reflections on the American Proposition*. New York: Sheed & Ward, 1960.

National Episcopal Conference of Cameroon. "Some Declarations of the Bishops on the Murders of the Clergy and on Insecurity in Cameroon." L'Effort Camerounais Archives, July 25, 2008, http://www.leffortcamerounais .com/2008/07/some-declaratio.html.

Nebechukwu, Augustine. "The Prophetic Mission of the Church in the Context of Social and Political Oppression in Africa." In *Evangelization in Africa in the Third Millenium: Challenges and Prospects: Proceedings of the First Theology Week of the Catholic Institute of West Africa, Port Harcourt, Nigeria, May 6–11, 1990*, edited by Justin S. Ukpon et al., 103–112. Port Harcourt, Nigeria: CIWA, 1992.

Neibuhr, H. Richard. *Christ and Culture*. New York: Harper, 1951.

"A New Balance: What the Pope's Interview Reveals." *Commonweal Magazine*, September 23, 2013, https://www.commonwealmagazine.org/new-balance.

"Nigerians Living in Poverty Rise to Nearly 61%." *BBC News Africa*, February 13, 2012, http://www.bbc.co.uk/news/world-africa-17015873.

Njoku, Francis. "An African Philosophy of Right: Basis for Leadership and Governance." In *Philosophy, Democracy and Responsible Governance in Africa*, edited by J. Obi Oguejiofor, 64–84. Studies in African Philosophy 1. Münster: Lit, 2003.

Novak, Michael. *The Spirit of Democratic Capitalism*. New York: Simon & Schuster, 1982.

Nwaigbo, Ferdinand, et al., eds. *Ethnicity and Christian Leadership in West African Sub-region: Proceedings of the Conference of the Fifteenth CIWA Theology Week Held at the Catholic Institute of West Africa, Port Harcourt, 29 March–1 April 2004*. Port Harcourt, Nigeria: CIWA, 2004.

Nwigwe, Boniface E. "Origin and Limits of State Authority." In *Philosophy, Democracy, and Responsible Governance in Africa*, edited by J. Obi Oguejiofor, 85–104. Studies in African Philosophy 1. Münster: Lit, 2003.

Nyasani, J. M. *The African Psyche*. Nairobi, Kenya: Theological Printing, 1997.

Nyerere, Julius. "The Church's Role in Society." In *A Reader in African Christian Theology*, edited by John Parratt, 117–30. London: SPCK, 1987.

Oborji, Francis Anekwe. "African Theology, Roman Catholic." In *Global Dictionary of Theology: A Resource for the Worldwide Church*, edited by William A. Dyrness et al., 15–20. Downers Grove, IL: InterVarsity, 2008.

Odey, John Okwoeze. *Nigeria, Search for Peace and Social Justice: The Relevance of the Philosophical and Theological Foundations of the Nonviolent Resistance of Martin Luther King, Jr.* Enugu, Kenya: Snaap, 1997.

Odozor, Paulinus I. "Africa and the Challenge of 'Foreign' Religious/Ethical 'Ideologies,' 'Viruses,' and 'Pathologies.'" In *Reconciliation, Justice, and Peace: The Second Synod*, edited by Agbonkhianmeghe E. Orobator, 214–25. Maryknoll, NY: Orbis, 2011.

———. "Truly Africa, and Wealthy! What Africa Can Learn from Catholic Social Teaching about Sustainable Economic Prosperity." In *The True Wealth of Nations: Catholic Social Thought and Economic Life*, edited by Daniel K. Finn, 267–87. Oxford: Oxford University Press, 2010.

Odumosu, Olakunle, et al. "Faith Based Organisations' (FBOs) Participation in Policy Process in Nigeria." Presentation at the Nigerian Institute of Social and Economic Research Seminar Series, Ibadan, Nigeria, June 2001, http://www.niseronline.org/downloads/PRSP_NRSS%20June%20 2011%20Paper.pdf.

———. *Religions and Development Research Programme: Mapping the Activities of Faith- based Organizations in Development in Nigeria*. Ibadan: Nigeria Institute of Social and Economic Research, 2009, http://www .religionsanddevelopment.org/files.

Ogbonnaya, Joseph. "The Church in Africa: Salt of the Earth?" In *The Church as Salt and Light: Path to an African Ecclesiology of Abundant Life*, edited by Stan Chu Ilo et al., 65–87. African Christian Studies Series 1. Eugene, OR: Pickwick, 2011.

———. *Lonergan, Social Transformation, and Sustainable Human Development*. Eugene, OR: Pickwick, 2013.

———. *Moral Integrity and Igbo Cultural Value*. Bloomington, IN: Xlibris, 2011.

Okere, Theophilus "Crisis of Governance in Africa: The Root of the Problem." In *Philosophy, Democracy, and Responsible Governance in Africa*, edited by J. Obi Oguejiofor, 3–11. Studies in African Philosophy 1. Münster: Lit, 2003.

Okolo, Chukwudum Barnabas. *The African Condition: Any Way Out?* African Survival Series. Enugu, Nigeria: Laurel Nigeria Enterprise, 1996.

———. "Liberation Theology: The Nigerian Connection." In *Religion and African Culture: Inculturation—A Nigerian Perspective*, edited by Elochukwu E. Uzukwu, 174–89. Enugu, Nigeria: Snaap, 1988.

Okoye, John I. "Foreword" to *Philosophy, Democracy, and Responsible Governance in Africa*, edited by J. Obi Oguejiofor, x–xi. Studies in African Philosophy 1. Münster: Lit, 2003.

———. "Governance and the Question of Virtue." In *Philosophy, Democracy, and Responsible Governance in Africa*, edited by J. Obi Oguejiofor, 12–21. Studies in African Philosophy 1. Münster: Lit, 2003.

Olarinmoye, Omobolaji. "Accountability in Faith-Based Organizations in Nigeria: Preliminary Explorations." Global Economic Governance Programme, University College, Oxford, GEG Working Paper 2011/67, http://www .globaleconomicgovernance.org/geg-wp-201167-accountability-faith-based-organizations-nigeria.

Bibliography

Onwubiko, Oliver A. *African Thought, Religion and Culture. Christian Mission and Culture in Africa 1.* Enugu, Nigeria: Snaap, 1991.

Onwuejeogwu, M. Angulu. *The Social Anthropology of Africa: An Introduction.* London: Heinemann, 1975.

Opongo, Elias Omondi. "Inventing the Creative Approaches to Complex Systems of Injustice: A New Call for a Vigilant and Engaged Church." In *Reconciliation, Justice, and Peace: The Second African Synod,* edited by Agbonkhianmeghe E. Orobator, 73–83. Maryknoll, NY: Orbis, 2011.

Orji, Cyril. *The Catholic University and the Search for Truth.* Winona, MN: Anselm Academic, 2013.

Ormerod, Neil, and Shane Clifton. *Globalization and the Mission of the Church.* Ecclesiological Investigations 6. New York: T. & T. Clark, 2009. Kindle edition.

Orobator, Agbonkhianmeghe E. "*Caritas in Veritate* and Africa's Burden of (Under)Development." *Theological Studies* 71 (2010) 320–34.

———. *The Church as Family: African Ecclesiology in its Social Context.* Nairobi, Kenya: Paulines Africa, 2000.

———. "Church, State, and Catholic Ethics: The Kenyan Dilemma." *Theological Studies* 70. (2009) 182–85.

Overseas Security Advisory Council. "Nigeria 2013 Crime and Safety Report: Lagos." April 19, 2013, Washington, DC, https://www.osac.gov/pages/ContentReportDetails.aspx?cid=13917.

Ozigbo, Ikenga R. *Igbo Catholicism: The Onitsha Connection, 1967–1984.* Onitsha, Nigeria: Africana-Fep, 1985.

Pape, John. "Black and White: The 'Perils of Sex' in Colonial Zimbabwe." In *African History,* edited by Chima J. Korieh and Raphael Chijioke Njoku, 289–305. San Diego: Cognella, 2011.

Parratt, John. *Reinventing Christianity: African Theology Today.* Grand Rapids: Eerdmans, 1995.

Parrinder, Edward Geoffrey. *African Traditional Religion.* Westport, CT: Greenwood, 1976.

Paul VI, Pope. "Apostolic Letter Issued Motu Proprio: *Apostolica Sollicitudo*: Establishing the Synod of Bishops for the Universal Church." Washington, DC: National Catholic Welfare Conference, 1965, http://www.vatican.va/holy_father/paul_vi/motu_proprio/documents/hf_p-vi-motu-proprio_19650915_apostolica-sollicitudo_en.html.

———. "Dogmatic Constitution on the Church: Lumen Gentium, Solemnly Promulgated by His Holiness, Pope Paul VI, on November 21, 1964." Boston: Saint Paul's, 1965, http://www.vatican.va/archive/hist_councils/ii_vatican_council/documents/vat-ii_const_19641121_lumen-gentium_en.html.

———. "Eucharistic Celebration at the Conclusion of the Symposium Organized by the Bishops of Africa: Homily of Paul VI." Kampala,Uganda, July 31, 1969, http://www.vatican.va/holy_father/paul_vi/homilies/1969/documents/hf_p-vi_hom_19690731_en.html.

————. "Gaudium et Spes: Pastoral Constitution on the Church in the Modern World Promulgated by His Holiness, Pope Paul VI on December 7, 1965." Washington, DC: National Catholic Welfare Conference, 1965, http://www.vatican.va/archive/hist_councils/ii_vatican_council/documents/vat-ii_cons_19651207_gaudium-et-spes_en.html.

————. "*Populorum Progressio*: Encyclical of Pope Paul VI on the Development of Peoples." Washington, DC: United States Catholic Conference, 1967, http://www.vatican.va/holy_father/paul_vi/encyclicals/documents/hf_p-vi_enc_26031967_populorum_en.html.

Pawlikowski, J. T. "Creating an Ethical Context for Globalization: Catholic Perspectives in an Interreligious Context." *Journal of Ecumenical Studies* 42 (2007) 363–72.

Pett, David. "Sub-Saharan Africa's Big Move up." *Financial Post*, March 12, 2011, FP1, http://www.financialpost.com/related/topics/Saharan+Africa+move/5389108/story.html.

Pew Forum on Religion and Public Life. "Global Christianity: A Report on the Size and Distribution of the World's Christian Population." Washington, DC: Pew Research Center, 2011, http://www.pewforum.org/uploadedFiles/Topics/Religious_Affiliation/Christian/Christianity-fullreport-web.pdf.

————. "Tolerance and Tension: Islam and Christianity in Sub-Saharan Africa." Washington, DC: Pew Research Center, 2010, http://www.pewforum.org/executive-summary-islam-and-christianity-in-sub-saharan-africa.aspx.

Pius XI, Pope. "Quadragesimo Anno: Encyclical Letter on Reconstruction of the Social Order." London: Catholic Truth Society, 1931, http://www.vatican.va/holy_father/pius_xi/encyclicals/documents/hf_p-xi_enc_19310515_quadragesimo-anno_en.html.

Rahner, Karl. *Foundations of Christian Faith: An Introduction to the Idea of Christianity.* Translated by William V. Dych. New York: Crossroads, 2007.

————. *Ecclesiology, Questions in the Church, the Church in the World.* Vol. 14 of *Theological Investigations.* Translated by David Bourke. NY: Seabury, 1976.

Rodney, Walter. *How Europe Underdeveloped Africa.* Washington, DC: Howard University Press, 1981.

Roof, Wade Clark, ed. *Religious Pluralism and Civil Society.* Annals of American Academy of Political and Social Science 612. Los Angeles: Sage, 2007.

Rose, Or N. "In the Footsteps of Hillel: Judaism and Religious Pluralism." *Tikkun* 23 (2008) 62–73.

Rosenhaus, Matthew, et al. "A Statement on the Lisbon Meeting by Officers of the Interreligious Peace Colloquium." *World Faiths and the New World Order: A Muslim-Jewish-Christian Search Begins,* edited by Joseph Gremillion and William F. Ryan, 230–38. Washington, DC: Interreligious Peace Colloquium, 1978.

Rostow, W. W. "The Stages of Economic Growth." In *The Globalization and Development Reader,* edited by Amy Hite and J. Timmons Roberts, 47–55. Malden, MA: Blackwell, 2007.

Bibliography

Roxburgh, Charles, et al. "Lions on the Move: The Progress and Potential of African Economies." *June 2010 McKinsey Global Institute Report*, 1–8, http://www.mckinsey.com/insights/africa/lions_on_the_move.

Rutagambwa, Elisée. "The Rwandan Church: The Challenge of Reconciliation." In *The Catholic Church and the Nation-State: Comparative Perspectives*, edited by Paul Christopher Manuel, Lawrence C. Reardon, and Clyde Wilcox, 173–90. Religion and Politics Series. Washington, DC: Georgetown University Press, 2006.

"Rwanda: How the Genocide Happened." *BBC News Africa*, December 18, 2008, http://news.bbc.co.uk/go/pr/fr/-/2/hi/africa/1288230.stm.

Ryan, William F. *Culture, Spirituality, and Economic Development: Opening a Dialogue*. Ottawa: International Development Research Centre, 1995.

Sachedina, Abdulaziz. "Advancing Religious Pluralism in Islam." *Religion Compass* 4 (2010) 221–33.

———. *The Islamic Roots of Democratic Pluralism*. New York: Oxford University Press, 2001.

Safari, Peter Celestine. "Church, State and Rwandan Genocide." *Political Theology* 11 (2010) 873–93.

Samartha, Stanley Jedidiah. "The Holy Spirit and People of Other Faiths." *Ecumenical Review* 42 (1990) 250–63.

Sanks, T. Howland. "The Changing Face of Theology: A Tradition in Progress." *America* 12 (2011) 13–18.

Sanneh, Lamin O. *Disciples of All Nations: Pillars of World Christianity*. Oxford: Oxford University Press, 2008.

———. *Whose Religion Is Christianity? The Gospel Beyond the West*. Grand Rapids: Eerdmans, 2003.

Schineller, Peter, ed. "September 10–13, 1996 Benin City Communiqué on 'Rays of Hope.'" In *The Voice of the Voiceless: Pastoral Letters and Communiqués of the Catholic Bishops Conference of Nigeria, 1960–2002*, 329–33. Ibadan, Nigeria: Daily Graphics, 2002.

Sen, Amartya. *Development as Freedom*. New York: Anchor, 2000.

Shorter, Aylward. "The Curse of Ethnocentrism and the African Church." In *Ethnicity: Blessing or Curse*, edited by Albert de Jong, 27–32. Tangaza Occasional Papers 8. Nairobi, Kenya: Pauline Africa, 1999.

———. *Toward a Theology of Inculturation*. Eugene, OR: Wipf & Stock, 2006.

Smith, Adam. *An Inquiry into the Nature and Causes of the Wealth of Nations*. Edited by Edwin Cannan. New York: Random House, 1937.

Smith, Jane. "American Muslims and Religious Pluralism." *Religion Compass* 5 (2011) 192–201.

Soédé, Nathaniel Yaovi. "The Enduring Scourge of Poverty and Evangelization in Africa." In *Reconciliation, Justice, and Peace: The Second African Synod*, edited by Agbonkhianmeghe E. Orobator, 181–92. Maryknoll, NY: Orbis, 2011.

Sölle, Dorothee. *The Silent Cry: Mysticism and Resistance*. Translated by Barbara Rumscheidt and Martin Rumscheidt. Minneapolis: Fortress, 2001.

Soyinka, Wole. *Of Africa*. New Haven: Yale University Press, 2012. Kindle edition.

———. *The Open Sore of a Continent: A Personal Narrative of the Nigerian Crisis*. New York: Oxford University Press, 1996.

Spadaro, Antonio. "A Big Heart Open to God: A Conversation with Pope Francis." *National Catholic Review*, September 30, 2013, http://www .americamagazine.org/pope-interview.

Stackhouse, Max L. *Globalization and Grace. Vol. 4 of God and Globalization*. Theology for the Twenty-first Century. New York: Continuum, 2007.

Stiglitz, Joseph E. *Globalization and Its Discontents*. New York: Norton, 2002.

Synod of Bishops. "*Lineamenta*: The Church in Africa in Service to Reconciliation, Justice and Peace." Nairobi, Kenya: Paulines Africa, 2006, http://www.vatican.va/roman_curia/synod/documents/rc_synod_ doc_20060627_ii-assembly-africa_en.html.

———. "The New Evangelization for the Transmission of the Christian Faith: Instrumentum Laboris." Vatican City: Libreria Editrice Vaticana, 2012, http://www.vatican.va/roman_curia/synod/documents/rc_synod_ doc_20120619_instrumentum-xiii_en.html.

Taylor, Charles. *The Malaise of Modernity*. Concord, Ontario: House of Anansi, 1991.

Thiong'o, Ngugi Wa. "Learning from Slavery: The Legacy of the Slave Trade on Modern Society." *UN Chronicle* 46 (2009) 6–7.

Tsele, Molefe. "The Role of the Christian Faith in Development." In *Faith in Development: Partnership between the World Bank and the Churches of Africa*, edited by Deryke Belshaw et al., 203–218. Oxford: Regnum, 2001.

Tyndale, Wendy. "Religions and the Millennium Development Goals: Whose Agenda?" In *Religion and Development: Ways of Transforming the World*, edited by Gerrie ter Haar, 207–229. New York: Columbia University Press, 2011.

United Nations Economic Commission for Africa. "Economic Report on Africa 2012: Unleashing Africa's Potential as a Pole of Global Growth." Addis Ababa, Ethiopia: United Nations, 2012, http://www.uneca.org/adf/ publications/economic-report-africa-2012.

———. "Economic Report on Africa 2013: Making the Most of Africa's Commodities; Industrializing for Growth, Jobs and Economic Transformation." Addis Ababa, Ethiopia: United Nations, 2013, http:// www.uneca.org/publications/economic-report-africa-2013.

United Nations Industrial Development Organization. *Economic Development in Africa Report 2011: Fostering Industrial Development in Africa in the New Global Environment*. New York: United Nations Conference on Trade and Development, 2011, http://www.unctad.org/en/docs/aldcafrica2011_ en.pdf.

United Nations Office on Drugs and Crimes. "Transnational Organized Crime in Eastern Africa: A Threat Assessment." Vienna: United Nations, 2013,

http://www.unodc.org/documents/data-and-analysis/Studies/TOC_
East_Africa_2013.pdf.

Uzukwu, Elochukwu Eugene. "The God of Our Ancestors and African Unity."
African Ecclesiastical Review 23 (1981) 344–52.

———. *God, Spirit, and Human Wholeness: Appropriating Faith and Culture in
West African Style*. Eugene, OR: Pickwick, 2012.

———. *A Listening Church: Autonomy and Communion in African Churches*.
Maryknoll, NY: Orbis, 1996.

———. "Re-Evaluating God-Talk from an African Perspective." *Currents of
Encounter* 4 (2012) 55–71.

Van Butselaar, G. Jan. "The Role of Churches in the Peace Process in Africa: The
Case of Mozambique Compared." In *The Changing Face of Christianity:
Africa, the West, and the World*, edited by Lamin O. Sanneh and Joel A.
Carpenter, 96–115. Oxford: Oxford University Press, 2005.

Venter, Denis. "Democracy, Good Governance, and Leadership: What
Prospects for an African Renaissance?" In *Philosophy, Democracy, and
Responsible Governance in Africa*, edited by J. Obi Oguejiofor, 229–75.
Studies in African Philosophy 1. Münster: Lit, 2003.

Visser, Margaret. *Beyond Fate*. Toronto: House of Anansi, 2002.

Weber, Max. *The Protestant Ethic and the Spirit of Capitalism*. Translated by
Talcott Parsons. Mineola, NY: Dover, 2003.

Wolfensohn, James D. "Foreword." In *Religion and Development: Ways of
Transforming the World*, edited by Gerrie ter Haar, xvii–xviii. New York:
Columbia University Press, 2011.

Zalot, Jozef. *The Roman Catholic Church and Economic Development in Sub-
Saharan Africa*. Lanham, MD: University Press of America, 2002.

Zambia Episcopal Conference Plenary. "Act Justly and Walk Humbly with Your
God: A Pastoral Letter from the Catholic Bishops of Zambia." Lusaka,
Zambia: Zambia Episcopal Conference, 2013.

Index

Note: When Church is capitalized it refers to the Catholic Church.

Index

Lightning Source UK Ltd.
Milton Keynes UK
UKOW06f1022130916

282860UK00002B/146/P